Angela Demasi
0427161176

The Austra

The primary appeal of *The Australian Metropolis* will be to students of planning theory and practice in planning, urban studies, social science, architecture and humanities courses at the tertiary level; to practitioners in the private and public sectors who are offered a distilled overview of where they've come from and where they could be going; and to historians of local and regional history, public policy and social change. But the breadth of the coverage will also appeal to anyone interested in understanding how Australia's cities grew.

Stephen Hamnett is Professor of Regional and Urban Planning at the University of South Australia. He is the author of *Bouwen en Wonen in Onzekerheid* (1978) with Andreas Faludi, *Flexibility and Commitment in Planning* (1983) with Andreas Faludi and others, and co-editor of *Urban Australia: Planning Issues and Policies* (1987) with Raymond Bunker.

Robert Freestone is Associate Professor of Planning and Urban Development at the University of New South Wales. He is the author of *Model Communities* (1989) and editor of *Spirited Cities* (1993).

Contributors include some of Australia's leading teachers, researchers and practitioners in planning, history and urban studies.

The Australian Metropolis

A Planning History

Edited by

Stephen Hamnett and Robert Freestone

ALLEN & UNWIN

First published in 2000 by
Allen & Unwin
9 Atchison Street
St Leonards NSW 1590
Australia
Phone: (61 2) 8425 0100
Fax: (61 2) 9906 2218
E-mail: frontdesk@allen-unwin.com.au
Web: http://www.allen-unwin.com.au

National Library of Australia
Cataloguing-in-Publication entry:

The Australian metropolis: a planning history.

Includes index.
ISBN 1 86508 053 5.

1. City planning—Australia—History. I. Hamnett, Stephen. II. Freestone, Robert.

307.12160994

Cover and title page artwork:
John D. Moore
Chaos, 1923
oil on canvas, 61.0 × 76.0 cm
Art Gallery of New South Wales, Sydney

Set in 11/13 pt Goudy Old Style by Midland Typesetters, Australia
Printed by South Wind Production, Singapore

10 9 8 7 6 5 4 3 2 1

Contents

Figures

Tables

Contributors

Ian Alexander is an activist/community planning advocate who also teaches part-time in the Department of Geography at the University of Western Australia, Perth.

Robert Freestone is an associate professor in the Faculty of the Built Environment at the University of New South Wales, Sydney.

Christine Garnaut is a research associate in the Louis Laybourne Smith School of Architecture and Design, University of South Australia, Adelaide.

Stephen Hamnett is professor of regional and urban planning at the University of South Australia, Adelaide.

Renate Howe is associate professor of Australian studies at Deakin University, Geelong.

Alan Hutchings is a commissioner of the South Australian Environment, Resources and Development Court, Adelaide.

Margo Huxley is a professorial fellow with the School of Social Science and Planning, RMIT University, Melbourne.

Michael Lennon is chair of the Australian Housing and Urban Research Institute, Melbourne.

Ian Morison is an engineer and planner in private practice in Canberra.

Helen Proudfoot is a historian and heritage consultant in Sydney.

Introduction

Robert Freestone and Stephen Hamnett

In 1969, Hugh Stretton could not find a publisher for a manuscript which has subsequently become a contemporary classic in Australian urban studies, *Ideas for Australian Cities*.[1] However, the publication in 1977 of Max Neutze's definitive *Urban Development in Australia*[2] signified a legitimacy for contemporary urban studies that over the past two decades has burgeoned into a diverse, multidisciplinary literature on cities and city life.

Urban history, focusing on the physical, demographic and cultural transformations of cities, has become established as an important strand with its own seminal texts.[3] The history of urban planning is conventionally seen as a sub-category of this historical mainstream, although interest in the field is confined to neither historians nor planners. Canberra, popularly regarded as the only genuinely planned city in Australia, for better or worse, has always had its own rather insular historiography.[4] But over the past quarter-century, planning history has quietly built up a respectable literature. Leonie Sandercock's *Cities for Sale*, a political history of planning in several state capitals published in 1975,[5] was the breakthrough contribution in marking a critical, scholarly departure from old-fashioned descriptive accounts. An intermittent stream of substantial books has followed, among them historical studies of state developments,[6] central cities,[7] metropolitan areas,[8] planning movements,[9] planned communities,[10] and notable individuals.[11] In fact, the wider literature in journal articles, conference papers, book chapters and commissioned histories is impressively diverse.[12]

What has not emerged, until now, is a single-volume introduction to the development of urban planning in Australia. This book is a first attempt to fill the need for such an accessible text: a convenient, initial resource for anyone interested in the broad evolutionary sweep of modern planning. Its primary appeal will be to students studying planning theory and practice in planning, architectural, social science and humanities courses at tertiary level; to practitioners in the public and private sectors who are offered a distilled overview of where they've come from and where they could be going; to historians of local history, public policy and social change; and to general readers interested in appreciating planning's role in Australian urban development.

The writing of planning history sits at odds with the action-orientated, forward-looking, and, of course, ahistorical character of most planning literature. Much planning history is unavoidably 'about failure', to quote Sandercock's disarming summation of her own findings.[13] Much of it can also be read as a chronicle of political failure, missed opportunities, blinkered visions, communication breakdowns, degraded ideals, technical foul-ups and redistributive impacts which were the exact opposite of what was intended. Such problems go with the territory (and the mark of great planning disasters is to have these flaws compounded in the one project[14]). At the same time, we can point to historical achievements, such as the securing of generous parkland reservations, the conservation of natural and built heritage resources, communications improvements, attractive design projects, saner arrangements of land uses, the dampening of land speculation, encouragement of housing choice and affordability, the closer integration of land use, transportation and general infrastructure decision-making, and a successful balancing of private and community interests in millions of development decisions at the local level.

Constructing a comprehensive, national win–loss scorecard of planning achievements is not our intention. Even when sensibly restricted to specific cities, time periods and policies, there have certainly been too few such studies, partly because of the prodigious analytical demands faced.[15] But several desiderata for a critical history of planning flow from these observations. The first is the importance of a balanced appraisal of positive, negative and, indeed, ambivalent legacies. Even this is difficult to do as the political and economic climate for planning changes restlessly and calls forth new responses before the old ones have been played out. Second, and related to this, is the fundamental fact that planning is a social product. Planning's origins, agenda, evolution, forms and impacts are best appreciated within a broader societal context. Without that bigger picture, histories of planning can soon degenerate into a celebration of heroic individuals, plans and places within a simplistic and deterministic view of history that reifies planners over the planned and assumes that more planning is better planning.

History can have many uses, some mischievous, ideological and obfuscatory; but the social utility of good planning history derives from intellectual, pedagogic and pragmatic values. A historical perspective offers 'a systematic way to understand the changing context of organisations, communities, and policies within which planners pursue their profession'.[16]

It can enlighten, inspire, humble and liberate. It can inform planning practice.[17] Peter Hall, one of the best known commentators to bring a historical dimension to planning studies, argues simply in *Cities of Tomorrow* that he finds the subject 'intriguing. As elsewhere in human affairs, we too often fail to realise that our ideas and actions have been thought and done by others, long ago; we should be conscious of our roots'.[18] While we cannot artificially inseminate planning with any ersatz glamour, we can at least hold out for intrinsic interest, if not the understanding and questioning that comes from a collective 'drawing breath'.[19]

Such positive goals at least implicitly underlie much recent writing in the genre. Australian enthusiasm for planning history has been linked to a recent 'self-questioning mood' in Australian planning education,[20] but it broadly mirrors increasing international interest since at least the late 1970s. Concern with understanding planning's role as part of the matrix of forces shaping urban development; the passing of old practices and the emergence of innovative forms of planning in response to new challenges faced by the modern state; tracking the international diffusion of planning ideas, ideologies and idealogues beyond the Anglo–American realm; revisionist probes of where gender, race and difference figured in the received wisdom; a rising tide of heritage consciousness and management issues for designed landscapes; and an inevitable end-of-the-millennium stocktaking mindset—these are some of the factors explaining this interest. The resultant global literature is voluminous, variegated and interdisciplinary.[21]

While *The Australian Metropolis* is the first synoptic survey of its kind in Australia, other countries can boast a more established tradition in this area. In the United States, for example, there is a library shelf of recent authored and edited volumes documenting urban planning's role in urban and national history from a variety of perspectives. The first and most important of these was Mel Scott's landmark *American City Planning since 1890* published in 1969.[22] This lengthy, albeit narrowly conceived institutional history, remains a benchmark reference work. Radically different interpretations are offered courtesy of marxism by Richard Fogelsong[23] and post-structuralism by Christine Boyer.[24] Leonie Sandercock's *Making the Invisible Visible* is an American-centric exploration of the 'noir' of planning history, aiming to liberate voices either overlooked or oppressed by establishment history.[25] Collections have successfully brought together diverse contributions. In 1983, Donald Krueckeberg assembled both a volume of biographical studies of planners from different eras and an introductory primer on American planning history.[26] In 1988, Daniel Schaffer's *Two Centuries of American Planning*[27] brought together a small number of substantive essays on topics such as park systems and post-war reconstruction, while a 1995 anthology edited by Sies and Silver dramatically expands the geographical and topical scope of the field.[28]

Books such as these offer models for constructing an introductory overview of the Australian experience: from readers based on previously published materials through conference-generated collections and professional history to stylised interpretations of particular places and events. Our approach has been to opt for a hybrid text, which involves a number of collaborators pursuing a collective sense of purpose and theme. Mindful of a potentially broad readership, and so for pragmatic rather than ideological reasons, we have decided upon a straightforward, chronological account. Planning theory and practice are interpreted as evolving through identifiable phases or eras characterised by distinctive and dominant packages of ideas, institutions and ideologies assembled to meet the challenges of the times.

This notion of a sequence of planning 'paradigms' is used to good effect in Peter Hall's *Cities of Tomorrow*. We could do worse than borrow such a conceptual framework from a best-selling book, and it does provide a useful heuristic device which captures well the notion of planning as a societal product whose goals as much as limitations are ultimately linked to a dynamic and ever-evolving economic, political, social and environmental backdrop. There are, of course, dangers in presuming any single definition of planning at any one point in time.[29] Used too dogmatically or simplistically, the paradigm idea can ossify into an idealist typology which can obscure the inherent complexity, fragmentation and contradictions of different eras, as well as shut out oppositional histories or interpretations. This is certainly not our intention, which is to enliven what might otherwise be a dogged decade-by-decade description of historical planning facts and to provide a more fluid exploration of evolving ideas and practices organised around the major themes and concerns—the *Zeitgeist*—of the day.

The accompanying table embodies, in summary form, the chronological–conceptual framework which underlines this recounting of Australian urban planning history. Modern planning emerges in response to the problematical state of late colonial cities. This move toward a coordinated, higher order approach to public intervention parallels international developments, although the federal capital project constitutes a uniquely Australian catalyst. Early American-style city beautiful dreams soon give way to British-connected garden city ideas which more directly address suburban realities at both macro- and micro-levels. Through this phase, an organised movement urging the state to make the required legislative adjustments comes together through public information campaigns, voluntary planning associations and national conferences. The 1920s sees the first practical outcomes of this propagandist phase, with an ever-widening scale of planning captured in the formation of the first metropolitan-level agencies to address growth issues. None of these is put on a permanent footing, so that the planning cause falters in the wake of the stock market crash of 1929.

A generational shift in the planning movement occurs through the years leading up to World War Two as new priorities are defined: housing, redevelopment, regional planning and the quest for professionalism. Propelled initially by the idealism of post-war reconstruction and the need to plan ahead for peacetime prosperity, the 1950s see the development of a number of statutory metropolitan blueprints in the British town and country planning tradition. In the 1960s, the accent shifts to new-look strategic 'structure' plans to best facilitate long-term growth but, with the end of the long post-war boom in the 1970s, many of the assumptions underpinning planning are challenged for the first time through social action. The mythology of planning as a politically neutral, land use arrangement exercise in 'the public interest' is exposed. New forms appear as a result: environmental, social, advocacy, heritage, cultural and participatory planning. The 1980s seek to assimilate this growing fragmentation into new strategies against a background of post-industrial economic restructuring and pressures on public finance. The early 1990s witness the emergence of yet another round of strategic plans underpinned by renewed aspirations for coordinated planning. But the latter years of the decade see the dominance of a market-led approach in which ecological and social concerns rest uneasily with a new paradigm of planning stressing deregulation and place marketing.

This shorthand history sits on top of numerous specific issues, trends and activities which a truly comprehensive account of Australian planning history might need to explore: the design of country towns and regional Australia, fashions in planning methodology, the making of environmental laws, the rise of specialised epithetical plannings, the founding of the profession, the development of planning education, the fate of those disenfranchised by planning, countless detailed studies of planning in action and so on. This book cannot attempt to cover everything, although we hope that its framework is robust enough to help situate such phenomena in temporal and contextual terms. But providing another layer of coherence in addition to the chronological organisation and paradigmatic conceptualisation is the adoption of metropolitan planning as a primary focus of the book. That is, we are interested in the ideas that have guided the planning and management of the largest cities in Australia since the nineteenth century—particularly in relation to their size, structure, functioning and quality of life. The result is largely a middle-ground view. With the Federal Government's direct involvement

Table A Basic chronological framework of Australian metropolitan planning

Core period	*Planning era*	*Major concerns*	*Major events*
Nineteenth century	Colonial town planning	Town founding and design Public infrastructure	Light's Adelaide Public health reforms
1900s	Emergence of planning concerns	City improvement City beautiful	1901 Melbourne Congress Federal capital
1910s	An organised planning movement	Garden cities Planned suburbs	Town planning associations National planning conferences
1920–30s	Experimentation, institutionalisation and legislation	Regulation Comprehensive town planning	Melbourne and Perth Town Planning Commissions Town Planning Acts in SA and WA
1940s	Idealism and reconstruction	Establishment of statutory planning systems Housing Emergence of regional planning	Commonwealth Housing Commission and state housing authorities Cumberland County Council
1950s	Mark One master plans	Town and country planning Professionalisation	Sydney, Melbourne and Perth metropolitan planning schemes Land use zoning
1960s	Mark Two master plans	Structure planning Corridor cities Planned suburban development	Transport–land use strategies Canberra's Y Plan
1970s	Reorientation and conflict	Rise of environmental and heritage concerns Public participation	Federal urban policy Green Bans and resident action
1980s	Revival of strategic planning	Urban management Ecological sustainability	Urban consolidation policies Joint ventures Better Cities
1990s	Competitive versus sustainable cities	Compact cities Entrepreneurialism Cultural planning	Deregulation, privatisation and planning systems reform Whole of government approaches Urban design

in cities intermittent, and local authorities burdened with the minutiae of day-to-day small area administration, we concentrate on the central role of state governments in metropolitan development. Even by the late nineteenth century, the states were the main metropolitan planners by reason of their involvement in the programming and financing of public infrastructure.

Nevertheless, while this book tells just one story, its narrative is driven by different voices. We have not attempted by ourselves to flesh out the bare bones of our historical pen-picture but have conscripted to the project other authors with a detailed knowledge of planning in certain eras. Their brief was to provide a national coverage, drawing on examples from across Australia, but to include more detailed case notes on selected events, plans, places or people as necessary. The coverage is both period-specific and thematic, but there is some unavoidable overlap between chapters in the scene-setting of core events and the tracking of outcomes and legacies of particular actions. We have not sought to impose an inert, crypto-encyclopaedic and homogeneous style. Our collaborators were encouraged to inject theoretical and personal perspectives to provide connections with wider fields of knowledge. While a unified sense of purpose provides a measure of integration, individual chapters were conceived as complete and meaningful statements in their own right.

The settlement forms and modes of thinking inherited from the nineteenth century were a fundamental influence on the course of metropolitan planning in the twentieth century. Helen Proudfoot looks at the transition from town planning as the laying out of town grids by colonial surveyors in the nineteenth century towards more multifaceted urbanistic interventions by the turn of the century. Robert Freestone carries this story forward into the Federation era, a period in which the formative ideas of modernist planning revolved around city beautiful notions. The two major products were the 1909 Royal Commission for the Improvement of Sydney and Its Suburbs, and the international Federal Capital Design Competition won by Walter Burley and Marion Mahony Griffin. Implementation of the Griffin scheme saw its richly symbolic and artistic content expunged in favour of garden suburbanism. In Chapter 3, Christine Garnaut examines the broader influence of the garden city movement, which hit its peak just as a formal town planning movement materialised in the 1910s. The garden city legacy resides largely in planned suburbs and other new communities, but there were other normative ideas about metropolitan spatial footprints which pointed the way towards the future containment of suburban sprawl. Alan Hutchings surveys the inter-war years. Far from constraining horizontal extension, growth management in the 1920s aimed at facilitating it. The agenda shifted toward coordination, efficiency and economy. This was the era in which the goals of the pioneers were first realised in legislation with comprehensive metropolitan planning exercises also initiated in three cities.

Planning innovation can be linked to the cyclical nature of the capitalist economy,[30] and out of the economic downswing of the 1930s arose bold new planning ideas about the desirable scale and nature of public intervention in urban land and housing development. The 1940s, outlined by Renate Howe, were a period of transition, not just from pre-war to post-war life, but—more fundamentally for planning—from idealism to institutionalisation; from housing welfarism to technocratic plan-making; and from the problems of post-colonial capitals to the reconstruction of modern industrial cities. The 1948 *Cumberland County Council Plan* for Sydney was the classic master plan of the period. Through the 1950s, metropolitan planning went into mass production, with major schemes following for Melbourne and Perth. The ideas of restraining the outward growth of cities and of establishing self-contained new communities can be found in these plans, but they were more significant in practice in establishing homogeneous land use zones, an expansive suburbia of detached houses, freeway corridors and, overall, a spatial structure seemingly in tune with the good times of Menzies-era Australia. Ian Alexander argues in Chapter 6 that, whatever the merits of this approach, it actually inscribed lasting inequities on the metropolitan landscape. Ian Morison takes the metropolitan planning impulse forward to the 1960s, when green belts and satellite town templates are displaced by growth corridor strategies. There is a remarkable homogeneity in planning documents through this period, although effectiveness in implementation varies widely. The 'Y Plan' for Canberra, the 'scientific' outcome of sophisticated land use–transportation studies, was comprehensively realised in a city where planners enjoyed extraordinary powers under a leasehold land tenure system. In the other capitals, the ability of land use planners to shape metropolitan form so precisely was more circumscribed (see McLoughlin's study of Melbourne[31]).

As Margo Huxley contends in Chapter 8, the significance given to alternative spatial forms seemed much less important in the 1970s. This decade ushered in a radically different environment for planning: an era of slow growth and rapid social change through which the tacit consensus which buttressed planning in the early post-war years collapsed and conventional planning practices were contested seriously for the first time. Enlivened at one end of the decision-making spectrum by outbreaks of resident action over unpopular redevelopment and freeway projects, and at the other by the unprecedented intervention of the Federal Government in urban affairs, the 1970s witnessed a significant round of revised and new planning legislation, the formation of specialist agencies, the arrival of new values of ecological and built conservation, and a move toward more participatory processes in plan-making and implementation. The latter part of the 1970s saw the emergence of a style of planning which came to be known as 'urban management', meaning trend-based planning preoccupied with the coordination of land release and infrastructure investments, but lacking the confidence to set out longer term visions of the 'good city'.

In Chapter 9 Michael Lennon argues that this style of planning persisted for most of the 1980s. However, the latter years of the decade and the early 1990s, saw a revival of interest in long-term, strategic metropolitan plans which sought to bring together economic and social concerns with the new imperatives of ecologically sustainable development, and to support these with 'whole of government' management structures—the apotheosis of the longstanding quest for better coordination. The South Australian Planning Review of 1990–92 was the benchmark for this new approach. The period also saw the Federal Government's interest in the cities briefly revived. But all of this happened against a backdrop of growing concern for economic liberalisation, smaller government, and a perceived need to adopt more competitive and entrepreneurial styles of planning. In the final chapter, Stephen Hamnett shows how these tensions have persisted into the closing years of the twentieth century. There are echoes of the last *fin de siècle*, as Australian cities compete for growth, status and prosperity, although the means are different. Pulled in different directions by local–state conflicts, small government ideology, mega-projects, joint ventures, environmental protection, and the demands of what have become culturally diverse cities, the *Zeitgeist* is hard to pin down. Most cities in the late 1990s have 'integrated' metropolitan plans which seek to provide for more 'compact' cities, but their persistent underlying notion of collective action in the public interest through government planning is stridently challenged by neo-liberal critics and also by post-modern ways of viewing the world. As there were at the beginning of the twentieth century, there are substantial challenges facing those who would seek to make our cities better.

Several themes emerge from this multi-authored survey. These include the continuity and circularity of much planning thought, the ongoing quest for coordination, the centrality of state governments in metropolitan planning and the difficulties of securing inter-governmental cooperation, the unavoidable politicisation of planning, the influence of global developments on theory and practice, the significance of Canberra as both a unique laboratory and mirror of twentieth-century planning ideas, the primacy of suburbanisation in Australian metropolitan evolution, and the not infrequent failures of planning in relation to both theoretical ideals and community needs. The history of urban planning which emerges from the ten chapters of this book is not a narrow professional saga of triumph and tribulation. Planning is not cast as an independently heroic activity unambiguously striving for the common good, as portrayed by some of its early advocates and myth-makers. This history of Australian urban planning is defined by the evolution of ruling economic, political, technological, cultural and environmental forces as much as by its own interventions.

As a first introduction to the history of urban planning in Australia, *The Australian Metropolis: A Planning History* stands as an authoritative rather than definitive interpretation. There must be the inevitable sins of omission and commission that accompany such ventures. But as typical forward-looking planners laying the groundwork for something better, our hope is that a future historiography of urban studies in Australia will value this book as a useful, interesting and timely collection which helped pave the way for many more detailed historical explorations of the Australian urban planning experience.

1 Founding cities in nineteenth-century Australia

Helen Proudfoot

In 1788, the scene was set for a great and irreversible change in the way land was perceived and managed in Australia. Until then, the indigenous people ranged over their defined territories according to a seasonal pattern, hunting, fishing and culling the fruits of the land, but not cultivating the soil or domesticating animals for meat consumption. After 1788, the land was claimed as being under the British Crown and a system of land survey was introduced. The land was measured, divided, and appropriated according to a very different system, at first by crown grant, and then by purchase. Though the indigenous people had been living in bands or small communities of fluctuating size, they had not established permanent settlements. Agriculture, pastoralism and urbanism were thus the radical innovations of British colonisation.[1]

The timing of settlement by European powers in colonies in far-flung empires had a crucial effect on the subsequent development of these colonies.[2] The spatial expression of towns in the colonies was determined by a dynamic process which had more to do with contact with the parent metropolitan power than with a perception of the geographical nature of the country settled. In fact, in Australia, only a cursory examination of the continent was carried out by James Cook before it was decided to send the cargo of convicts to Botany Bay. The continent, in all its bulk, variety and extent was unknown, except in outline.

The timing was crucial, according to Louis Hartz, in other ways. He postulates that the preoccupations of the age in which colonies are founded are transferred to colonial offspring and become the guiding principles of their foundation ethos.[3] Thus, the English Enlightenment was the guiding hand for Sydney and New South Wales, but by the time Adelaide and Melbourne were founded, nineteenth-century capitalism and utilitarian doctrines were on the ascendant, and the complexion of these cities became different.[4]

The English had been establishing colonies vigorously since the Restoration period in the late seventeenth century. From their small European island, they expanded first into Scotland and then into Ireland. Then the attractions of the New World enticed them to plant colonies along the east coast of North America. When these colonies prospered, a program of emigration was embarked upon. After the American colonies rebelled, the British colonising zeal turned eastwards towards India and the Pacific.

There was an underlying program for the administration of British colonies. These were controlled from London, first under the Board of Plantations, and then under the Colonial Office. Governors, appointed for a fixed term, were to be vice-regal, administrative heads. They were assisted by the army, on the one hand, and a small bureaucracy of public servants on the other.[5] Chief among the public servants was the surveyor-general, who was charged with the mapping and subdividing of the territory settled.

Though Sydney was founded in 1788, it was 30 years before inland exploration of any extent was seriously embarked upon, and the pattern of Australian capital city foundation—the potential metropolitan urban centres—was not to emerge until the middle of the nineteenth century. It was linked to the foundation of separate states, three of which hived off from New South Wales (Van Diemen's Land, Queensland and Victoria), with the other two, South Australia and Western Australia, founded as entirely separate ventures.

Maher has pointed out that the capital cities, when they did emerge, were based on a new economic order evolving under capitalism, driven by Europe's industrial revolution.[6] Economic potential and administrative structures created a settlement system based on very few principal sites. Each of these was separated from the others by large distances, so the capital cities from the beginning dominated their particular state territories. The port cities, as capitals, were points of contact with England, and became the channels through which the produce of the developing hinterland—wool, timber and beef—was despatched to Europe. The production of these staples, in turn, was able to generate capital inflows to sustain further development.

The colonial urban grid

The key to English colonisation policy was the establishment, in the first instance, of a planned, orderly, principal town. It was a deliberate policy of urbanisation. Towns were to be centres for trade and defence, and a civilising influence. Towns were established along the same conceptual lines, though some had a free settlement base, and town plans were variations on a similar grid pattern. The grid basis, with its *cardo-decumanus* orientation, was the underlying physical structure, and was markedly similar in each city.[7]

The plan of the Australian colonial town had descended from the earlier 'Grand Modell' put forward by Lord Shaftesbury and John Locke for the colonies in Ireland and America.[8] It was based, even further back, on Roman and Greek colonial models in the Mediterranean, which relied on the symmetry, proportion and regularity of the grid layout. The colonial grid had re-emerged as the most straightforward and flexible planning instrument for the founding of Australian cities. The first nucleus of Sydney, Parramatta, Hobart Town, Port Macquarie, Brisbane and Albany, for example, was the central strip of the Parade Ground, where the soldiers (and convicts) were assembled and reviewed. This very early stage was soon blended into the grid system as the settlement grew and changed complexion.[9]

In London, Granville Sharp, in his role as philanthropist and anti-slavery agitator, had reformulated the symbolism of the colonial grid for use in Sierra Leone, the colony where the resettlement of American slaves in Africa was being tried. He published an influential book on the plan of the proposed town of Freetown in 1794. Sharp advocated the plan's adoption in the East Indies, America, and 'elsewhere'. It was an ideal plan, in the Platonic tradition.[10] His suggestion that this egalitarian plan could be useful in the settlement of lands colonised by Britain came at a crucial time for Australian settlement. It is interesting to note that Sharp was a frequent visitor to the country house of William Oglethorpe, who went back to England after he had founded and planned Savannah in North America.[11] Savannah's plan became the archetypal model for American cities, a textbook example of a formal colonial grid. Sharp, who worked in the Ordnance Office in the Tower of London, and who was in close contact with.a body of trained surveyors, saw obvious virtues in Oglethorpe's Savannah.[12]

The principles outlined by Sharp were adopted by Governor Darling in 1829 in New South Wales and put into practice in the towns planned by Surveyor-General T.L. Mitchell and his team of surveyors. Each town section was to be identical: streets were to be 66 feet (20.1 metres) wide, with the main streets in some cases 80 feet (24.4 metres) wide, and allotments were to be the same size, with a balance between public and private land. In the plan of Melbourne, surveyed as a potential city by Robert Hoddle in 1837, the principles of symmetry, balance, regularity, standard-sized allotments, and squares for internal open space or for administrative buildings were used to good effect, along with surrounding open space parklands in the Township Reserve. In the Australian context, these reserves were used for various purposes: for the development of urban parks, for special land uses attracted to the town and for the extension of the town.[13] The emphasis on identical-sized allotments might be considered, in a political context, as a 'democratic' rather than a merely 'regular' arrangement.

Mitchell had been trained in the demanding school of military surveying, gaining experience in the Peninsular Wars against Napoleon. The surveying technique was developed by the English Board of Ordnance at the Drawing Room in the Tower of London where the English National Survey was planned, and taught at naval and military schools. Mitchell took some pride in his map-making and had a meticulous drafting style. His Australian town plans fitted into the surveying framework he had laid down for the division of the Twenty Counties which constituted the settled portion of Australia in 1826. His great achievement was his 'Map of the Colony', engraved in 1834.[14] This was the context of all the subsequent town plans in the colony; town reserves were set aside for potential towns within the county structure.

As settlement grew, and Europeans established themselves on the coast and across the mountains, the time came for marking out potential towns which were seen as crucial centres for the local administration of their districts. A surveyor was sent to make a preliminary survey of the site before settlement was firmly established, noting the lie of the land, indicating rivers, hills and any particular features, as well as existing buildings and huts, river crossings and roads, and the local vegetation and type of soil. The plan was set within a larger Township Reserve. It was sent back to Sydney for examination by Mitchell or his deputy Perry, and placed before the Legislative Council. When approved, the town was marked out on the ground: streets and sections were the backbone, town allotments were of standard size. In the larger plans, sites were set aside for a courthouse and a gaol, for churches and schools, and some peripheral sections were marked for 'suburban allotments' at a larger size than the standard allotments.[15]

The colonial surveyors, as a body of men, led strenuous and hard-working lives, often in trying conditions, working in pairs or sometimes isolated in the field. Their rewards were often meagre. They were key figures who, largely unacknowledged as they were part of the public service, were responsible for far-reaching decisions in land matters.[16] The misleading legend that their town plans were not made on the site of the town, resulting in roads running straight uphill and other absurdities, is patently not typical, although, as alluded to later, John Sulman would use it for propaganda purposes when he was arguing, 50 years later, for a looser, anti-grid street system.

Small town plans can be considered as the germ of capital city planning. A typical one of these is illustrated here: Goulburn was planned as a larger 'gateway' town, a stopping place and centre on the way into the interior (Figure 1.1). Bathurst, as another example, had echoes of early American plans, with its central square reserved for public use. Its almost Vitruvian layout has five simple sections arranged around a central square. The first plan (1831) of Port Macquarie shows the penal settlement

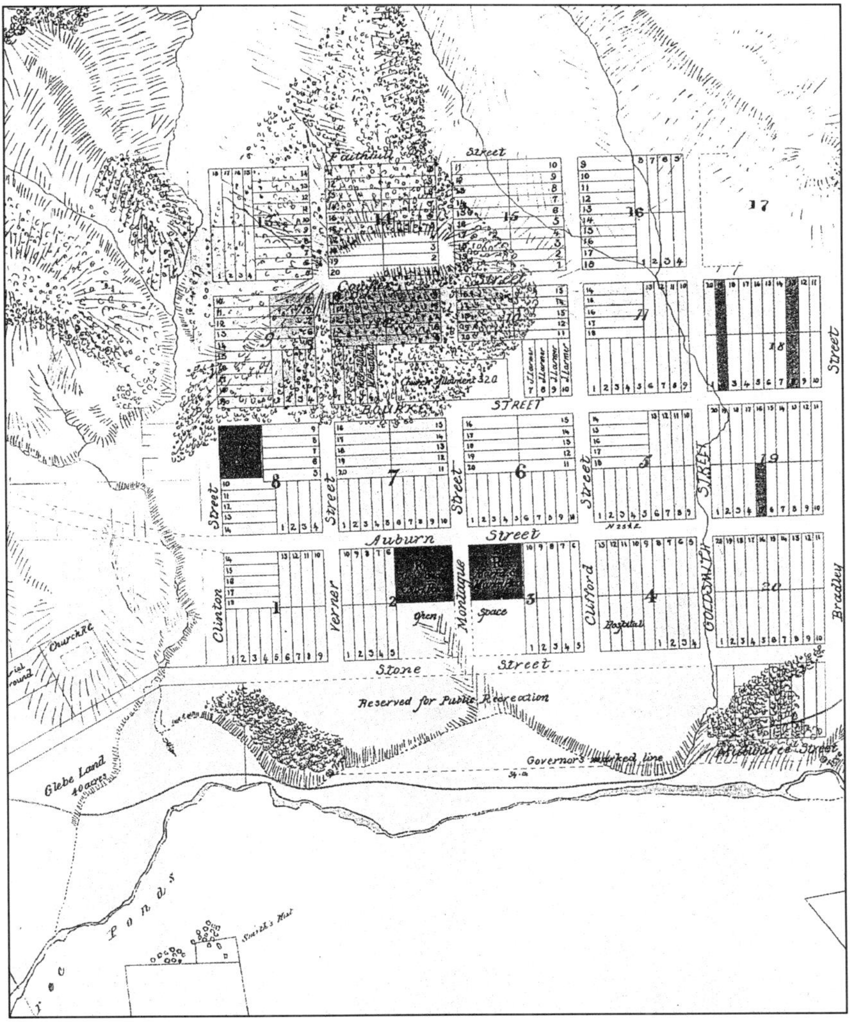

Figure 1.1 Plan of the Town of Goulburn (1833)

Source: Map No. 2789, Archives Office of New South Wales, Sydney.

being re-planned as a town for free settlers, the change of pattern announcing its different function.

It is these town plans of the 1830s, rather than that of Sydney itself, that indicate more clearly the pattern of the potential cities of the other states. Robert Hoddle worked on Goulburn a few years before he was sent down to plan Melbourne. Goulburn was also influenced by Governor Bourke in its final siting and dimensions, as were the details of the plan of Melbourne, with its back lanes added at Bourke's suggestion (Figure 1.2). Sydney's plan was less distinct, formed as it was by the contours of its harbour and the confusion of the earliest years (Figure 1.3).

The other five capitals were founded early in the nineteenth century: Hobart Town in 1804, as a deterrent to the French interest; Brisbane as a convict centre in 1825; Perth as a free venture in 1829; Adelaide and Melbourne in 1837. Adelaide had a 'model plan' devised by Colonel Light (Figure 1.4) that has been hailed since as the epitome of the 'Grand Modell', an influence on Ebenezer Howard and the garden city movement (see Chapter 3 in this book), and Australia's best known textbook plan.[17] Melbourne also was a very successful planned vindication of the grid system. All became the capitals and key administrative centres of their states, the largest city and the contact point for goods and services from London and Liverpool.

Emergent problems of urban growth

After the 1850s and the beginning of the gold rushes, when the accepted town form was in place, there were other pressing questions to be dealt with. With the expressed policy being the formation of a central urban place or city for each state, there were great problems of health and congestion to be solved: how to service a large and growing immigrant population, how to arrange for water to be available for every household, how to cope with the disposal of sewage, and how to allow circulation into and out of the central city

These problems took years to address, and much argument preceded their gradual solution. Discussions were started in the 1850s and carried on in the fledgling learned societies which were emerging in the cities. In Sydney it was the Philosophical Society of New South Wales, where scientific-minded Governor Denison was a catalyst. In Melbourne, it was the Victorian Philosophical Society, founded about the same time. There was a strong sense of the need to contribute to the making of a society, both moral and liberal, among what was seen as a discordant and heterogeneous population.[18]

A major cause of the delay was the reluctance of legislatures to put

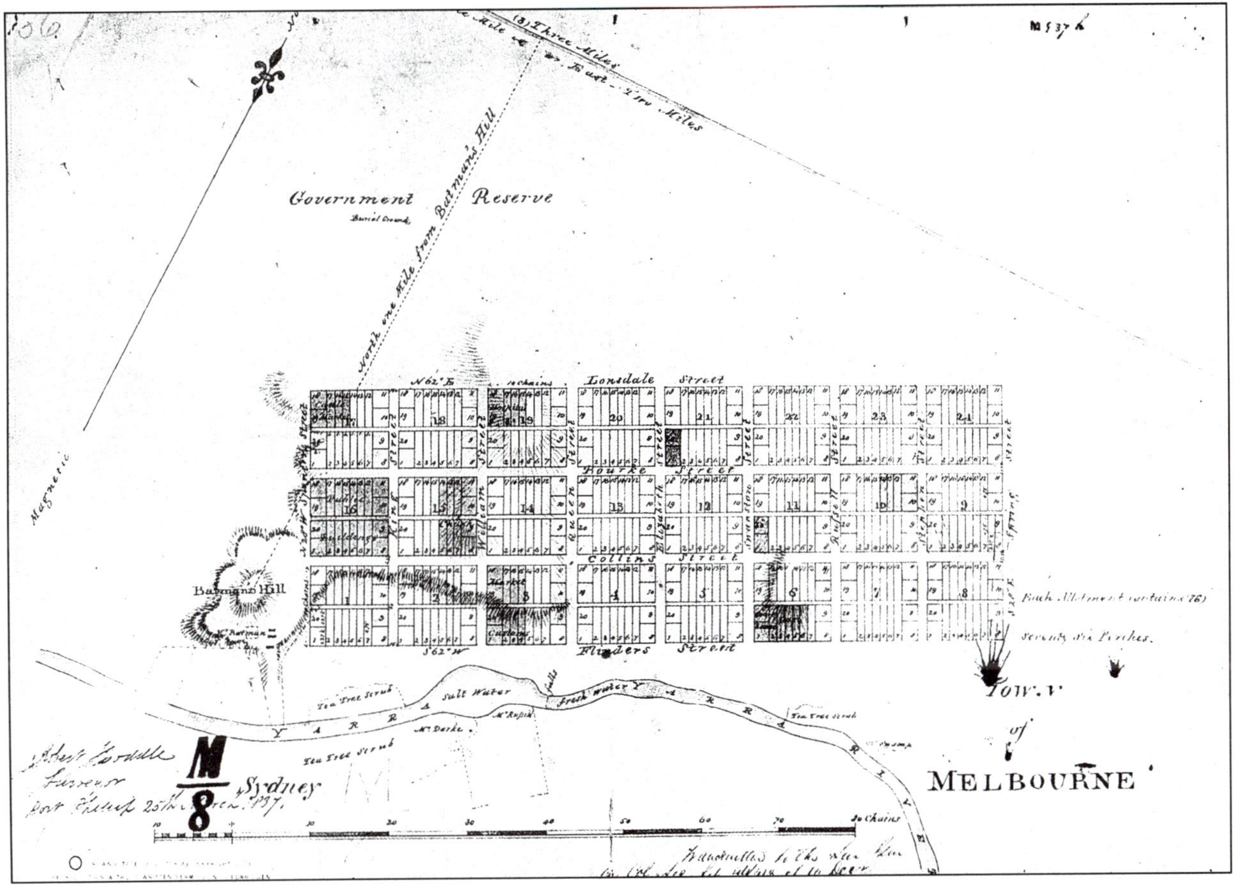

Figure 1.2
Robert Hoddle,
Town of Melbourne,
25 March 1837

Source: Original held in the Central Plan Office Melbourne: marked Sydney M8.

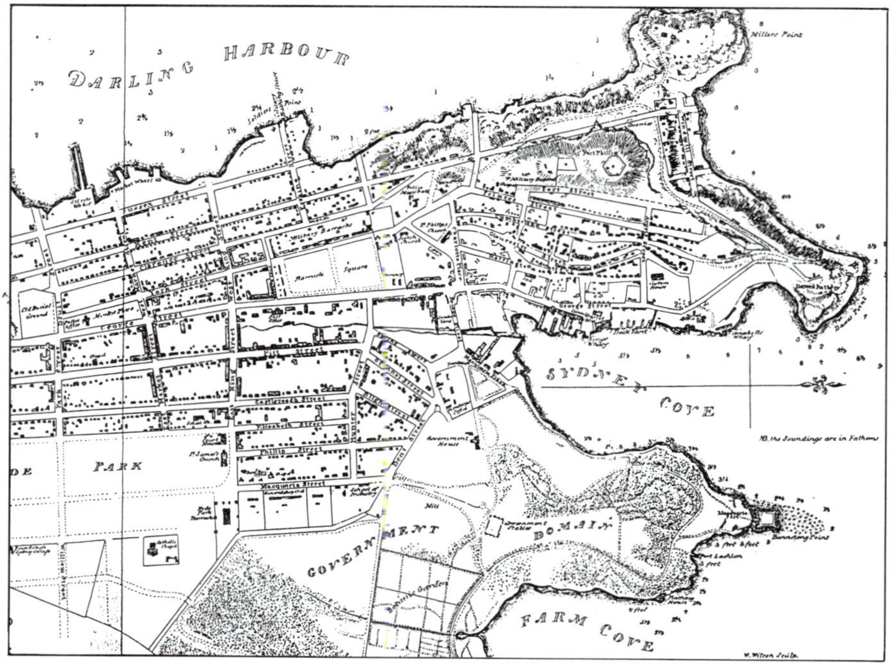

Figure 1.3 Map of the Town of Sydney (1831)

Source: Part only. W. Wilson, drawn and engraved for the *New South Wales Calendar and General Post Office Directory, 1831.*

in train effective water and sewerage systems, and their hesitation to entrust the newly formed local government bodies to carry them out. Several decades were to pass before it was decided to set up state bodies to deal with servicing the city. Major capital works were involved; the costs had to be borne by the state by borrowing from Britain. The need to undertake the great expense of supplying services for the public welfare, and the political will to enact and administer firmer regulations of private building activity, did not emerge until the 1880s and 1890s.

In the meantime, the suburbs surrounding the central city core had been subdivided by private developers, without strong central control. They became crowded, tightly built, badly serviced terrace precincts, unhealthy for their inhabitants. Infant mortality in Sydney, for example, was scandalously high. Further out, however, at the edge of the urban perimeter, the promise of a 'healthy' lifestyle on a suburban block was made possible by the establishment of public tramways and then railways, a transport network which did good service for the city.

As for the water and sewerage services in the two main cities, the problems were not solved for some decades after this period of complaint.

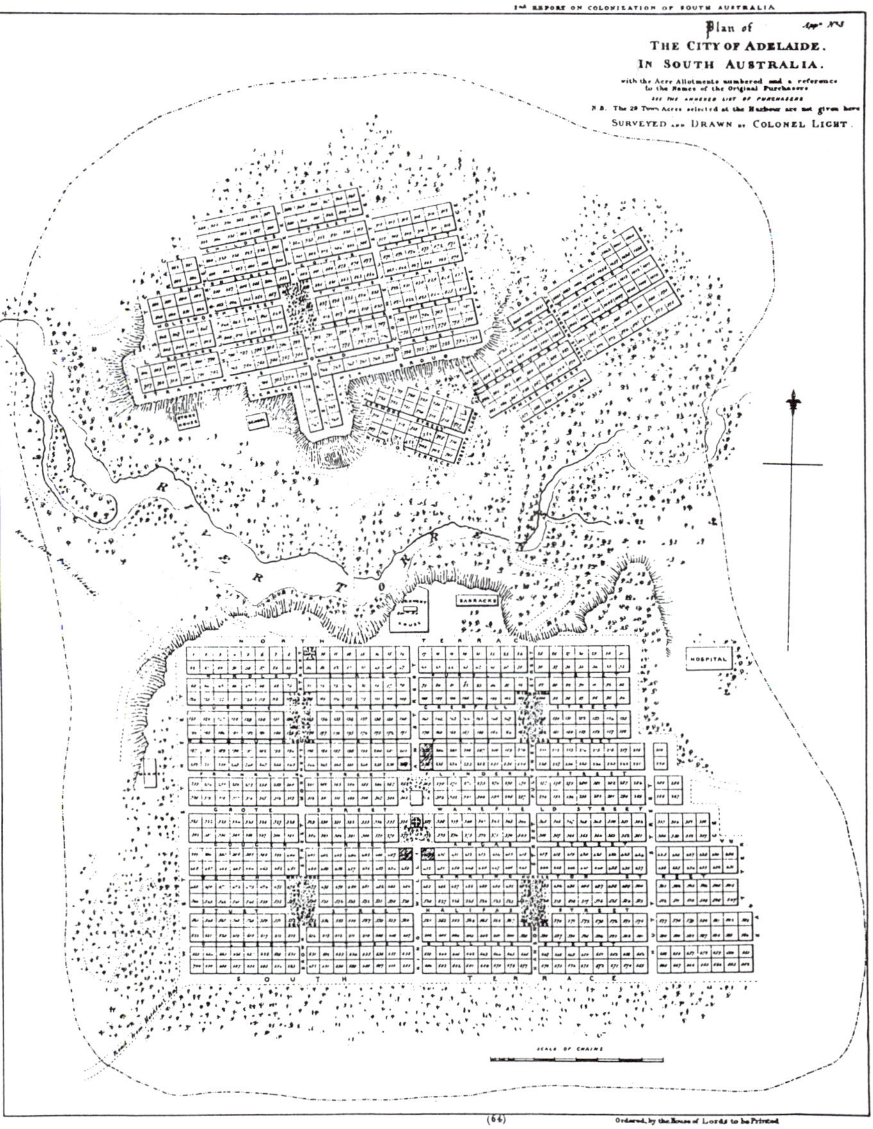

Figure 1.4 Plan of Adelaide (1837)

Source: South Australian Colonization Commissioners, *Third Annual Report 1838.*

To service Sydney with water, after the Lachlan Swamps and the city springs and wells grew more stressed, a Commission of Inquiry in 1869 recommended the tapping of the headwaters of the Nepean and its tributaries in the rocky Woronora Plateau south of Sydney. The water was to be transported by gravity flow to a central dam at Prospect, and from there to the pipe head at Guildford to be reticulated throughout the metropolitan area. An army of men began work in 1880 on this ambitious scheme, which was in operation by 1888.[19] Melbourne's water supply was secured earlier than Sydney's, with the commencement of the Yan Yean reservoir and the laying of the pipes for reticulation. After some controversy about the lead content in the pipes, the system was in operation by 1857 in the city and in the suburbs a few years later.[20]

The disposal of sewage was less straightforward. It was not until 1889 that the first steps were taken in Melbourne to provide an efficient sewerage system for the city. In Sydney, also, sewerage disposal has been a recurrent problem even after the first ocean outfall system was put in place at Bondi in 1890.[21]

Urban reform at mid-century

In the middle years of the nineteenth century, some notable individuals emerged who concerned themselves with the problems of the towns. Christopher Rolleston, William Bland and William Stanley Jevons were three Sydney advocates for the better organisation of city services, which were lagging far behind the immigration program.

Governor Denison had appointed Christopher Rolleston (1817–88) as the first registrar-general for New South Wales. Rolleston launched a program of compulsory registration of births, deaths and marriages. He followed the path taken in Melbourne by W.H. Archer, who was a disciple of the English statistician William Farr. Rolleston arranged to hold the New South Wales census at the same time as the Victorian census, coinciding with the English census, so that comparisons could be made.[22] Rolleston's first paper to the Philosophical Society in 1857, 'The sanitary condition of Sydney', opened the debate about what should be done about the sorry state of urban water supply and sewage disposal. The census figures Rolleston quoted in his paper were a shock to the members. They discovered for the first time the appalling rates of children's deaths in the city, in a country where there was ample space and a supposedly healthy climate. The childhood death rate in Sydney in 1856 was proportionally higher than that in London in 1845, which was a year of cholera.

Later in the century, another gifted statistician, T.A. Coghlan, extended the range of information to be included in the census, thus making possible an overview of living standards in New South Wales, with the inclusion of the sorts of dwellings built and the materials of their construction. The surprising thing in those end-of-the-century times was the number of people who were still living in tents. These figures became vital information for improvers to work with.

William Bland (1789–1868) was born in London, trained in medicine, and became a naval surgeon by 1812. Transported to New South Wales after a duelling affair, he began a private practice and was soon immersed in Sydney life and politics with participation in the Emancipists Association, which championed the petition for self-government, a cause mounted with some fervour in the 1830s. In 1842, the British Government responded and enacted a measure to allow for partial self-government by the appointment of twelve nominees and 24 elected members in the Legislative Council of New South Wales. In the first election, held in 1843, Bland was elected as the member for Sydney. He joined the Philosophical Society of New South Wales when it formed in 1856. When Rolleston delivered his paper to the society, Bland was ready to take up the campaign for reform. He followed it up with his own paper, *Sanitary Reform of Towns and Cities*, published in book form. He envisaged a hierarchy of parks and reserves around Sydney.[23] The pollution of Sydney Harbour had been increasing from early colonial times and the need to treat sewage had become urgent.[24]

The papers by Bland and Rolleston acted as a stimulus to the young William Stanley Jevons (1835–82), a scientifically minded scholar who was employed as an assayer at the Sydney Mint. While Jevons was training to be a chemist, he was impressed by the work being done in the London slums by Henry Mayhew. Jevons had determined to study the rise of the new Australian towns and examine their populations and social characteristics while the colonial societies were forming and growing rapidly. He was well known for his 'Sydney by night', a series of articles about his nightly rambles about The Rocks district. He published various accounts of Sydney life in Henry Parkes' newspaper, *The Empire*, and in the columns of the *Sydney Morning Herald*, one with the alarmist title of 'The social cesspools of Sydney'.[25] His accounts of Sydney have become classic studies. He had a fresh and lively eye, completely dispassionate, and he was intrigued with the way the city was shaping up. Despite his years (he arrived in Australia when he was only nineteen), he was a skilled observer of colonial life. A compulsive walker, he made long journeys on foot to the Blue Mountains, the Illawarra region, around Sydney and to the goldfields, and was an avid reader and chronicler of places, people and events.[26]

The writings of Jevons foreshadowed some interesting later developments in city planning theory. He wrote the first 'social survey' of Sydney, and the technique he developed anticipated a long line of Australian town and city surveys carried out during the mid-twentieth century. He noted the types of houses and streets, the distribution of occupations, the arrangement of residential and industrial uses, and the classes of people who lived in the various districts. He sought ways to understand the process of growth. In the town of Goulburn, as an example, he was at a loss to understand how a town appeared there at all. Nevertheless, he plotted a social map of the town, indicating the different classes of buildings then appearing.

Bland, Rolleston and Jevons appeared in Australia at a crucial time when things were changing rapidly in the growing cities. There was serious consideration of what kind of society was forming and how its ideals could be formulated. They seem collectively to represent a practical critique of the direction of urban life and development after the first half century of imperialist settlement and town founding. They put into succinct form the concerns expressed by the members of the philosophical societies of both Sydney and Melbourne as they began to evolve as bodies able to comment on the need for local public intervention to improve urban life in the larger cities. It is noticeable that town planning (though it was not named as such), and the questions raised by the need to improve the infrastructure and workings of the capital cities, were dominant themes among the papers contributed to the meetings of the societies in the mid-nineteenth century. Charles Nicholson, president of the Philosophical Society, remarked that colonial life was made tolerable as it gave every individual of quality the opportunity to affect the course of history.[27] Members of the learned societies became involved in the tasks of writing, agitating, and then making political decisions to try to sort out the more pressing problems.

Towards the metropolis

The surge of migration that the gold rushes had triggered off meant that the cities had to cope with a vastly increased population. The simple components of the colonial town plans were severely tested and the servicing of the cities became compellingly urgent. Even so, services lagged badly behind population growth.

Slum clearance became an issue in the 1870s, and in Sydney the City Corporation began to pursue a policy of repair and demolition. By 1892, well over 2500 insanitary buildings had been repaired and nearly 2000 demolished. A smallpox epidemic in 1881 made the problem more urgent. It was not until 1896, however, that the colony's first Public Health Act granted the corporation firm authority to order the demolition of buildings.[28]

The years leading up to the turn of the century were characterised by steady growth in the two main metropolitan centres. Population in Melbourne grew enormously, from 268 000 in 1881 to 473 000 in 1891, reaching half a million by 1901. In 1890, Melbourne could boast that she was the twenty-second largest urban agglomeration in the world.[29] Sydney, on the other hand, jumped from 137 586 in 1871 to 224 939 in 1881, 383 333 in 1891, and 481 830 in 1901.[30] Its rise was not quite as spectacular as Melbourne's, and certainly not quite so self-congratulatory. The rivalry between the two cities grew endemic, and did nothing to foster inter-city cooperation.

The vigorous growth of the two major capital cities in the closing decades of the nineteenth century was applauded as a sign of progress, energy and enterprise, despite the problems that began to appear. The enterprise of their citizens in harnessing market forces in the creation of wealth was admired. Melbourne, in its buildings and services, was cited as a triumph of the market principle in the optimistic days of the boom of the 1880s.[31] Both Melbourne and Sydney began to assume the title of 'metropolis', and they began to evolve into more segregated, impersonal and competitive patterns. Even the governments were starting to behave in a 'mercantile' manner, in the way increased charges were made for their services. The capitals of the other states too, though not so large and not so metropolitan in feeling, were, from the beginning, centres of government as soon as they became centres of trade.[32]

Melbourne's growth, outstripping that of the first-founded and initially slow-growing Sydney, was based on three main factors. The first was its attraction of immigrants from Great Britain and the rush to the goldfields which were within a radius of 100–200 kilometres from the city. Second was the growth, in classical capitalist style, of import-replacing industries which generated a variety of trades and diversified products. A third critical factor was the will of the Victorian Government to protect local industries by high tariffs. The city assumed an overwhelming economic and political hegemony in its region. Pastoral products, though still important for export, were not crucial components of the city's growth. It is interesting to note that Hoddle, who planned the city in 1837, wrote that from the beginning it was assuming an 'upstart appearance of a metropolis'. Sydney, however, though not enjoying as great a surge of growth as Melbourne, was also prospering from the New South Wales goldfields. Though the goldfields were not as spectacular and were more remote from the city, the mining was sustained over a drawn-out period. The goldfields attracted a migrant population, most of which eventually drifted back to the city, boosting the skills of the urban population and swelling numbers to a critical threshold.

Both Melbourne and Sydney, like other Far Eastern cities developed by Great Britain—Singapore, Bombay, Calcutta and Hong Kong—were in the process of becoming 'existential cities', that is, providing in themselves both goods and services, and a strong internal market economy.[33]

Their positions were initially strategic, but when they began to grow as centres for their immediate regions, there arose a dynamic within them which utilised the sale of town land, the building of houses and central city buildings, and the provision of the servicing infrastructure, all based on opportunistic borrowing, to create an apparent climate of circulating wealth.

In the case of Melbourne, the city's economic influence reached beyond Victoria itself. The Riverina district of New South Wales looked to Melbourne as its main market and port. Victorian capital was invested in pastoral stations, in railways, and in electricity in other states. The sheer size of booming Melbourne and Sydney reflected their roles as centres of political life, financial organisation and communication networks. In each case, they had truly assumed the role of 'metropolis', in its modern sense, a word now used to denote a principal city of a state, a word which has largely displaced the older 'capital'. Both Melbourne and Sydney were founding metropolitan institutions in the second half of the nineteenth century. Both built universities, museums, art galleries and libraries; both built stock exchanges, insurance houses, large opulent banking chambers, churches and courts; and both set aside land for public parks and urban spaces. Professional bodies were forming in each city, and free education was becoming more widely available.

A new milieu for urban reform

The end of the century was a time for earnest self-appraisal. Previous patterns of metropolitan expansion were beginning to be questioned; new suburban patterns were seen as the way forward and new social groupings were hardened into distinct classes of workers. The union movement began to form, protecting individual gains. It was a time for theorising, and its achievement was, almost surprisingly, the collective decision of the six states to join into a united Commonwealth.

Late in the century, a new critique of urban problems began to surface, allied with a renewed look at the basic physical planning model. John Keily, a Melbourne surveyor, gave a paper to his institute in 1889 criticising the conventional extensions of towns as timid, ad hoc additions lacking any 'pre-existing design'. John Sulman, one year later, gave a seminal paper to the Australasian Association for the Advancement of Science (a body which had succeeded the previous philosophical societies) on town layout, advocating a spider's web design in place of the grid template and functional land use zoning for different purposes.[34]

In parallel with the trough of the 1890s, when the new suburban theories were circulating, there was a counter-movement to embellish the city core with dignified and stately parades and classically derived buildings. These ideas led to schemes for city improvement and re-planning streets, especially in Sydney.[35] In Melbourne, some streets were planted with trees from the 1880s, and a series of tall commercial buildings went up utilising the American invention of internal lifts. There were some non-utilitarian architectural styles, such as Art Nouveau, enjoying a brief, tentative beginning.

Model suburbs were being talked about. Experiments were being made with street widths, both wider and narrower. Annandale (1878) in Sydney was one of master builder John Young's schemes. The plan drawn up by F.H. Reuss Jr featured wide streets and lots, a waterfront crescent, reserved public building sites and small reserves. Another was the Kensington subdivision plan, aptly titled 'Rus in Urbe' by designers W.L Vernon, Howard Joseland and G. Voss Mocatta. Their ambitious plan for 1000 acres in Sydney's eastern suburbs, however, with services and roads being built before settlement, came at a bad time, just before the 1890s depression. It was abandoned, as was Hopetoun, a similarly ambitious planned suburban community in Melbourne.[36]

The most hopeful, if flawed, examples of a reforming impulse, can be found in more modest schemes in the outer suburbs of the growing cities, rather than in theoretical models on paper. After the northern suburbs railway was built in Sydney in the early 1890s, house-and-garden suburbs were planned by developers at various stations along the route, and there was an effort to establish all-residential communities, extolled for their healthful qualities. This proved to be a restricted vision, however, as it consciously excluded industry; minimal sites were set aside for public services, and further outward movement was encouraged. These northern suburbs became potential dormitory suburbs without a strong local economic or social life, where the journey to work dominated the movement pattern along the main spinal rail and highway link.[37]

Conclusion

The tendencies in nineteenth-century town planning can be briefly summed up as follows: it laid a solid basis for further development. Australian cities drew upon a revitalised colonial grid for their plans, and tempered them with the arrangement of parklands surrounding the city core. Physical planning settled down to a straightforward ground plan, which nevertheless implied a public commitment hedged about with an aura of special conditions which modified the simplicity of the grid and gave it a local and practical character suited to the Australian environment.

The watershed decade of the period was the 1890s, when economic depression hit the commercial life of the cities. This was the time when the system, so buoyantly created in the late nineteenth century, began to falter. Among the inhabitants of both city and country, there was disbelief, made harder by the former successes. Confidence, so easily gained in the 'long boom' of the 1870s and 1880s, was very easily lost in the unemployment and distress of the 1890s.

By the end of the nineteenth century the influence of the 'Grand Modell' was waning as utilitarian theories and laissez faire practices preceded the flood of immigration from the United Kingdom. The regularity of the streets and town blocks was criticised; new ideas from Britain and Europe were in the air. Ideas about healthy suburban life as a model were put against 'urban' congestion. John Sulman, hailed as the chief advocate of town planning in Australia, came out against the grid system. The ordered, standardised, predictable grid, its virtues forgotten, became relegated to the past, and an emerging town planning consciousness claimed it held the key to order, amenity and beauty through new techniques tailored for modern times.

2 From city improvement to the city beautiful

Robert Freestone

The 'Congress of Engineers, Architects, Surveyors, And Members of Allied Professions' held in Melbourne in May 1901 to consider 'Questions relating to the Laying Out and Building of the Federal Capital, and matters of Professional interest generally' was not only the first real opportunity for interested professionals to intensively discuss the planning of a new national capital, but also the first conference on post-colonial town planning staged in Australia. The proceedings were infused with an idealistic fervour deriving from the timing of the Congress: at the start of a new century, at the onset of a technologically informed modernist quest for the ultimate twentieth-century city, and in the earliest days of Federation—the Congress coinciding with the first sitting of Federal Parliament. With the return of economic health after the 1890s doldrums, interstate urban rivalries were rekindled; all the south-eastern capitals, it seemed, were bidding to be the 'Queen City of the South'. Competition was particularly intense between Sydney and Melbourne, each heading towards half a million in population. The relevance of the conference to the restructuring of these established cities, in order for their physical image to match their growth aspirations, would not have been lost on delegates.

Across twelve papers which varied widely in scope, intellectual rigour and technical content, an extraordinary array of issues were canvassed, including traffic flows, public transport, water supply and waste management, provision of parks and public gardens, controls on residential densities, building covenants, fire-proofing, and air-conditioning.[1] The importance of aesthetic elements relating to the location of public buildings, 'picturesque features' and 'schemes for architectural adornment' also emerged from the deliberations.[2] Many of these issues had been inherited from the milieu of nineteenth-century urban reform (see Chapter 1). The layout of new commuter suburbs, land subdivision, the breaking from gridiron street patterns housing quality and affordability, the development of network infrastructure, traffic improvements, the aesthetics of city building, and the impact of population growth on public health and environmental quality, were all current issues. The importance of the 1901 Congress was in beginning to pull these disparate threads towards a common goal: the planning of total urban environments.

While the Melbourne Congress indicated that Australian improvers were confident about enumerating components of a planned approach to urban development, there was less confidence about the overall package. The ideal city visualised was a dreamy concoction of grand public buildings, homogeneous townscapes, distinguished residences, noble boulevards, parks and parkways. The sources were both old and new world cities: Paris, imperial London and other European capitals; Washington DC, Chicago and other boom cities in the United States. The impulse toward a new civic art was global, but adapted to diverse cultural settings. This was what Charles Reade meant when he stated that in Australia 'the early conception of town planning . . . manifested itself not at all dissimilarly to antecedent developments in America and Europe'.[3] Each nation 'drew according to its own needs and possibilities',[4] with American responses to urban beautification codified most formally into a 'city beautiful movement'.[5]

Australians, as always, were alive to these overseas models, but comprehensive homegrown statements on urban improvement were few and far between. The cupboard was not completely bare, as the previous chapter has noted. Melbourne surveyor John Keily's suggested approach in 1899 to the 'harmonious whole' was for each planned community unit to have its own 'distinct character' and landmarks. John Sulman in 1890 had invoked the intersecting radial and circumferential lines of a spider's web as the preferred alternative to the colonial grid. This template offered both functional convenience and intrinsic potential for town decoration through placement of buildings. Other possibilities for beautification lay in curved streets, tree planting and open space. Sulman resuscitated this same influential model years later in connection with the federal capital (Figure 2.1). Surveyor–statistician George Knibbs developed Sulman's radial city into a rigorous mathematical statement in 1901.[6]

Despite these theoretical contributions, most contemporary distillations of the ideal urban environment assumed an empirical character. Sydney architect George Sydney Jones' emphasis on the need for 'some uniformity of spirit of design' was widely supported. But what did that actually mean? Jones himself ventured towards a consensual definition at the 1901 Congress:

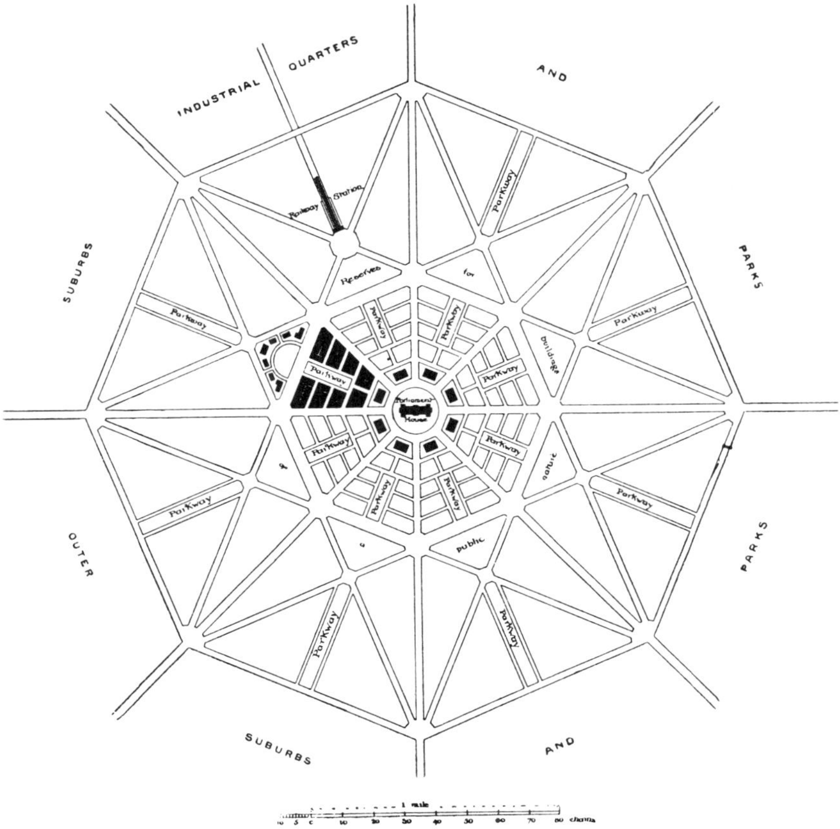

Figure 2.1 John Sulman's suggested plan for a federal capital of Australia (1909)

Source: J. Sulman, *The Federal Capital of Australia*, John Sands, Sydney, 1909.

> We are probably all agreed on general principles as to what the plan should be—for instance—that the streets should be wide and tree-planted, that the circus, the square and the boulevard, straight and curved lines, park lands, gardens and the like should find their proper places; that the public, semi-public and private building blocks should be disposed in due relation one to the other on sites best adapted for each, and with due regard to the future expansion of the City.[7]

Such statements reflect the way in which an aesthetic vision was a vital force in the emergence of modern town planning consciousness in Australia. The relevance of the principles listed by Jones to the design of completely new greenfields cities was readily apparent. There was also potential in the re-planning of older cities. How they might be systematically assembled and extended into a regional vision for an existing metropolis was less certain, but by the end of the 1900s that goal, at least, was closer to hand. The two major projects to advance the notion of metropolitan planning were the 1909 Royal Commission for the Improvement of Sydney and Its Suburbs, and the international competition for the design of the federal capital in 1911–12. These two events were preceded by a spate of piecemeal city improvement schemes. They were followed by an acceptance of the need for a kind of comprehensive planning in which civic art would be just one rather than the major objective.[8]

The ideology of civic beautification

At the turn of the century, informed opinion in architectural and artistic circles held that Australian cities had squandered opportunities to become refined, virtuous and artistic centres of urban civilisation. Most considered assessments were pejorative. For all their brash dynamism, Australian cities seemed ugly, dull, and lacking civic pride. They boasted few noble vistas, architectural squares or open space systems. The emerging central business districts were a chaos of uncoordinated building designs and heights, fire escape stairs, street awnings, advertising signs, and tram, telegraph and telephone wires.

C. Bogue Luffman described Melbourne as having 'the most uninteresting streets and surroundings of any great town in the world—convenient and clean—nothing more. No view points, no internal spaces, no dignity.'[9] There were snatches of urban beauty: individual public buildings, botanic gardens, avenues of trees, elite suburbs, and the serendipity of river and harbour settings. But of the capital cities, only Adelaide with its ring of parklands dating from the 1830s had a memorable urban form and made a strong case for the benefits of comprehensive civic design.

The hallmarks of the artistically planned city, which crystallised in the early 1900s, were order, harmony, formality and symmetry. The preferred architectural styles reflected establishment tastes, with a penchant for the neo-classical. Ruling tastes were captured fleetingly in the elaborate triumphal arches and other decorations erected along commercial streets on major state occasions such as visits by British nobility.[10] These networked, ephemeral displays were also important in seeding the idea of a wider scale of aesthetic-driven public intervention. Major civic buildings were preferably showcased on freestanding sites surrounded by parkland, squares or wide streets. Where there was the potential for several related government buildings, grouping in civic centres, rather than scatteration, was considered most desirable. Commercial skyscrapers were frowned upon. Harry Kent, when president of the Institute of Architects of New South Wales, expressed concern at the looming skyscraper problem on 'humanitarian, artistic, and precautionary principles'.[11] Securing uniformity of height emerged as a feasible strategy to inject some measure of aesthetic uniformity in business districts and helped sanction building height regulations exemplified in the New South Wales *Height of Buildings Act 1912* and Melbourne Building Regulations in 1916. Physical objects of desire included gateway and landmark features, parks, gardens, riverside drives and artistic street embellishments such as statuary and fountains. While the designed landscape was self-consciously mannered, remnant naturalistic environments along watercourses and around harbour foreshores were also valued.

For artistic inspiration, Australians looked to Europe as much as the United States. British hegemony meant that Australian designers were less constrained by the École des Beaux-Arts tradition which had such a stranglehold on American civic architecture and planning.[12] However, Australian improvers were clearly impressed and influenced by the efforts of the United States to come to grips with the problems of rapid urbanisation. Architectural and building journals from the 1890s carried frequent references to Washington, printed images of American park systems and park-like streets, and, increasingly through the 1900s, reproduced quotations from city beautiful advocates such as Charles Mulford Robinson, author of *Modern Civic Art* (1903), and Daniel Burnham, the influential chief architect of the Chicago World's Columbian Exposition (1893), member of the Senate Park Commission re-planning Washington DC (1901) and co-author of the seminal *Plan of Chicago* (1909). The latter plan not only represents the zenith of city beautiful thought, with its sumptuous images of a sophisticated, Europeanised city centre, but a crucial transition towards metropolitan-scale urban design, with its regional road network, parks and parkways.[13]

The beautification of the city was not conceived as an end in itself. Beauty had to be more than skin deep. A major premise of the American city beautiful movement was 'beautility', the idea that reform had to be useful as well as beautiful. The same practicality, and in particular the economic value of aesthetic improvements, was rarely forgotten in Australia. The maxim 'town planning pays' was frequently heard, often with reference to likely positive impacts on property values.[14] Utility itself had different connotations. For example, at a practical level, governmental civic centres not only delivered an attractive grouping of public buildings but also delivered improved communication within the bureaucracy. At a more ideological level, the fusion of artistic design and rational physical improvement targeted, if somewhat more nebulously, nationalism, citizenship, social cohesion and quality of life. In this sense, city beautiful aspirations were the first coherent encapsulation of the enduring environmentalist values associated with the town planning movement.

The logic of re-ordering and embellishing cities was ultimately linked to the promise of economic betterment. In essence, a beautiful city was also a progressive and prosperous one. Australian cities in the Federation era were keen to establish their competitiveness and attractiveness in a new political landscape in which positive foreign opinion and world city status were also at stake. In Hobart, for example, the city beautification movement was transparently linked to efforts to sell the city as a tourist destination.[15] The wisdom of Daniel Burnham was widely acknowledged: 'The delightfulness of a city is an element of first importance to its prosperity, for those who make fortunes will stay, and others come if the attractions are strong enough; and the money thus kept at home added to that freely spent by visitors, will be enough to ensure continuous good times.'[16]

Selling the city beautiful

The goal of a city beautiful was articulated primarily through professional and bureaucratic discourse rather than through any organised populist movement. Local 'progress associations' may have pursued a spectrum of parochial improvement issues, of which beautification might have been just one, but there appear to have been no formal citywide city beautiful–type bodies. And by the time voluntary town planning associations emerged in the second decade of the twentieth century, a more eclectic array of goals were in place. The theme of improved urban aesthetics as an integral element of town planning reform was most closely associated with a handful of local government reformers and architect—planners who sought, like their American contemporaries, to mediate 'tensions between civic ideals and commercial pursuits'.[17] Prominent in government circles were the politician John Fitzgerald (1862–1922) and the civil servant William Bold (1873–1953).

Sydney lawyer, trade unionist, alderman and state parliamentarian Fitzgerald was the most powerful political figure associated with the early planning movement. A politician in the progressive mould, he was planning's most urbane spokesperson, pitching his message to many groups, but in particular the 'citizen who wants to realise the best possibilities of the city beautiful'.[18] Fitzgerald had been involved in organising the New South Wales exhibits at the World's Columbian Exposition. Thereafter, he was able to highlight the valuable lessons in urban improvement to be learnt from America. But his ideas were eclectic. Drawing on British and continental precedent, he was equally at home preaching the necessity for public housing and state socialism as for ennobling artistic advancements. His life-long obsession was metropolitan government and the formation of 'greater' cities in the interests of coordination, efficiency and regional-scale design which were all hampered by balkanised local government. British-born Bold was Perth's leading public figure as town clerk for nearly half a century. A prime mover in securing a 'City Improvement Plan' for Perth in 1911, he was later active in the formation of the local town planning association and principal author of Australia's first comprehensive town planning legislation. Bold was 'anxious to mould Perth into a model city' and adopted the ideas and rhetoric of the city beautiful movement in pursuit of this ideal.[19] He played a key role in the beautification of inner areas of Perth and was instrumental in securing playgrounds, parks and parkways for his adopted city.

Architects formed the majority of artistically inclined urban improvers. From their ranks came the frequent suggestion that the goal of aesthetic improvement was best achieved by state governments establishing advisory bodies—'art commissions', 'courts of design' or 'councils of taste'—to advise on urban design matters.[20] The guru of the architect–planners was expatriate Briton John Sulman (1849–1934). As cities were composed primarily of buildings, it followed logically for Sulman that 'city planning was essentially an architectural problem'. Sulman was the leading planner of his generation, an influential teacher, commentator and practitioner who was close to the only truly genuine national figure in a state-segmented planning movement.[21] His influential writings on the design of the federal capital, the improvement of Sydney and principles of civic design culminated in the seminal *An Introduction to the Study of Town Planning in Australia* (1921).

The sphere of influence of other architects was more limited, but collectively their voices indicate the many early facets of artistically inclined design. John Barlow was a leading light in the New South Wales Institute of Architects and, as foundation editor, ensured the Institute's journal became a mouthpiece for city beautiful idealism and specific improvement suggestions. Barlow's most original musings centred on his attempts to reconcile the axiality of the full-blown city beautiful idiom with the informal beauty of natural environments and competing charms of pre-industrial cities.[22] On the other side of the continent, George Temple Poole was an active campaigner for an authority with powers over 'the improvement of the rivers and their banks . . . the formation of a civic centre from which branch or radiate the principal thoroughfares and streets and encircling boulevards . . . [and] provision of parks at various points'.[23] In 1915, Melbourne architect Harold Desbrowe-Annear won a competition to design a new campus for the University of Western Australia with a formal beaux-arts plan which guided development until the 1920s. In 1921 he applied similar principles in an ambitious project for the siting and design of a national war memorial in Melbourne, which aspired to a more fundamental reworking of street arrangements, park planning, and the location of public institutions.[24] As chief architect for the Commonwealth Government, John Smith Murdoch was involved in important civic design projects in Canberra, Brisbane and Perth.[25] Finally, many of the enduring images now associated with the city beautiful strand in Australian planning were the work of one individual, architectural draftsman R.C.G. Coulter. As early as 1901, Coulter had envisioned a waterside federal capital and over the next few years he painted a series of imagined cities for various federal capital sites investigated by the Commonwealth Government. His work on the federal capital culminated in his being awarded a consolation prize for an entry in the design competition submitted jointly with Charles Caswell and Walter Scott Griffiths. Coulter was also responsible for translating into pictorial form many of the improvement ideas considered by the Sydney Royal Commission in 1908–09, and he later provided attractive renderings for J.J.C. Bradfield's suggested improvements for the approaches to the Sydney Harbour Bridge, and at Lavender Bay and Circular Quay.[26]

City improvements: the Sydney experience

Privately floated improvement schemes have a long heritage. The various schemes which surfaced in all Australian cities during the 1900s continued a nineteenth-century tradition of reform generally stimulated by impending celebrations and unforeseen crises. The Sydney experience exemplifies this pattern and the evolution towards more comprehensive concepts. Two early catalysts were the search for appropriate civic projects to commemorate the centenary of British settlement in 1888[27] and the outbreak of bubonic plague in the summer of 1900. Ideas were promoted and debated but then abandoned because there was no overall framework for action. A City Improvement Board had been appointed in 1879, but it functioned mainly as an appeal body in relation to enforcement of building regulations rather than as a proto-planning agency.[28] Sydney architect–journalist Florence Taylor was the queen of the improvement scheme tradition into the 1940s and 1950s, but by that time her often eccentric visions of redeveloped precincts, tunnels and central city airports were seen as increasingly marginal to mainstream planning concerns.[29] In the early twentieth century such schemes were the virtual building blocks of planning agenda.

Through the 1900s, private improvement schemes continued to be discussed in daily newspapers and at professional meetings. Three trends were evident: more and more proposals surfaced as the new century brought a heightened appreciation of the city's problems and potentialities, the scale of proposed action increased as piecemeal suggestions were synthesised into more complex packages across broader geographical areas and an aesthetic dimension became prominent as the creed of beautility took hold: functional improvements could be attractive; attractive improvements must be functional.

Two of the more prominent discussants were Norman Selfe (1839–1911) and the ubiquitous John Sulman. Selfe was a distinguished engineer who, in various professional and public lectures from the turn of the century, incrementally fashioned a synoptic plan with many of his ideas being picked up by others. Among other things, Selfe called for the opening of new streets, the widening of old ones, intersecting both with 'garden spaces' and opening up 'noble vistas ... terminated by stately edifices'. The northern frontage to the new Central Railway Station would be redeveloped as 'a grand city centre adorned with lawns, flower gardens, fountains and bandstand'. A grand University Avenue would connect the Town Hall precinct to Sydney University. Observatory Hill would score a landmark building, waterside terraces would beautify the harbour foreshores, and new 'picturesque and sanitarially perfect' suburbs would be developed.[30]

Sulman's major statement was in a series of articles that appeared in late 1907 in the *Daily Telegraph* and were published early the next year as *The Improvement of Sydney*. The main objective of his plan, he told his readers, was to 'consider the needs of the City as a whole'. The centrepiece of the plan, which focused on the inner city, was a cruciform arrangement of two major streets, one running north–south down the axis of Elizabeth Street, the other east–west down a widened and extended Park Street. Addressing two of the most pressing contemporary accessibility problems, a new approach road to Central Station from the eastern suburbs was envisaged down Foveaux Street, while a waterfront drive around the eastern side of Darling Harbour to Dawes Point was proposed. The plan form is relatively simple, but would have required extensive cuts and tunnels to deal with topography. Sulman saw his traffic-orientated plan as embodying intrinsic aesthetic potential, but also suggested other possibilities such as the creation of a civic centre at Town Hall involving the relocation of St Andrew's Cathedral, the remodelling of Macquarie Street, arcaded streets and, wherever there was the space, 'a garden bed, a tree, or a few shrubs'.[31]

Such musings were set against a background of ongoing street widenings and resumptions by the City Council and other key statutory authorities, notably the Sydney Harbour Trust.[32] There was obviously no shortage of plans, both theoretical and practical, many responding to the potential of new technologies and construction materials. What was lacking was overall coordination—a general plan to integrate all the various facets of improvement. The idea of town planning in its modern sense emerges with this comprehensive goal in mind, driven overwhelmingly by an urban growth coalition: professionals with a stake in the built environment, business interests concerned with the movement of goods, senior public servants, local officials and politicians.

The state government politicians were the most reluctant players, as they were concerned about the financial cost and social ramifications of introducing new forms of state intervention into the market-driven city. But even they began to realise the need for an overall plan of attack. In October 1906, E.W. O'Sullivan, a former minister for public works, moved in State Parliament for a Select Committee to report upon 'the best suggestion for the improvement and ornamentation of Sydney, the suburbs and environs'. In the 'Federation euphoria' of 1901, O'Sullivan had proposed to redevelop Fort Denison for a 230 feet (70 metres) high memorial, 'Australia Facing the Dawn', as Port Jackson's answer to the Statue of Liberty.[33] It was precisely this kind of project which convinced commentators that development 'in a becoming manner' required some form of coordination.[34] O'Sullivan's idea lapsed, but by 1908 Sydney City Council was urging parliament to prepare the kind of strategic plan which was beyond its resources and limited area of governance: one which would vet all the various improvement schemes in the air and embrace the entire metropolitan region.

Sydney, 1909

The outcome of this lobbying was the first real systematic canvassing of city beautiful–type ideas in Australia: the Royal Commission for the Improvement of the City of Sydney and Its Suburbs. Established by the Wade Government in February 1908, the eleven-person body (all male, of course) was chaired by Lord Mayor Thomas Hughes, and included Norman Selfe and E.W. O'Sullivan. The Commission's mandate was to 'examine and investigate all proposals that may come before [it] for the Improvement of the City of Sydney and its Suburbs, and to fully inquire into the whole subject of the remodelling of Sydney', looking ahead 25 years. It was specifically directed to consider 'ornamentation and improvements as will tend to add to the attractions and beauty of the City and adjoining Suburbs'. The modus operandi adopted was a serial interviewing of all individuals keen to promote their own ideas. The Commission met 90 times to interview 40 witnesses, including luminaries such as Sulman, Fitzgerald, Barlow, government architect W.L. Vernon and the commissioner of railways, T.R. Johnson.[35] A final report was issued in June 1909.

The Royal Commission's final report should not be typecast as a city beautiful plan. The main preoccupation was traffic movement, particularly freight flows to and from the port zone. The overriding goals were a physical form and public infrastructure commensurate with Sydney's aspirations as the major economic powerhouse and trading centre of the British Empire in the South Pacific. The Commission eventually produced 60 specific recommendations (see Figure 2.2), heavily weighted towards new and reconstructed roads, but also encompassing improved public transportation, remodelling of slum precincts, provision of children's playgrounds, improved building regulations and endorsement of suburban living.

'Beautification of the City' was a significant though secondary component of the Commissioners' brief, although it was accepted that aesthetic improvements were fundamental to the dignity and future prosperity of Sydney. As Florence Taylor put it, Sydney had the potential to become 'the richest city in the world' so it was only proper that it be 'expected to dress for the occasion'.[36] The so-called 'decorative point of view' was a recurrent theme in evidence taken. The commissioners felt that the 'scheme of improvement' would generally contribute 'to the attractiveness of the city'. But numerous specific aesthetic projects were endorsed, such as a remodelling of the Central Railway Station precinct, an elevated railway station at Circular Quay, the replacement of Darlinghurst Gaol by a 'public building of national importance', conservation of 'natural beauty' and extensive tree planting where this did not interfere with traffic flow.

While the recommendations of the Commission were not implemented *in toto*, a schedule of public works had been drawn up for the following half century.[37] The Commission remains significant on other grounds. It helped articulate the dominant goals and values of modernist urban planning. Despite the neo-classical garb, the images associated with the Commission were indisputable expressions of modernity. The recurring underlying values were of linearity, uniformity, spaciousness, harmony, specialisation, order, efficiency and placelessness.[38] The Commission was also the first significant planning inquiry for any Australian city. It provided the first major public forum for informed planning debate in Sydney. And it effectively legitimised planning as an unavoidable obligation of the modern state.

However, the 1909 Sydney plan fell short of a truly comprehensive metropolitan strategy. It was more akin to the pragmatic 1907 plan of the New York City Improvement Commission than the contemporaneous Burnham and Bennett plan for Chicago. The Commission said that it did not attempt an 'ideal plan of city re-construction' for cost reasons

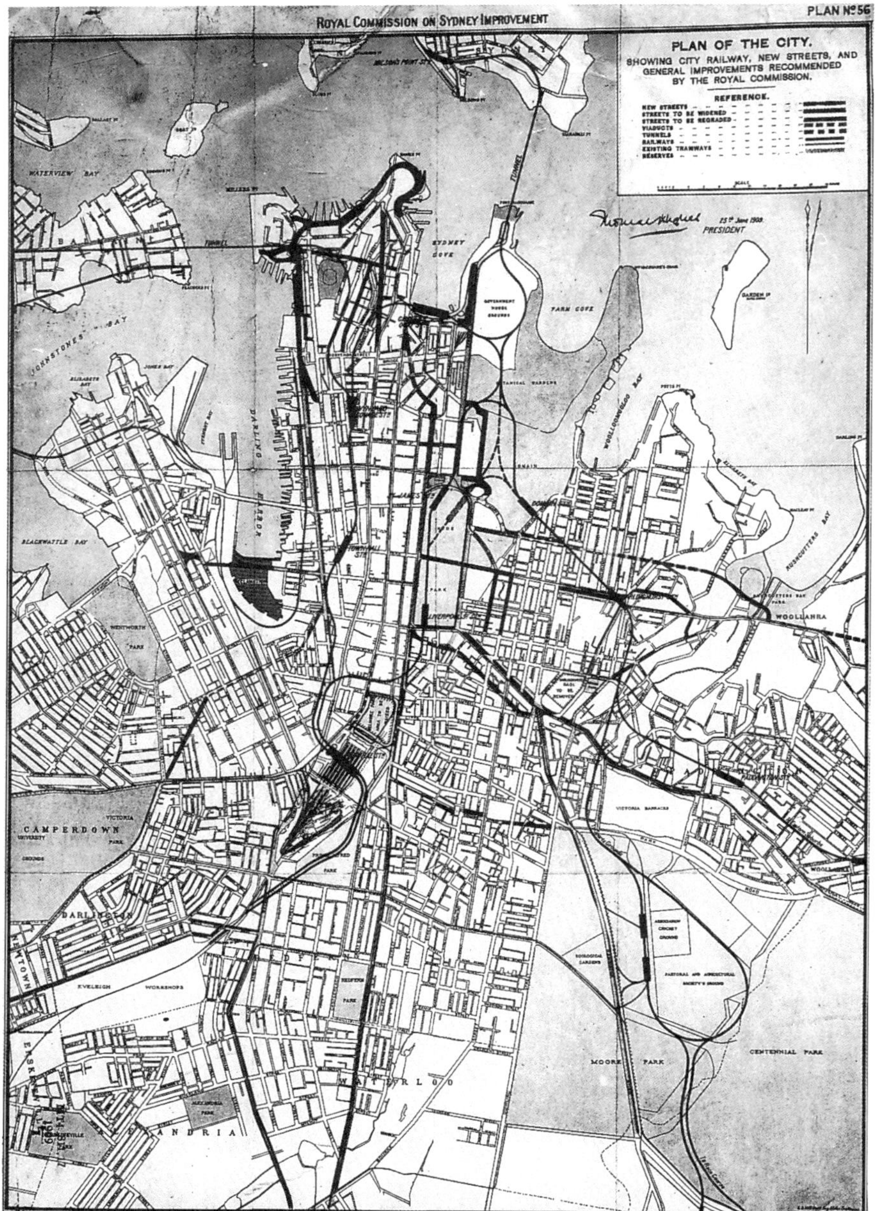

Figure 2.2 General plan of improvements for Sydney recommended by the Royal Commission (1909)

Source: New South Wales Parliamentary Papers, vol. 5, 1909.

and, as a result, the final inventory of individual recommendations lacked 'any ruling idea or organic coherence'.[39] An electrified suburban rail system extended into a city underground loop was endorsed. There was also enthusiasm for local authorities to be able to prepare the kind of statutory planning schemes that the British Parliament was considering at that time. Such legislation might ensure suburban development 'along harmonious lines'. But that was all. There was no holistic spatial vision. The hopes held by *The Bulletin* seem realistic: 'In the end, Sydney will be only a patchwork metropolis, but there is no reason why it shouldn't be a very beautiful patchwork.'[40]

Canberra, 1912

The federation of previously independent colonies as states, the formation of a new national tier of government and intense rivalry between the two major cities resulted in the idea of a new federal capital on the lines of Washington DC. The site on the Limestone Plains near Yass was confirmed in December 1908 only after a protracted 'battle of the sites'. Interest in the planning of a completely new city continued the process, commenced at the 1901 Congress, of coming to grips with precisely what was involved. It also opened up opportunities for more developed set-piece 'ground plans' of which Sulman's was the best known (Figure 2.1). At the same time, the Commonwealth Government began to look overseas for advice.[41] An international competition announced in April 1911 was the logical outcome of this process.[42]

While the competition was ignored by most of the big names of world planning at this time, 137 plans were submitted for judging by early 1912. They provide a kaleidoscopic overview of the state of town planning on the eve of World War One. The timing meant that city beautiful ideas would surface in many submitted entries and they are certainly there in the magnificent winning entry by Chicago landscape architect Walter Burley Griffin (1876–1937) and his wife Marion Mahony Griffin (1871–1961), albeit skilfully adapted to the 'irregular amphitheatre' of the site. The sources of the Griffins' remarkable plan are both complex and fascinating, intermingling artistic, sociological, philosophical and morphological ideas from an array of antecedents including Patrick Geddes, Christopher Wren, German Expressionism, and ancient and oriental cultures. Griffin was notoriously guarded about his influences. Incredibly, the fully developed, workable and brilliantly executed Canberra plan arrived with nothing in his past remotely approaching the same metropolitan scale, bar a mysterious 1906 extension plan for Shanghai.[43]

The city beautiful connections in the Griffins' Canberra were most evident in the central governmental core. The plans convey a monumental city dominated by grand axes and vistas, ensembles of monolithic buildings, terminal landmarks, citadels and 'cumulative massing'. Griffin had visited the World's Columbian Exposition as a high school student and it made a lasting impression, giving him his 'first lesson in town planning'.[44] The influence of the Exposition can be discerned in both the configuration of space at the core of his plan, with a formal grouping of uniformly scaled buildings set around a water court, and the inclusion of specific structures, such as a 'casino' and 'watergate' feature. Griffin described the major structures in this federal group as having a 'connected park or garden frontage . . . as in the case of the Mall at Washington'.[45] Lessons gleaned from the *Plan of Chicago* (1909) were arguably more influential. The 'dominating architectural feature' of the Capitol in the Griffins' plan was reminiscent of Burnham's towering civic centre. There was the same boulevardisation of waterfronts and accentuation of water-based leisure. Marion's brilliant artistic presentations recall the renderings of Burnham's illustrator, Jules Guerin, and amplify the intellectual linkages between the two plans.

The Griffins' plan was imbued with more obvious democratic ideals, complex geometry and symbolism than was typical of most city plans, even city beautiful ones.[46] It still embodied values and design elements which connect it to the evolution of a distinctive vocabulary of mainstream modernist planning: the holistic, organic approach to urban form and function; the predilection for specialisation of land use functions; the penchant for segregated residential spaces; and the idea of road hierarchies. The feature which really distinguishes the plan in this sense was its metropolitan scale. This was a plan which anticipated the long-term growth of the city. Few entries did likewise, although second prizewinner Eliel Saarinen submitted a remarkable satellite town plan in the image of Ebenezer Howard.[47] The critical diagram is the 'City and Environs' plan (Figure 2.3), a plan for a suburban metropolis structured around a triangulated series of specialised sub-centres and three times as large as the town of 25 000 population required for the competition. Predictably, British and European critics aligned to the picturesque planning associated with Raymond Unwin and Camillo Sitte saw only endless repetition of star-points and gridiron streets.[48] This misconstrued what was actually an innovative application of German-style extension planning—a general rather than detailed framework for orderly suburban growth. Here was a glimpse of the kind of comprehensive metropolitan master planning still lacking in metropolitan Australia.

The Griffins' plan in the fullest sense—as a three-dimensional urban environment, if not a work of art—remained a theoretical project.[49]

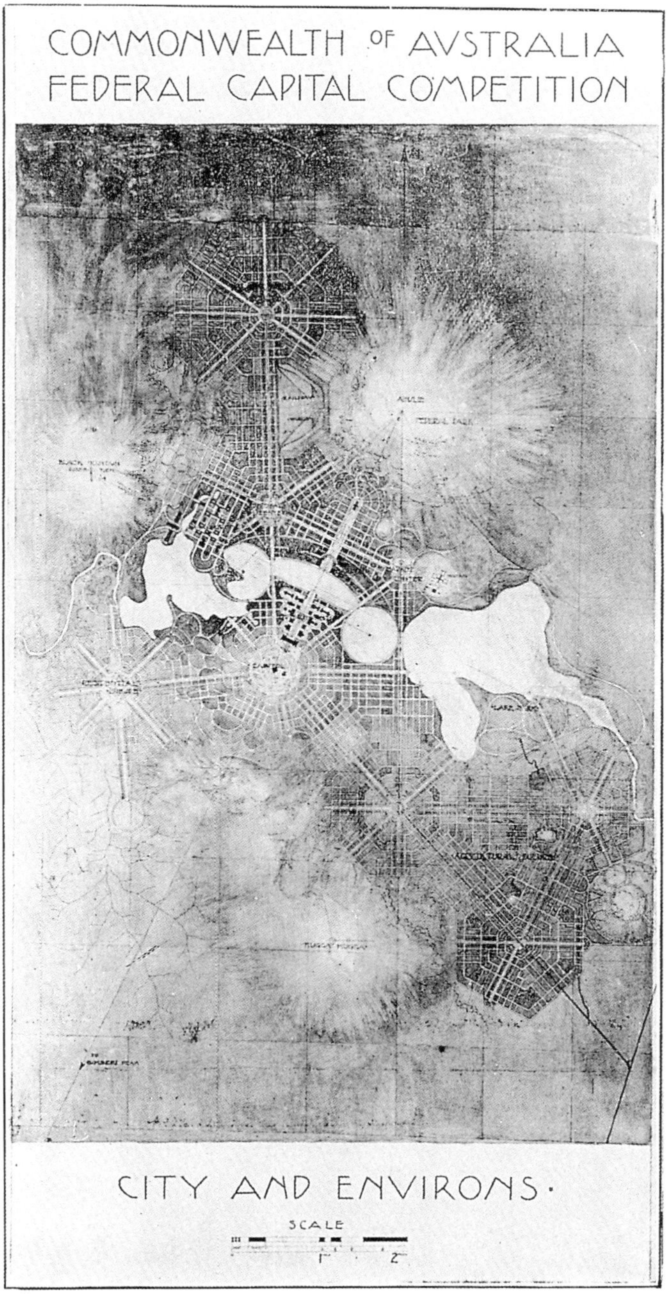

Figure 2.3 'Provision for Extension' in the Griffins' winning design for Canberra (1912)

Source: Commonwealth Parliamentary Papers, vol. 2, 1912.

The legacy in present-day Canberra is mainly restricted to the axial geometry of the central 'parliamentary triangle'. In 1921, John Sulman's Federal Capital Advisory Committee officially put the early quest toward the 'city beautiful of our dreams' on hold. Walter Burley Griffin resigned as federal capital director of design and construction, the need for 'utilitarian development and economy' became paramount and more cost-effective garden city concepts took hold. From that point until the late 1950s, the significance of Canberra as a planning achievement waned. Indeed, the struggling, sprawling town was to attract damning criticism from leading world planners such as Thomas Adams.[50] It had been very different a decade earlier. The federal capital project was an enormous catalyst in the emergence of an organised planning movement. Some of the crucial initiatives came from Sydney-based George Taylor rallying around Griffin and the Canberra plan when it was first under threat.[51] But, as discussed in Chapter 3, the organised planning movement would develop its own agenda divorced from the early seeds of urban beautification.

Beautifying the planned urban landscape

Clearly, Canberra was a special case. The rectilinear-polycentric form of the Griffins' plan had no significant contemporary influence, although it surfaced in one-off projects such as A.J. Macdonald's ideal soldier-settlement town for the Victorian Mallee.[52] But the winning entry glowed with powerful imagery suggesting how architectonic design could be injected into established cities for landmark status, sensory pleasure, and moral redemption. The notion that such aesthetic uplift alone was what town planning was all about was flittering away even as the Sydney Royal Commission got down to business in 1908. But beauty was now recognised as an integral component of planning along with other goals such as efficiency, economy and equity. Even as the touchstone of planning quickly moved onto ever more functional and legislative concerns through the 1920s and 1930s, urban beautification survived in what inter-war planning reports referred to as the issue of 'civic art and amenities'.

Paradoxically, aesthetic improvements still proved easier to achieve than social or legislative reform and many small-scale aesthetic improvements implemented by local and capital city councils were often the most visible outcome of planning in practice. There are numerous examples, from the design and setting of individual public buildings, planned civic spaces, foreshore and riverbank improvements, street widenings, parkways, street tree planting and war memorials, to the design of bridges and other engineering works such as electricity sub-stations and power houses. As in the United States, the city beautiful impulse was not always about state power or showcasing privilege but often touched humbler, more utilitarian planning exercises. Nevertheless, there were many ambitious plans never consummated, along with other schemes first aired in the 1900s which took an eternity to realise. An example in the latter category would be the protracted saga of dealing in design terms with the railway land which bifurcates central Perth and the related goal of grouping cultural institutions north of the tracks.[53]

Table 2.1 summarises some of the more notable developments whose origins lie partly in schemes for urban adornment. City beautiful theorising took on its own local character. For example, Melbourne's long-running obsession has been for a civic square, centre or landmark of some kind to compensate for absent natural environmental advantages. The Shrine

Table 2.1 Showcase planned precincts in the city beautiful tradition

Feature	*City*	*Key agents and designers*	*Project*
Boulevards	Melbourne	Melbourne City Council	St Kilda Road (1901)
	Sydney	Sydney City Council	Anzac Parade (1917)
	Perth	Perth City Council; Hope and Klem (town planners)	Oceanic Drive and The Boulevard (1930)
Public squares	Perth	Commonwealth Government; J.S. Murdoch (commonwealth architect)	Forrest Place (1923)
War memorials	Melbourne	Hudson and Wardrop (architects)	Shrine of Remembrance (1934)
	Brisbane	Commonwealth Government; S.H. Buchanan and Cowper (architects); J.S. Murdoch (commonwealth architect)	Anzac Square (1930)
Parks	Sydney	N. Weekes (town planner)	Hyde Park (1926)
Civic centres	Geelong	P. Everett, with Laird and Buchan (architects)	Johnstone Park (1916)

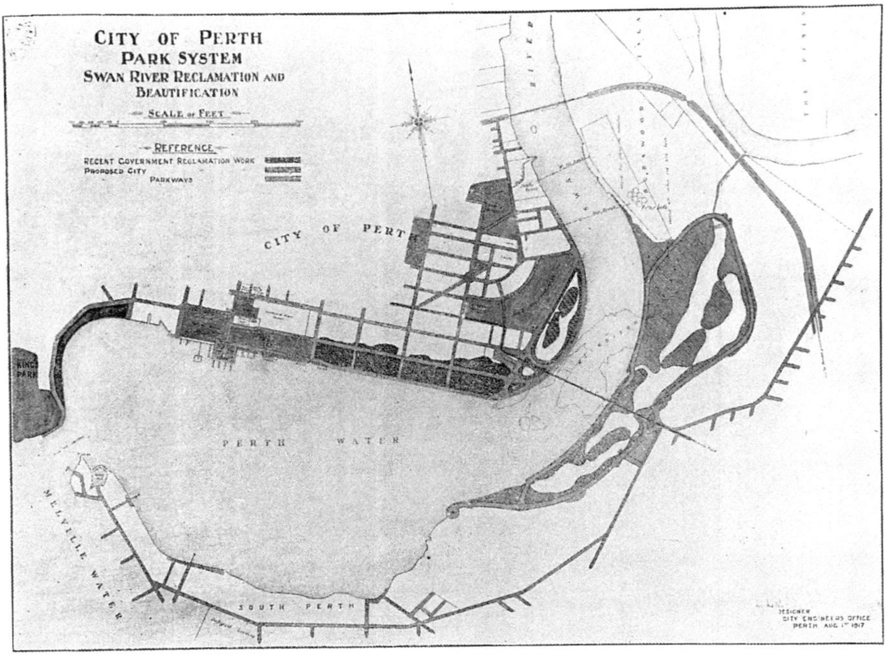

Figure 2.4 Suggested City of Perth park system (1917)

Source: Proceedings of the 1917 Australian Town Planning and Housing Conference and Exhibition, Vardon & Sons, Adelaide, 1918.

of Remembrance was the first edifice to deliver that objective in the 1930s (though the quest continues with Federation Square and at Docklands). In Perth, under the leadership of William Bold, a major concern was the provision of parkland and parkways, and even before the end of World War One the city had made the breakthrough towards the park system concept (Figure 2.4). Both in Perth and in Brisbane aspirations towards the central public squares largely ignored by the colonial surveyors were eventually realised in connection with Federal Government office plans. Although there were various schemes for the remodelling of Victoria Square,[54] the city beautiful ethos was more muted in Adelaide, still basking in its status as the original parkland city and with the local planning agenda set by Charles Reade more orientated to administrative concerns. It is easy to dismiss these various projects, big and small, as design determinism, but as Rybczynski reminds us, the goal of urban beautification was rarely an end in itself and did leave a legacy of usable and valuable spaces, buildings and environments.[55] By contrast, the treatment of the public realm in the renaissance of entrepreneurial urban design in the 1990s is far more problematical.

Conclusion

For a short time in the 1900s, the city beautiful movement seemed to best express the aspirations of urban reformers and progressive civic authorities. The aesthetic ethos, which helped catalyse modern planning consciousness in Australia, was a rather eclectic one, with both elite and utilitarian connotations, and drawing on American and British influences. There were always formidable obstacles to the wider realisation of city beautiful dreams. Beyond traditional Australian apathy towards 'utopian' schemes, the costs of implementing proposals were usually regarded as prohibitive by politicians already nervous about the state's direct involvement in urban development matters. The power of private capital to frustrate physical reconstruction involving freehold property holdings was well established. Even when aesthetic-based physical reform was sold as functional, cost-effective improvement, it ultimately failed to directly address more pressing and practical planning needs such as better roads, improved subdivision plans and adequate housing.

The idea of the city beautiful lingered on. For a time it seemed synonymous with the garden city in defining the quintessence of reformers' dreams.[56] But garden city concepts were cut from a different cloth—placing home near the centre of planning theory yet also carrying ideas about the desirable size, shape and direction of growth of cities not even hinted at by the city beautiful approach. As what the journal *Architecture* called in 1918 the 'veritable beacons of progress to all mankind' were redefined as places like Letchworth and Hampstead rather than Washington or Vienna, the cutting edge of planning moved away from civic beautification. The general closeness of traditional cultural ties with Britain and its planning movement became far more evident in the 1910s.

3 Towards metropolitan organisation: town planning and the garden city idea

Christine Garnaut

During the 1910s, an eclectic cohort of politicians, professionals, private citizens, and state and local government officials focused on pragmatic measures to improve the physical and social condition of the Australian city, remove its 'worn-out system of development'[1] and create a vision for its future. Campaigning individually and collectively in state-based town planning associations, these reformers heightened awareness of modern, overseas trends in city planning and management, instilled public confidence in the reforming potential of town planning and acted to address 'the whole problem of the proper organisation of city life'.[2]

The reform imperative of the 1910s—to 'improve the condition of urban life for the mass'[3]—dictated a broader agenda than that which had previously inspired the city beautiful movement. Nationally, a range of ameliorative action groups continued to lobby, as they had over several decades, in relation to specific issues such as public health, roads, transport, home and workplace conditions, civic design and eugenics; but other voices now entered the debates. Their particular concern was the detrimental effects of laissez faire capitalism and haphazard, unchecked development on land use, transport, housing, economic efficiency and the general wellbeing of the metropolis and its residents. They argued for an end to the piecemeal, 'happy-go-lucky' approach that had shaped the nineteenth-century city and its suburbs.

Reformers of the early twentieth century metropolis had a vision of holistic, as opposed to issue-by-issue, reform that encompassed not only physical improvement of the metropolis but also control of its administration and development. They sought an administrative mechanism with expertise to anticipate and prepare for the future, the authority to 'guide and regulate . . . growth . . . [and] coordinate the varied uses of the city',[4] and the legislation to bring their objectives to fruition. Thus, during the 1910s, the complex matter of city organisation and management and its realisation became part of the reform agenda. While the quest for metropolitan organisation was new for Australia, it was one that had already been embarked upon in other parts of the world. As was their predilection, Australian reformers looked to Britain for example and found it in the nascent movement for comprehensive town planning and the *fin de siècle* garden city paradigm of urban growth.

Town planning and garden city ideas

The subject of town planning more widely captured Australians' attention following the announcement in 1911 of the international competition to design a federal capital 'on Town Planning lines'.[5] With their country thrust onto the world stage, Australian reformers were forced not only to take stock of the state of the metropolis but also to acknowledge a 'world wide movement for the more effective planning of towns'.[6] Initiated in the 'old world', the movement responded to the physical and social problems precipitated by the rapid industrialisation and expansion of cities.[7] Town planning emerged as a tool for urban reform, and a set of clearly defined social, environmental and administrative goals was established. Broadly, these encompassed improved housing, sanitation and amenity to raise living and working standards, and to make people 'cheerful, hopeful and healthy'.[8] A 'guiding oversight and direction'[9] was perceived as essential to efficiently and effectively organise and control urban growth. Inspired by the example of Continental municipal reform, town planning advocates in Britain proposed legally sanctioned authorities to regulate, coordinate and control public facilities, utilities and metropolitan land use, present and future. In short, they called for anticipatory, comprehensive planning. The British *Town Planning and Housing Act 1909* embodied the goals of the town planning movement and became a benchmark for legislative efforts elsewhere.

Coterminous with the town planning campaign, the London-based Garden City Association (GCA) advanced social revolutionary Ebenezer Howard's garden city idea as a model for city planning and organisation, and as a way of giving 'new life and direction to suburban growth'.[10] Howard's vision of 'a healthy, natural and economic combination of town and country life'[11] offered a means to control overcrowding and expansion, redress rural depopulation, improve residential and workplace environments, and affirm the role of the individual and the home in the urban landscape. In his proposed model of urban reform—'Social City'—he demonstrated a means to check overpopulation and ill-regulated growth, reserve open space in order to shape and contain the city, and establish fully planned, self-contained communities.

Howard's argument for comprehensive planning and his suggested methods of residential development were a contemporary and enduring influence on international planning thought. The renowned exemplars, Letchworth Garden City (1903) and Hampstead Garden Suburb (1907), represented an environmental ideal readily embraced by the town planning movement. The principles that shaped the two- and three-dimensional form of these sites typified planning 'on garden city lines' and were popularly accepted as the suburban norm.

Architect–planner and leading garden city practitioner Raymond Unwin played a central role in both translating the 'detailed' site planning aspects of the garden city idea onto the ground and in marketing its 'larger', metropolitan aspects—decentralisation, satellite communities and reserved public land to keep the metropolis 'always within reasonable touch of open country'.[12] He suggested that if an 'unbuilt-on zone' was reserved around suburban extensions, then 'the Garden City method of development would be largely attained'.[13] Unwin illustrated this view, 'The garden city principle applied to suburbs', in his 'strategic'[14] monograph *Nothing Gained by Overcrowding: How the Garden City Type of Development May Benefit Both Owner and Occupier* (1912). Composed essentially of suburbs constellated 'as satellites revolving around the central sun town and separated by open park spaces',[15] Unwin's adaptation of Howard's idea also found favour in contemporary planning thought and, together with Letchworth and Hampstead, helped take the garden city idea to the world.

Metropolitan cities without metropolitan plans

The Royal Commissions for the Improvement of the City of Sydney and Its Suburbs (1909) and on the Housing of the People (Melbourne, 1913–15) heightened public and municipal awareness of the physical condition of the early twentieth century Australian metropolis. Official reports filed by local government authorities, including transport, municipal health and medical officers, provided ample evidence of the disarray. Typically, the metropolis was characterised as 'a metropolitan city without a metropolitan plan'.[16] The boundaries of the original capitals had shifted to encompass a stew of suburbs and subdivisions that oozed from the fringes. Suburban extensions comprised streets, building blocks and dwellings but were largely devoid of natural features or public recreation space. Apart from Adelaide, with its much admired encircling ring of parklands, 'the city and suburbs [were] continuous, forming a vast area of streets and dwellings without any ready access to open country for public use'[17] (Figure 3.1).

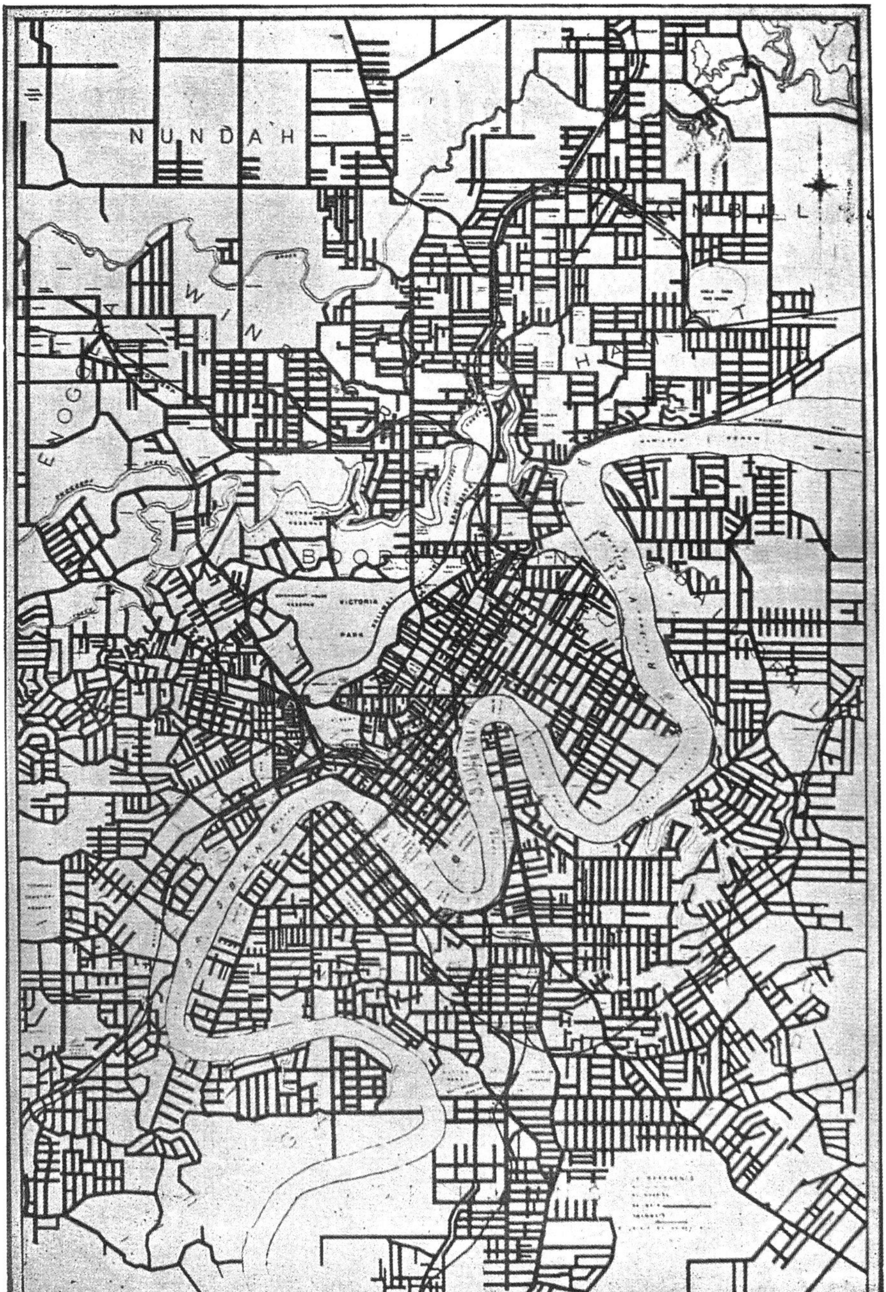

Figure 3.1 Map of the City of Brisbane (c1917)

Source: C. Reade, *Report on Planning and Development of Towns and Cities in South Australia*, SA Government Printer, Adelaide, 1919.

'Go-as-you-please' development had led to private investors controlling the location and practices of industry, and the construction and condition of factories and houses. Factories 'invaded residential areas',[18] contributing to visual, noise and air pollution. 'Excessive subdivision of land and ... low-quality housing'[19] was common for the working classes. Prior to the 1910s, the state played no part in housing its citizens. Individuals either constructed their own homes or rented privately. There were limited local regulations controlling the height, design and placement of dwellings (and other building types), and no controls over rent. Landlord exploitation of tenants was rife.

Transit routes—roads, tram tracks and railway lines—had seemingly evolved as and where they were needed, and by the 1910s many were rendered inconvenient or inefficient. In the city centre, dead-end, narrow, incorrectly graded or uneconomically wide streets were common. The increasing use of trams and motor vehicles aided suburbanisation as the former became the principal means of public transport to the suburbs. But convenient automobile cross routes and circumferential or ring avenues were generally lacking.[20] The misplacement of railways also caused concern. For example, in Perth their siting was considered

> a most flagrant example of disregard of city well-being. There in the midst of its way of communication, disconnecting nine-tenths of the citizens from the centre of civic life in rude severance, are the railways, and the great area of yards and squalid sheds ... Night and day trains, conveying goods from and to the Port, are dragged shrieking through the heart of the city and all amenities are subordinated to this form of traffic.[21]

'City muddling'[22] arose in the absence of a formal system of metropolitan management. There was no overseeing government authority and cities were divided into numerous separate and independent councils. For example, in Adelaide in 1919 there were three city corporations, including one for the City of Adelaide, six municipal corporations and sixteen district councils. Sydney and Melbourne each had a city council and 53 and 22 municipal councils respectively.[23] 'Every one of them had its mayor or chairman, its ... [councillors], its town or district clerk, its officials and its labourers, all housed in a town or district hall.'[24]

Councils had limited powers and little control over development within their boundaries. The consequence was a tangle of statutory authorities and local councils variously responsible for public utilities such as railways, trams, harbours, roads and bridges, water supply, lighting and sewerage; constructing public buildings; maintaining roads; and attending to matters related to health and sanitation.[25] There was considerable dissatisfaction with this disorder and 'a growing consciousness ... that some comprehensive machinery, some wider conceptions of municipal life were needed to control the suburban growth'.[26] In that milieu, town planning and garden city ideals gained popularity.

Towards an organised town planning movement

In the 1910s, city beautiful advocates introduced in Chapter 2, notably John Sulman, John Fitzgerald and William Bold, turned their interest and attention to the wider subjects of town planning and garden cities. Together with other reformers[27] they gleaned information about international developments from publications, study trips, conferences and world tours, and transferred their knowledge to the populace via professional and community connections, and local government affiliations. But the inspiration and challenge of the federal capital competition and the 1914 Australasian Town Planning Tour by Charles Reade (1880–1933) and William Davidge provided the impetus for like-minded individuals to unite in collective, organised action through state-based town planning associations. Although no national association emerged, the state bodies effectively constituted a town planning movement that provided the ground swell of support for modern city planning ideas and methods, and for legislation to effect them.

The Town Planning Association of New South Wales was formed in October 1913 under Sulman's presidency. By the end of 1916 there was a similar body in every state.[28] Membership was open and voluntary and reflected the broad base of support for town planning—private individuals, professionals, politicians, and representatives of community and welfare groups. Adopting largely propagandist and educative roles, the associations sponsored and arranged lectures, circulated planning literature, lobbied parliament and local government, and occasionally involved themselves in specific projects. While the New South Wales Association could claim status as the inaugural town planning body, the South Australian Town Planning and Housing Association, constituted in 1915, developed a local and national profile due to the fervour and tenacity of its propaganda campaign. Among its more ambitious publicity projects was *The Light Journal of Town Planning*, a slim, one-off volume published in June 1920 largely in support of the *Town Planning and Development Bill 1919*. While each town planning association pursued locally pertinent objectives, they all championed comprehensive legislation to eliminate the free rein of private investors, to address the physical problems of the city and to remedy the fragmented nature of metropolitan governance. A variety of implementation models were suggested, including larger metropolitan councils such as 'Greater Brisbane', state government appointed central town planning authorities and advisory commissions of experts.

The South Australian Government took the lead in initiating legislation when it appointed Charles Reade to assist in drafting a Town Planning and Housing Bill. The South Australian Town Planning and Housing Association rallied behind Reade in 1916 and again in 1919–20 when the Town Planning and Development Bill 1919 was mooted to replace its unsuccessful predecessor. In Brisbane, the *City of Brisbane Improvement Act 1916* was directly influenced by the Queensland Town Planning Association's campaign for city improvement.[29] Legislation informed by the South Australian Bill was proposed in Perth and Hobart, and supported respectively by the Town Planning Association of Western Australia and the Southern Tasmanian Town Planning Association.[30] Outcomes of this legislative drive initiated in the 1910s are discussed in Chapter 4.

Support for town planning reached its crescendo towards the end of the 1910s when delegates from town planning associations around Australia, state and local government representatives, and members of the professions and the general public conferred at national conferences in Adelaide (1917) and Brisbane (1918). As the number of delegates suggests—over 250 attended the first and 600 the second—both were major, focal events in the life of the town planning movement. The two conferences gathered reformers from around Australia in the one location to air their concerns, deliberate over ways in which these concerns might be addressed and challenge one another to action. The conferences were an invaluable means of disseminating information and knowledge not only through the presentation and publication of papers but also via exhibits of photographs, plans, maps and drawings associated with town planning schemes around the world.

John Fitzgerald presided over both meetings. His stirring opening speeches addressed the mission and potential of town planning to 'change the destiny of the urban population'.[31] In 1917, prominent town planning advocates, including George Temple Poole and William Saw (from Western Australia), Edward Rigby, T.G. Ellery and James Morrell (Victoria), Crawford Vaughan, Albert Conrad and Charles Reade (South Australia), John Sulman, George Taylor and J.J.C. Bradfield (New South Wales), Thomas Price (Queensland), and Walter Burley Griffin, contributed ideas, visions and strategies about how change could happen. Their papers dealt with the issues of the day: housing, sanitation, amenity, roads, traffic, expansion and layout of suburbs and subdivisions, parks, development control and town planning legislation. The speakers (and their audiences) were clearly imbued with enthusiasm for, and confidence in, the redeeming powers of town planning and in its social, civic and financial dividends: slum eradication; housing equity; clean and efficient workplaces; healthy, comfortable, visually appealing living environments; ample public recreation space; effective transport routes; morally uplifted, happy and contented citizens; improved land and property values; and 'the economic conduct of trade and commerce'.[32]

Although one year later, delegates' enthusiasm and confidence remained high, the idealism of Adelaide was tempered and the tenor of the Brisbane meeting was more pragmatic. Municipal administration and legislation remained on the agenda but were addressed less frequently. Matters relating to the functional effectiveness of the city were dominant with Sydney surveyor and real estate agent Henry Halloran presenting the objectives and benefits of land use zoning while others raised the classification of roads, traffic flows and the coordination of public services as priorities. Repatriation emerged as a major theme in 1918 as the nation and individual states faced the reality of housing and employing World War One veterans. Concrete proposals were forwarded for schemes that accommodated soldiers and civilians, for example, Darra Industrial Garden City near Brisbane and the Mitcham Garden Suburb on the outskirts of Adelaide. The very title of these projects suggested the influence of garden city ideals; such ideals were also obvious in William Bold's discussion of the type and distribution of open space around Perth.

Metropolitan applications of the garden city idea

The 1914 Australasian lecture tour by Davidge and Reade was an invaluable tool for alerting Australians to town planning and garden city ideals and to the potential suburban and metropolitan applications of Howard's idea.[33] The two lecturers were well qualified for their mission. Architect, surveyor and civil engineer Davidge was a member of the executive of the London-based Garden Cities and Town Planning Association (GCTPA), successor to the GCA. Prior to the tour's commencement, he spoke, by invitation, about town planning and the garden city movement at the Melbourne meeting of the British Association for the Advancement of Science. New Zealand–born Reade, a journalist turned town planning advocate, was one of the leading propagandists for the garden city movement outside Britain. His training and duties in the offices of the GCTPA honed his understanding of the theoretical and practical components of the garden city idea and exposed him to a range of international developments planned 'on garden city lines'.[34] The Australasian tour launched his career as a town planner.

In the wake of the success of the tour, Reade was appointed adviser on town planning to the South Australian Government and, two years later in 1918, government town planner. An able administrator, he headed the drive for legislative reform, prepared designs for public and private commissions, and was the leading figure behind the Adelaide and Brisbane conferences. Reade actively encouraged, supported and affirmed the efforts of town planning associations across the nation, frequently corresponding and meeting informally with key state advocates.[35]

Prior to the 1914 tour, news of the garden city idea filtered into Australia through a variety of channels.[36] It was publicly introduced in newspapers, journals such as *Salon* and *Building*, addresses to professional bodies associated with town planning, local government reports, and plans for pioneering experiments such as the model suburb of Daceyville (1912) in Sydney. Initially, the focus of its application was on the garden city as an environmental ideal and on the 'site planning "principles" to realise that ideal'.[37] However, the Davidge–Reade tour alerted Australians to the 'larger' aspects of Howard's idea and these helped 'local planners and reformers articulate certain ideas about the desired shape, structure and size of the metropolis'.[38]

Reflecting the influence of garden city thought, Australian reformers began to focus on ways in which reserved open space—an element largely ignored in newly developed suburbs and subdivisions—could be incorporated into the existing and expanded metropolis. Proposals utilised agricultural or green belts in the form of parklands, parkbelts, parkways, radial parks or green girdles for various ends: to contain urban expansion, to frame development, to provide contact with nature, to create a *rus in urbe* character and secure recreation areas or land for agricultural production. As Table 3.1 indicates, there was variation in the preferred location, type and function of metropolitan open space. None of these schemes was executed but several examples point to the diversity of ideas and schemes.

West Australian architect George Temple Poole's 1911 plan for 'Perth as it should be' proposed to bring the populace into contact with nature by linking existing parks, public gardens and unimproved open land in a half-mile (0.8 kilometre) wide, twenty mile (32 kilometres) long 'girdle of forest or parkland'[39] encircling the city. Initially a supporter of Poole's green belt, Town Clerk Bold later suggested a series of boulevards connecting existing suburbs. The boulevard concept derived from the United States (which Bold visited in 1914) and, like the parkway, was conceived 'as a means of making the parks accessible to the people and of connecting one park with another . . . they are of ample width . . . and the space not required for traffic purposes is laid out in lawns, flower gardens, plantations, shrubberies'.[40]

A call for open space as a tool for metropolitan containment came in 1913 from South Australia's Intelligence and Tourist Bureau director

Table 3.1 Proposed metropolitan applications of the garden city idea, 1910s–20s

Date	*City*	*Proponent*	*Proposal*
1911	Perth	G. Temple Poole	Girdle of parklands around city centre linking up existing reserves
1911	Perth	W. Bold	Green belt around the city
1913	Adelaide	V. Ryan	Outer ring of parklands
1914	Perth	W. Bold	Wide ring of boulevards around the city
1914	Sydney	J. Sulman	Reserved green belts between suburbs
1917	Adelaide	C. Reade	Metropolitan plan for Adelaide
1922	Canberra	J. Sulman	Planetary suburbs model
1923	Melbourne	Victorian Town Planning and Parks Association	Girdle of parklands and agricultural belt beyond the suburbs
1925	Sydney	Sydney Regional Plan Convention	Satellite towns separated by agricultural strips
1928	Brisbane	William Earle	Agricultural belt surrounding the city

Source: Based on R. Freestone, *Model Communities*, Thomas Nelson, Melbourne, 1989.

Victor Ryan. Although predating the Davidge–Reade tour, Ryan's suggestion of a conference of municipal councils to consider 'securing, in the near future, an outer belt, or circle, of Parks and Open Spaces . . . [to] protect . . . against future crowding'[41] was clearly informed by the garden city message. The circle of green was not achieved but resurfaced as a major element in Reade's 1917 plan for metropolitan Adelaide, discussed later in this chapter.

Agricultural belts were also favoured by proponents of some schemes. The Victorian Town Planning and Parks Association suggested one for Melbourne in a 1923 proposal to the Metropolitan Town Planning Commission. The belt was suggested as a way of limiting the size of the metropolis and of securing agricultural land in close proximity to the city. In 1928, Brisbane City Council's town planner William Earle drafted a metropolitan plan that featured an agricultural belt as a frame for the city.[42] Each of the examples noted applied one larger aspect of the garden city idea to the metropolis. There were, however, two schemes that drew more extensively on the ideas of Howard and Unwin—Reade's plan for metropolitan Adelaide (1917) and the Hope–Klem Perth Endowment Lands project (1925).

The 1917 metropolitan plan for Adelaide

Reade's 1917 master plan for metropolitan Adelaide (Figure 3.2) further informed Australians about the concept and advantages of comprehensive planning. In particular, it showed how decentralisation, satellite communities and reserved open space could be applied to guide the future development of the metropolis. Reade emphasised that his scheme was not a complete proposal but rather a 'preliminary programme of development and improvement, anticipating the probable future needs and growth of the . . . city'.[43] He regarded such a program as an essential reference document. Fulfilling its educational function, the plan was placed on public display at the First Town Planning and Housing Conference in 1917 and was later published in official documents.

Apart from the original drawing, a short commentary in Reade's 'Report on planning and development of towns and cities in South Australia' (1919), and references in Liberal parliamentarian Henry Barwell's speech on 'Soldiers' Settlements' at the 1918 Brisbane planning conference, no contemporary documentation survives. However, these sources are sufficient to compile a summary of the major elements of Reade's plan. They included:

- a separate industrial and factory zone at Port Adelaide with an adjacent model housing area for workers
- an outer ring of parklands combined with a parkway boulevard located on the suburban fringe
- a parkway of public parks and reserves following the line of the River Torrens from the hills in the north-east to the sea at Henley Beach west of the city
- new arterial roads from the city to the suburbs and to Port Adelaide
- new roads between the suburbs
- a major rail link from the city to the docks and factories at the port
- garden suburbs as satellite residential communities on the outskirts of the city
- new seaside suburbs beyond the outer ring of parklands
- undeveloped suburban areas earmarked for town planning schemes
- foreshore improvements including a marine boulevard between Marino

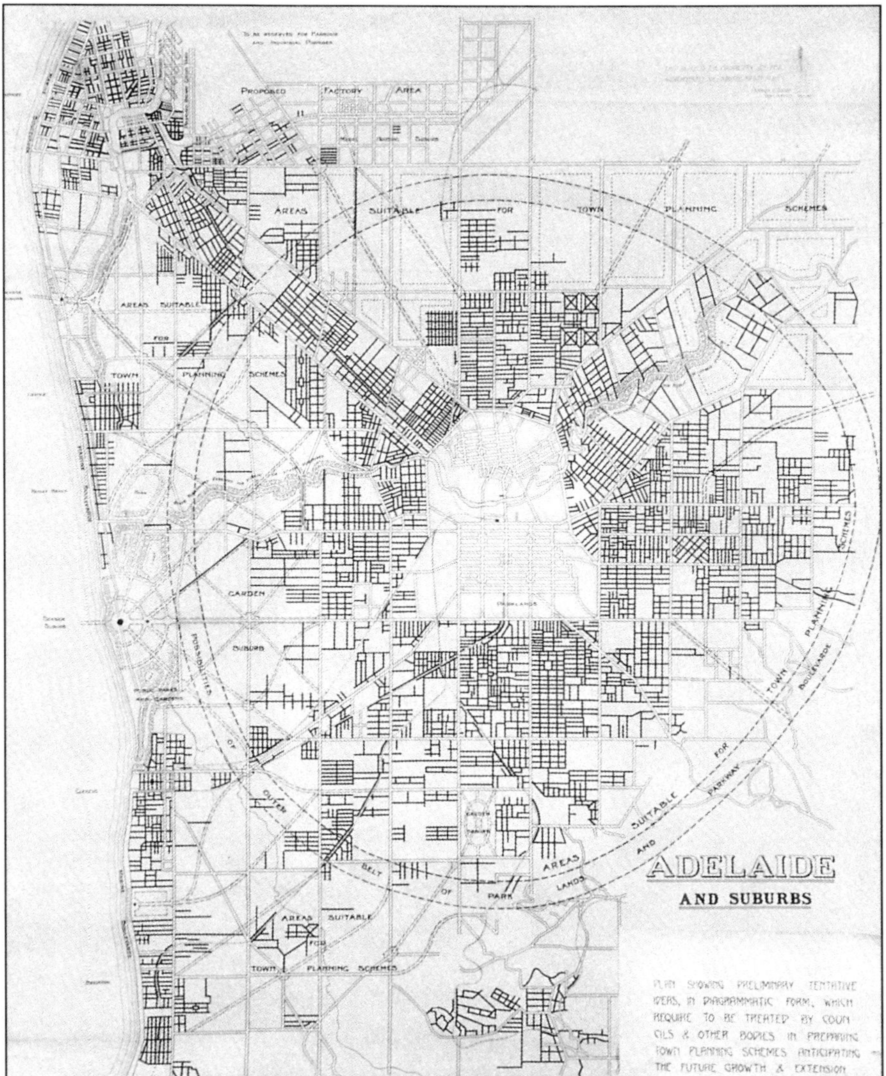

Figure 3.2 Adelaide and suburbs plan by Charles Reade (1917)

Source: Original plan held by City of Mitcham local history collection. Photograph from a transparency held by Colonel Light Gardens Historical Society.

in the south and Outer Harbour in the north to create public reserves and link existing with new coastal development.

Overriding Reade's scheme was a sense of imposing a spatial order that contrasted sharply with the 'muddlement'[44] of the existing metropolis. In a rudimentary way he was following Unwin's goal of bringing form into formless space. Reade recognised the existing functions and activities of the city and integrated them into a cohesive plan that clearly allowed for future growth. After Unwin, he reserved open space between residential communities to keep them in contact with nature and prevent their merging as one undefined mass. The River Torrens parkway and the coastal boulevard of public reserves reinforced the theme of linking people and nature.

At the time of its exhibition, the 1917 plan attracted little attention or public comment, apart from Sulman's favourable reference to its parkland and open space provisions.[45] There was no similar attempt in the 1910s to develop a comprehensive capital city master plan, let alone one that incorporated the larger aspects of the garden city idea. Nonetheless, Reade's scheme captured the direction in which reformers of the Australian city wished to move—towards a holistic approach to city planning—and should be recognised as the inaugural 'conscious attempt [in Australia] to plan land use and transport patterns at metropolitan scale'.[46]

Although no other blueprints emerged, an alternative model of metropolitan expansion could now be crystallised by Sulman in his planetary suburbs scheme, a model 'on a par with Unwin's "garden city principle applied to suburbs"'[47] (Figure 3.3). Sulman foreshadowed the idea in 1890 but gave it more complete expression in 1914 in a paper delivered to the British Association for the Advancement of Science Conference. Among his suggested improvements for Sydney was one similar to Unwin's earlier proposal: 'the reservation wherever possible

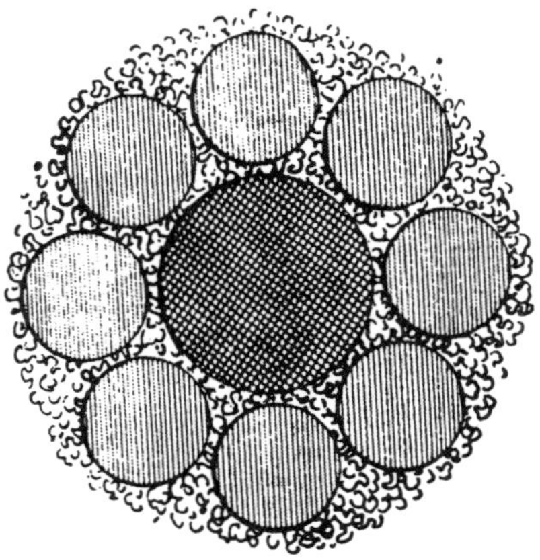

Figure 3.3 Sulman's planetary suburbs scheme

Source: J. Sulman, *Town Planning: A Sketch in Outline*, NSW Government Printer, Sydney, 1919. Digitised image courtesy P. Knight.

of belts of open land in perpetuity between suburb and suburb, so that the Greater Sydney of the future may consist of the city proper and a number of subordinate but economically self-contained and independent centres, and thus avoid the formation of a single large congested city area'.[48] Sulman did not translate the idea into schematic form, but illustrated the general principle in *Town Planning: A Sketch in Outline* (1919), also advancing it in the early 1920s as a basis for the planning of Canberra.

The Perth Endowment Lands scheme

In Perth the garden city idea had a significant influence on plans for the Endowment Lands, an estate of approximately 3500 acres (1417.5 hectares) owned and administered by the City Council under the *Perth Endowment Lands Act 1920*. The large unimproved tract lay west of the city and extended to the coast. It was first made a subject of public discussion in 1901 with the garden city a predominant theme from 1902.[49] At the 1917 Town Planning and Housing Conference, Poole referred to a plan to lay out the Endowment Lands as 'an extension of the city, as a garden suburb for residential purposes with a seaside, watering pleasure town on the ocean front'.[50]

In 1925, Perth City Council invited the local surveying firm of Percy Hope (1883–1952) and Carl Klem (1885–1979) to prepare a design using guidelines established in 1917 by the Perth Endowment Lands Committee and informed by Bold's 1914 world study tour.[51] Hope and Klem planned for two physically self-contained satellite communities, one on the coast and the other inland[52] (Figure 3.4). The two suburbs were generously separated by parkland—described by Poole as 'wooded hills and valleys'—but connected by two boulevards. The suburbs were built in satellite relationship both to each other and to the central metropolis, and in that regard represented a 'close approximation'[53] of Howard's 'Social City' model. Each had its own distinct layout and character determined by its primary function as either the inland residential town (Floreat Park) or the coastal recreational resort (City Beach).[54] Although the recommended physical plan of both townships was altered, the dividing green belt of parkland survived and today exposes 'the amenity value of breaking up continuous suburban sprawl with belts of open country'.[55] The Perth Endowment Lands scheme was deliberately planned to demonstrate how the garden city idea of satellite suburbs and reserved open space could be used to shape and control the expansion of metropolitan Perth. It was the only on-the-ground example of its kind to emerge in Australia in the 1910s.

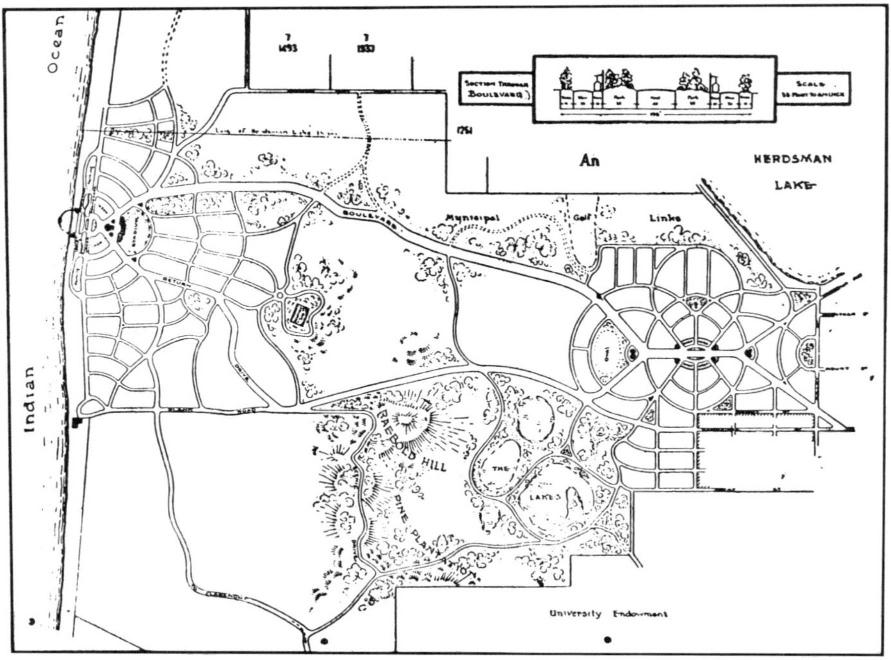

Figure 3.4 Master plan for the Perth Endowment Lands (1925)
Source: Perth City Council, *Lord Mayor's Report*, Perth City Council, Perth, 1926–27.

'Town planning on garden city lines'

Although the garden city idea made negligible impact at the metropolitan level, it did noticeably affect the layout of suburbs and subdivisions in metropolitan areas as well as regional and rural towns. Through its influence, 'the allocation of extensive urban open space as a way of creating a *rus in urbe* became a mandatory part of the planning process'.[56] The garden city idea challenged existing methods of residential development by advocating systematic, comprehensive planning in preference to subdividing, that is, merely cutting land up into streets and the maximum number of housing blocks. Garden city site planning principles offered an alternative to the usual gridiron pattern of street layout as well as 'greater opportunities for social intercourse'[57] through the provision of sites not only for housing but also for recreation, learning, worship, administration and commerce.

Inspired by the garden city campaign, the social imperative to improve housing conditions, the post-war shortage of homes and financial opportunism, the state as well as corporations, companies and private investors in every Australian state established residential environments 'on garden city lines'. These took the form of garden suburbs, subdivisions,

Table 3.2 Suburban examples of environments planned 'on garden city lines', 1910s–20s

Project type	*Name*	*City*	*Sponsor/original designer*
Garden suburb	Daceyville (1912)	Sydney	NSW Government/ J. Sulman
	Colonel Light Gardens (1917)	Adelaide	SA Government/C. Reade
	Garden City (1925)	Melbourne	Victorian Government/ F. Cook
	City Beach/Floreat Park (1925)	Perth	Perth City Council/ P. Hope and C. Klem
Garden subdivision	Mount Eagle Estate (1916)	Melbourne	Peter Keam/W.B. Griffin
	Linden Gardens (1920)	Adelaide	Peter Wood/W. Earle
Garden village	Matraville (1918)	Sydney	NSW Voluntary Workers Association/J. Sulman
	Gallipoli Garden Village (1919)	Adelaide	SA State Bank/C. Reade
Industrial garden village	Claremont (1921)	Hobart	Cadbury Brothers/ W. Earle

Source: Based on R. Freestone, *Model Communities*, Thomas Nelson, Melbourne, 1989.

towns and villages. Freestone's research locates them and recounts their history, design and influence.[58] Some notable suburban examples are summarised in Table 3.2.

The Australian garden suburb shared the basic site planning features of its British parent, although the local preference for detached, single-storey dwellings meant larger block sizes and more ample yards. Typically, in Australia, a residential environment planned 'on garden city lines' was a separate physical and social entity characterised by low density development; classification of roads (collector, secondary, residential); zoning for residential, commercial, administrative, educational, religious and industrial (in the case of towns and villages) purposes; recreational spaces of various types and size; preservation of existing natural features; architectural unity but not uniformity; and a park-like environment created by tree-lined streets, and public and private gardens.

Australia's most complete and accurate metropolitan example of a garden suburb planned 'on garden city lines' was the Mitcham Garden Suburb (now Colonel Light Gardens) south of Adelaide (Figure 3.5).

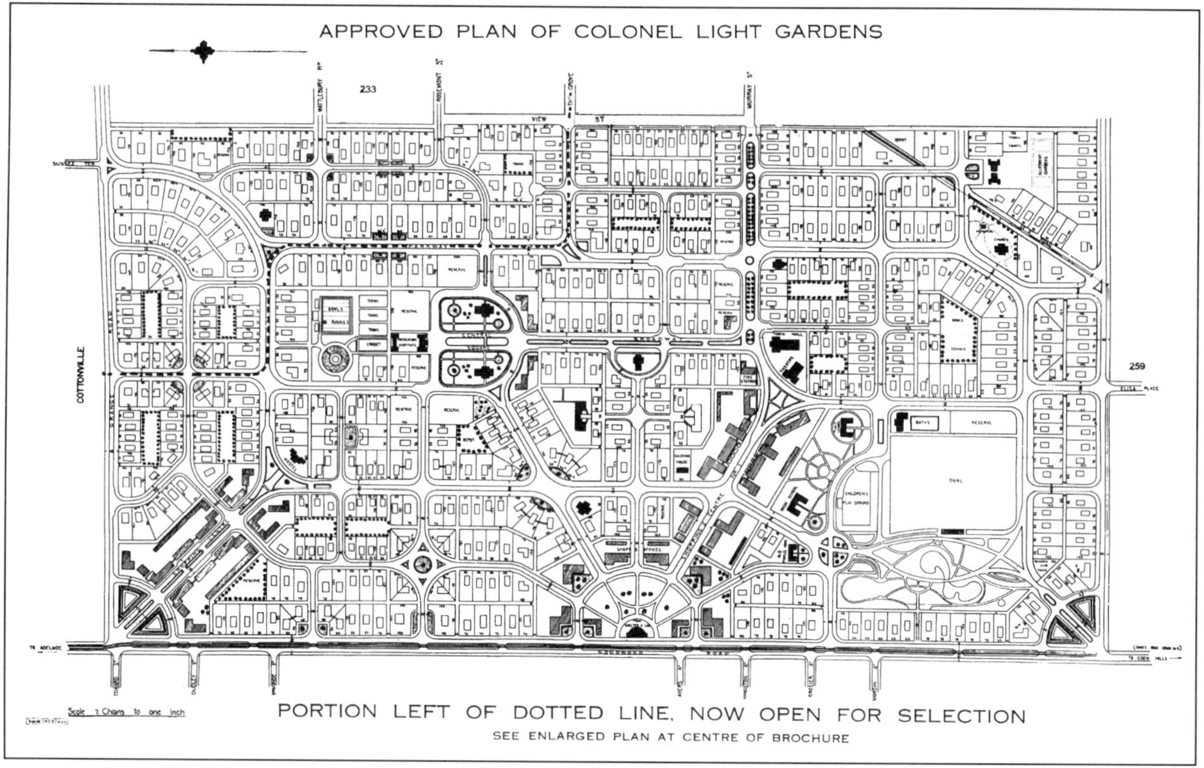

Figure 3.5 Approved plan of Colonel Light Gardens (1921)

Source: South Australian Government, *Comfort, Convenience, Beauty: Colonel Light Gardens, a Model Garden Suburb*, SA Government, Adelaide, 1921. Digitised image courtesy P. Knight.

Reade designed it in 1917 for the state government as a 'model garden suburb'. Aiming to demonstrate the theoretical and practical aspects of the garden city idea at a suburban level, he based his plan on Unwin's exemplar, Hampstead Garden Suburb.[59] Reade also drafted enabling legislation, the *Garden Suburb Act 1919*, to establish the suburb under the administration of the Garden Suburb Commission, a unique authority responsible to parliament.[60] Land sales commenced in August 1921 and the suburb was completed in 1927, largely in accord with the original design.[61] A sole commissioner administered the suburb until 1975, when the founding Act was repealed. Colonel Light Gardens stands today, virtually intact, a mature and enduring example of the garden city idea expressed 'at the level of home and the residential environment'.[62]

Conclusion

Town planning and garden city ideals initiated a new direction in Australian planning thought. Discussion and debate in the 1910s was focused on both the physical and organisational reform of the metropolis. The notion of comprehensive planning was introduced and ideas forwarded about how that might be achieved. A state-based town planning movement contributed to the 'propaganda of education and enlightenment',[63] raising popular consciousness about town planning and garden city methods. The garden city idea offered a paradigm of metropolitan growth and control to address contemporary social, physical, aesthetic and economic needs and, at the same time, offered an attractive suburban environmental ideal. While the latter was achievable, the larger goals of decentralisation—cities of limited size, satellite communities, agricultural and green belts—were more problematic; their attainment necessitated a shift away from the norm of a central business district surrounded by suburbs. Such a fundamental shift was unlikely since Australian reformers aspired to initiate change only within the existing economic and social framework. Moreover, at the time when the garden city idea was first advanced, there was no authority in any Australian city with the power to instigate change at the metropolitan level, and none evolved in the 1910s.

As the decade drew to its close, reformers' discussion increasingly turned towards the American-inspired city functional paradigm. James Morrell, architect to the Victorian Public Works Department, succinctly encapsulated this focus when he declared:

> Town planning ... concern[s] the planning of a city ... the improvement and extension in such a manner as to provide for the free movement, safety and control of traffic and transportation,

> segregation of buildings and activities, of specific types, to restricted areas . . . together with a sufficient percentage of parks and other open spaces for securing economic, convenient, healthful and pleasant conditions.[64]

While town planning ideals obviously remained high on Morrell's agenda, there was no specific reference to the garden city idea. But it would remain alive in Australia in subsequent decades in residential environments planned 'on garden city lines', in discussion over how best to create legal sanction for the town planning ideals espoused in the 1910s, and in debates about the future of the Australian city that centred on creating 'order in urban physical development, [bringing] the city government and its citizens together in preparing for their present and future needs and to provide for the requirements of their commerce and industries'.[65] Later, in the era of new and satellite towns, the garden city idea emerged as a significant influence on post–World War Two planning thought. That was perhaps its coming of age.

4 From theory to practice: the inter-war years

Alan Hutchings

The period between the two world wars was the time when the ideals of the town planning movement were tested in the legislatures of the states and in their expanding metropolitan capitals. After the terrible loss of life and well-being in World War One, the nation turned its mind to reconstruction and the new administrative invention of comprehensive town planning was seen as an important tool. During the 1920s, as the economy grew and cities expanded, there was considerable experimentation in how town planning could be used to guide the long-term growth of metropolitan areas and how it could be used as a means to improve the amenity of towns and suburbs. However, with the ending of the good years by the Great Depression of the 1930s, planning was, by and large, cast aside except for experiments in the provision of public housing.

As an operational system to effect the objectives of reform, comprehensive town planning came to be seen in the early decades of the twentieth century as consisting of the coordination of the supply and location of public facilities, the organisation of urban functions into systematic patterns and the regulation of the use of land.[1] This chapter illustrates how an increasing awareness of these matters influenced the way in which town planning came to be practised and how the administrative arrangements, legislative instruments and plans of the period were shaped accordingly.

A pivotal event

Chapter 3 discusses the town planning conferences of 1917 and 1918. If any event can be said to mark the transition from the days when the pioneers promoted ideals to the time when they and those who followed them began to turn their minds to the practicalities of implementation, it was the 1917 Conference. It is useful to consider its proceedings in terms of organisation, coordination and regulation. As an illustration of *organisation*, Reade's plan for metropolitan Adelaide (Chapter 3) is an exemplar—setting out, as it did, an inspirational but nevertheless basically achievable long-range plan.

Coordination loomed large in Reade's plan. South Australia's attorney-general, Crawford Vaughan, had expressed the need to coordinate public agencies—especially those dealing with transport—which were going 'their own separate ways', and this became an important theme of the 1917 Conference.[2] Moreover, there was a strong representation by senior officials from agencies across the states responsible for infrastructure such as water and sewerage, harbours, railways, roads, electricity supply and public works. In lesser numbers, but still forming a presence, were those from community-orientated bodies dealing with matters such as parks and gardens, and the provision of childcare centres. The professions also were represented—architecture, surveying, engineering and building—but with none of the obvious jealousies evident in the planning of Canberra.[3] Indeed, there was a sense that a separate profession would be needed, a view articulated later by one of the delegates, H.W. Uffindel. A solicitor and chairman of the South Australian Town Planning and Housing Association, Uffindel said: 'A Town Planner need not necessarily be a surveyor, architect or engineer, but he should be able to co-ordinate their work, and should have a larger vision than any of these other men.'[4] Completing the picture were experts on housing. Their presence underlined the reformist essence of town planning. For them, the coordination of infrastructure and synthesis with other urban elements into long-term plans, were, at the end of the day, secondary or 'derived concerns'.[5] Their primary purpose was to advance the public interest, defined in terms of equity and amenity.

Regulation—the drafting of legislation to force public agencies to coordinate, to ensure the adoption of metropolitan plans and to control activities on private property—was, of course, not ignored by the delegates at the 1917 Conference. Papers were given and information about emerging legislative initiatives was exchanged between the states. To inform their discussion, delegates were fortunate in that before them was a full-blown Bill, promoted by the government of the host state, which—at the very time of the Conference—lay before the State Parliament. South Australia's Town Planning and Housing Bill 1916, drafted by Charles Reade and refined by the parliamentary draftsman, was truly comprehensive and stood head and shoulders above those instruments that would follow both in South Australia and elsewhere. Reade read widely and drew on both British and North American examples, although the proposed administrative structure at least was clearly North American.

A three-member 'technically skilled' Central Town Planning and

Housing Commission was proposed which would 'pursue a consistent, a continuous and also a comprehensive policy' for Adelaide.[6] In some instances, the Commission would act alone; in others, with local government. Planning strategies would be expressed through schemes and implemented through zoning by-laws; that is, a parallel to the North American 'general plan' system. The scope of schemes across both built-up and greenfields areas would have been breathtaking even in today's terms, with the Commission also having powers to implement them through promotional means such as land reservation, land banking, parklands management, the provision of community facilities and the like. The housing provisions of the Bill would also have established the Commission as a public development corporation with a 'housing fund' to construct public housing estates. Not only that, 'societies of public utility' would be enabled to implement those parts of planning schemes aiming to provide 'dwelling houses for persons of small income'. No wonder there was a formal motion of acclamation by the delegates in support of the Bill!

Legislation

The delegates departed from Adelaide, reassembled in Brisbane in 1918 and then dispersed to their various states—some to pick up the threads of the initiatives they had already set in train, others to become involved themselves for the first time and to motivate others. In parliamentary democracies, legislation creates the frameworks for policy development and associated administrative systems. So the writing of planning law was high on their agendas.

In South Australia, the momentum for all-embracing legislation continued but the emphasis changed. Local government opposed the 1916 Bill's central commission. Reade sought a modification which balanced an 'administrative' viewpoint, whereby elected councillors were charged with administering a local government area, and a 'technical' viewpoint, in which a central authority, consisting of experts in the functional, financial and legal aspects of urban administration, would oversee the metropolis as a whole.[7] In the upshot, the *Town Planning and Development Act 1920* created the government town planner as the 'central authority' supported by a Central Advisory Board of Town Planning with both technical and local government members. Although in its scheme this Act was comprehensive, with the 'central authority' to have wide powers, in the end most of the Act was never promulgated. The government town planner was left high and dry with broad responsibilities for advising the government of the day on the wisdom of metropolitan planning but with few substantive responsibilities except for the laying out of government towns and the control of subdivision. Housing was considered to be a 'separate and distinct matter' by the then planning minister, H.N. Barwell,[8] and was made the responsibility of the State Bank. Nevertheless, within the Colonel Light Gardens suburb, which was created by way of the *Garden Suburb Act 1919*, housing was joined with land use organisation and administrative coordination to develop at least one small part of the Adelaide metropolis as a showpiece of comprehensive town planning (see Chapter 3).

Despite the emasculation of the 1920 Act, Reade's successors—William Earle and Walter Scott Griffiths (a member of the team that won the minority prize for Canberra's plan)—were able to make some progress. The last of the frontier government towns were planned for the wheat belt and for the Murray River irrigation area, model estates on garden suburb lines were initiated and reports about the basics of 'unified' metropolitan planning were issued. As the 1920s progressed, however, parliamentary support for planning ran out of steam. Town planning came to be seen as little more than a fancy name for land subdivision and Scott Griffiths' attempts to bring into play the yet-to-be promulgated sections of the 1920 Act were thwarted. In 1929, this view of planning as subdivision prevailed and the Act was replaced by a so-called *Town Planning Act* which reduced the role of the government town planner to nothing more than the state's chief subdivision processor.

In Western Australia, the story was happier. At the 1917 Conference, the small group of delegates from the west were able to report that they too were advanced in drafting a statute, albeit not to the stage of government acceptance and parliamentary debate as in South Australia. On their return home, and mainly through the Town Planning Association of Western Australia, these delegates persisted with their advocacy and in November 1929, the *Town Planning and Development Act* was promulgated.[9] This Act contained most of the concepts sought in the earlier South Australian statutes. There was a 'central authority', that is, a Town Planning Board with technical membership chaired by a full-time town planning commissioner. Its responsibilities included advising the minister responsible for town planning who would, in turn, be the approving authority for schemes prepared by local government, preparing schemes itself for Crown Land and approving subdivisions. Schemes would encompass a similarly wide range of matters as in South Australia and be implemented by both promotional and regulatory means. In addition, the schemes could 'provide for [the] planning, replanning or reconstruction'[10] of a locality, the first time that the notion of 'renewal' appeared in a substantive way in Australia.

Section 14 gave a town planning authority extremely wide powers to act as a public development corporation; for example, subject to a scheme and land ownership, an authority would be able to 'improve and make use [of land] as [it] may deem best'.[11]

This Act, then, brought together many of the planning ideas not only as they had evolved in the west but throughout Australia since the heady days of the 1917 and 1918 conferences. But the 1929 Act was not the only initiative. In 1920 the *City of Perth Endowment Lands Act* received assent. It enabled the city to become a development corporation with powers—similar to those of South Australia's Colonel Light Gardens commissioner—to plan and develop new urban areas on the Endowment Lands in the public interest. These powers were sweeping and enabled the council to survey, plan, construct and manage such areas and also 'to invite competitive designs for the laying out of lands'.[12] As described in Chapter 3, the garden suburbs of Floreat Park and City Beach resulted. Finally, in 1928 a *Metropolitan Town Planning Commission Act* was passed, which will be discussed later in this chapter.

In the more populous states of the eastern seaboard, with their faster growth, the situation was significantly different. Despite the strong representation at the national conferences of delegates from the eastern states, including influential law-makers such as J.D. Fitzgerald, the minister for local government in New South Wales, crucial legislative initiatives were weak. Fitzgerald declaimed that 'the period of Australian reconstruction after the war will . . . call for the experience and skill of the Town Planner'.[13] Perhaps so, but the town planner would have to apply it with little back up from the law. In New South Wales in 1919, in Victoria in 1921 and in Queensland in 1923, respective local government acts were amended to regularise the administration of subdivision, to classify roads by function, to fix building lines, and to declare residential districts in which 'trades, industries, manufactures, shops, and places of public amusement'[14] could be prohibited. The language was virtually interchangeable between each state, but this was hardly a recipe for town planning, comprehensive or otherwise. New development control powers were scattered through the legislation cheek by jowl with matters such as the 'temporary herding of cattle' (Victoria), the 'supply by the council of privy pans' (New South Wales) and 'electoral rolls' (Queensland). Little wonder the acts had little impact. It is also not surprising that local government planning took decades to rise above being a minor municipal technicality. Nevertheless, in these states a distinctly separate stream of administrative and legislative initiatives evolved to deal with metropolitan organisation and growth.

Metropolitan planning

Throughout the early decades of the twentieth century, Australian cities, particularly Melbourne and Sydney, grew rapidly. In 1906, 35 per cent of the nation's population was in the capital cities; by 1921, the proportion was 43 per cent.[15] This growth offered opportunities—taken up in one form or another in all of the mainland capitals—for planning advocates to demonstrate how comprehensive town planning could be used to guide metropolitan growth.

In Adelaide, Reade's 'ideas' plan, as the first demonstration in Australia of a possible all-encompassing metropolitan strategy, doubtless enthused delegates at the 1917 Conference. In its home town, however, the plan faded quickly from view. While Reade's successors promoted it as the basis for 'unified' metropolitan planning,[16] their views, as noted earlier, did not prevail and it faded from memory. Nevertheless, in the long term Reade's plan resurfaced to tacitly influence the shape of the 1962 *Metropolitan Development Plan*.[17] Paradoxically, despite the absence of a general legislative framework, in Melbourne and Sydney interest in this 'unified' approach to metropolitan planning grew rather than diminished.

A strong contingent from the Melbourne City Council attended the national conferences in 1917 and 1918. One was Frank Stapley, who besides being lord mayor, also presided over the Victorian Town Planning and Parks Association and the Victorian Institute of Architects at the turn of the decade. In 1920, he led the City Council in proposing a comprehensive approach to the planning of the Melbourne metropolis which was at the mercy, he opined, of statutory authorities, such as those responsible for transport and harbours, and of the 26 individual councils in the metropolitan area. Supported by his town clerk, T.G. Ellery, meetings were convened, resolutions passed and the Victorian state government persuaded to legislate by way of the *Metropolitan Town Planning Commission Act 1922*.[18] Although general town planning law for Victoria barely made a mark, the burgeoning metropolis of three-quarters of a million people was given an Act which embodied the latest in administrative and technical practice. In the swings and roundabouts of British vis-à-vis North American influences on Australian planning, Melbourne in the 1920s typified a period when the influence of the North American 'city functional' approach, which emphasised 'business-like, technocratic and survey-based planning', was at its height.[19] The concept of a city planning commission combining a local government, public utilities and (sometimes) business membership charged with preparing a comprehensive plan was at the core of North American practice.

It could be said that Reade's vision of a 'central authority', which was an essential element of the 1916 South Australian Bill, had at last found a home. Charged with preparing 'general plans and recommendations with respect to the better guidance and control of . . . development'[20] which were to be underwritten by 'estimates in reasonable detail of the cost involved', the Commission proceeded vigorously. By 1925, it had prepared progress reports on traffic, the master planning of the Fishermens Bend industrial area and development of the Glen Waverley suburban growth area. Its first technical chief was Alexander Macdonald, an architect and examiner of patents, who had submitted an entry to the Canberra competition and later assisted Walter Burley Griffin.[21] Well received by the minister of public works, these reports led to the Commission's tenure of office being extended until 1929 when its *Plan of General Development* was completed under the technical leadership of Fred Cook, a surveyor who had replaced Macdonald.[22] As 'Australia's first comprehensive metropolitan plan',[23] it aimed for a population of two million and emphasised transportation and land use zoning (Figure 4.1) with an open space system, primarily based upon natural features, being used to structure the expanding metropolis. Public housing was barely mentioned, however, because considerable opposition to this being considered a planning issue had developed among some members of the Commission.

The plan was well supported by extensive surveys and studies and contained recommendations for the implementation of its metropolitan-wide 'general plans' by way of improvement schemes, detailed zoning and legislation. There is no doubt that such a plan would have achieved most of what the pioneers of 1917 and 1918 had sought. Indeed, in 1930 a Bill was introduced into the Victorian Parliament, in effect, to legitimise the Commission by establishing a statutory state authority which would oversee the preparation of local government schemes within the framework of the 'general plan'. However, the Melbourne City Council changed its tack of a few years earlier. Faced with the reality of an overarching metropolitan authority, it saw its power and status threatened, drummed up opposition and the Bill lapsed.

In Sydney, there was a similar story of early enthusiasm. In 1922, under the presidency of the Sydney lord mayor William McElhone, a 'Sydney Regional Plan Conference' was formed. It brought together the rich, the influential and the technically expert 'to guarantee continual progress by fostering financial, physical, economic, moral and intellectual efficiency'.[24] But, in the end, little was achieved and in 1924 the Conference was disbanded. John Sulman, indisputably the leading technical expert in New South Wales and arguably in Australia, nevertheless persisted.[25] With the support of the Town Planning Association of New

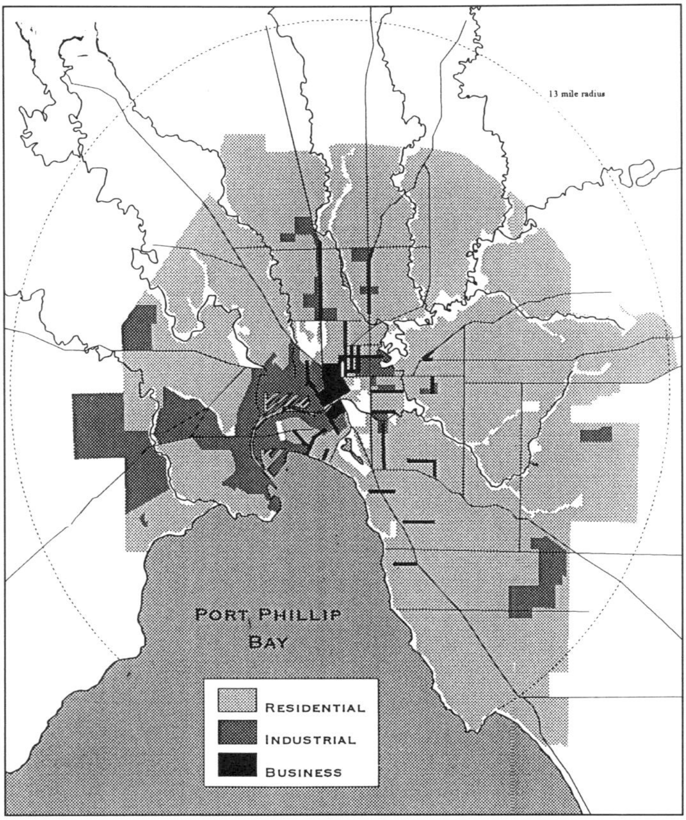

Figure 4.1 General land use zoning recommendations of the *Plan of General Development* for Melbourne (1929)

Source: R. Freestone and M. Grubb, 'The Melbourne Metropolitan Town Planning Commission, 1922–30', *Journal of Australian Studies*, no. 57, 1998. Drawing by A. Hardie.

South Wales, he offered his services, gratis, as the town planning commissioner for the City of Sydney to prepare a comprehensive plan. Although such a plan would have resulted in proposals for the metropolis' core only, surveys of the wider Sydney urban area would have been required. However, nothing came to pass and the notion of a 'unified' metropolitan plan for Sydney was stillborn.

In Adelaide, Melbourne and Sydney, then, attempts were made to view the metropolis comprehensively, to set out long-term development goals and to establish the administrative mechanisms to achieve them. In Brisbane, much was made of administrative arrangements and the coordination of public works, but there was no suggestion of any organising physical framework. The *City of Brisbane Act 1924* established one super council for the expanding urban areas from Sandgate in the north to

Yeerongpilly in the south. It enabled the Council to promote just about every form of enlightened human endeavour from education, morals and food supply to the 'planning and embellishment of the City',[26] and the organisation of public works and transport. But to where would the sewers run and the tramways lead?

Western Australia, having been the only state to succeed in promulgating a complete form of general planning legislation, also had reasonable success in the business of comprehensive metropolitan planning during the 1920s. W.E. Bold, the town clerk of the City of Perth for 43 years, argued soon after his appointment in the early years of the century that a town plan was the 'keystone' of good governance.[27] By the 1920s, this view spread more widely through local government which put its weight firmly behind a development plan for the metropolitan area.[28] In 1927, under its own Act, an eight-member Metropolitan Town Planning Commission was established to advise the government on a general plan for the metropolis, costs of associated public works, administration, transport, zoning, parks, distribution of warehouses and shops, and all of the other complex detail of day-to-day urban planning. Its report was issued in 1930.[29] In addition to advising on the foregoing matters, it recommended creation of more parklands, a system of main roads and railways running in parallel, and saw the metropolis as having one million people by 1980. Its work done, the Commission was disbanded. Efforts were made in the early 1930s to give its report—albeit it did not contain an encompassing metropolitan plan—the force of official policy, but to no avail. As elsewhere in Australia, the Great Depression brought development to a halt. The drive for coordination disappeared as did that for an overarching physical planning strategy within which it would occur. The idealism and enthusiasm for social reform and environmental improvement that underlay moves toward comprehensive town planning also dissipated.

The 1930s: A return to reform

The Great Depression was a severe shock to the Australian nation. Unemployment rose to the unprecedented level of 20 per cent in 1930. Manufacturing, which was fuelling the growth of the cities, fell away and unemployment in that sector reached 33 per cent.[30] Poverty became an urgent problem as did substandard housing and inadequate provision for public health. The cities began to slip back to the condition they were in during the early years of the twentieth century when the planning pioneers first sought answers to physical and social problems.

In the first years of the 1930s, little was heard from those either advocating planning as a philosophy or those administering the systems that had been put into place. Indeed these systems, such as they were, shrank to minor offices where functionaries rubber-stamped subdivision applications or checked rudimentary residential zoning by-laws. Nevertheless, by mid-decade, there was a resurgence of some of town planning's reformist ideals, particularly with regard to public housing.[31]

In Melbourne, Oswald Barnett, a school teacher and accountant, formed a group to advocate for the abolition of slums and improved public housing.[32] The group's campaign received strong support from influential sections of the Melbourne community and in 1936 the Victorian Government set up a Housing Investigation and Slum Abolition Board whose recommendations led, in turn, to the establishment of the Housing Commission of Victoria. The Commission's principal enabling act was the *Slum Reclamation and Housing Act 1938* which granted it far-reaching powers not only for housing improvement and construction but also as a planning authority in its own right. The Commission could (and did) require local councils to prepare planning schemes covering the full range of uses and activities occurring in urban areas. Upon this basis, the Commission became a powerful planning authority and development corporation and it changed the face of the inner suburbs of Melbourne over ensuing decades.

In Sydney, there was also public agitation for improved public housing throughout the second half of the 1930s which led to the establishment of a Housing Conditions Investigation Committee in 1936, a Housing Improvement Board in 1937, and the New South Wales Housing Commission in 1941.[33]

South Australia took a somewhat different tack in that public housing was not seen so much as a welfare measure but rather as a means by which low-rental housing could be supplied for workers and hence form part of the support base for the state's industrial expansion.[34] Established in 1936, the South Australian Housing Trust became a cornerstone of the enlightened corporatism of Premier Thomas Playford's conservative (at least in outward trappings) government. Chapter 5 describes how the Trust strongly influenced Adelaide's growth in the post–World War Two years. However, it is important to note here that the manner of its formation and organisation in the late 1930s exemplified the coordination principle. It quickly saw itself as a planning and development corporation charged with the task of providing houses and associated community facilities, shops and parks set out along the most up-to-date suburban design principles. Not only that, led by the premier and Cabinet, the Trust's leaders—along with senior officials from other agencies—became part of a strategic team charged with urban development in the public interest.

In Queensland, the search for ways and means to use town planning for reformist ends led not to public housing but to public works. The *State Development and Public Works Organisation Act 1938* promulgated with the purpose of 'improving the general economic welfare of the State and ... of encouraging employment generally' created the Office of Co-ordinator General with enormous powers:

> His initial tasks were to coordinate public works across the state, so as to create additional avenues of employment, to maintain continuity of employment throughout the state, to proportion expenditure equitably, [to] gain maximum public benefit from public expenditure, to coordinate departmental and local government activities, to prevent overlapping of functions, and to cooperate with industry.[35]

However, there were no long-term physical plans or strategies to organise and guide the location of works and their interlocking with other urban functions within Greater Brisbane or indeed Queensland's regional centres (except one).

The exception was the City of Mackay, an expanding industrial port on the central Queensland coast some 950 kilometres north of Brisbane. Reference was made earlier in this chapter to how planning in its general sense faded away during the 1930s. Nevertheless, the City of Mackay in the early 1930s commissioned Ronald McInnis, a surveyor who had strongly advocated town planning for many years, to prepare a plan.[36] It was put into effect as the *City of Mackay and Other Town Planning Schemes Act 1934*. In the second reading speech, E.M. Hanlon, the home secretary, made a distinction between mere 'residential planning' and expansive 'city planning'. The latter, he said, should be 'far seeing' and was necessary to avoid the problems plaguing Brisbane, Sydney and Melbourne. He referred to Britain's *Town and Country Planning Act 1932* which had engendered schemes throughout the United Kingdom and he saw the day when 'every town in the Commonwealth will have embarked on a town planning scheme'.[37] Hanlon stressed that schemes should look well ahead and, as well as providing for utility, amenity and convenience, should form the framework 'for the effective and inexpensive provision of municipal service'.[38] Town planning, at least as the means for improving amenity and functional effectiveness, was reaffirmed.

By way of a subsequent amendment to the *Local Government Act* in 1936, the City of Mackay scheme was to be the prototype for all of Queensland. With its zones, definitions and use group charts, areas for public purposes, proposals for parks, main roads and the like (Figure 4.2), it must also be seen as the prototype for the thousands of authorised policy statements, official strategies, development plans, statutory town

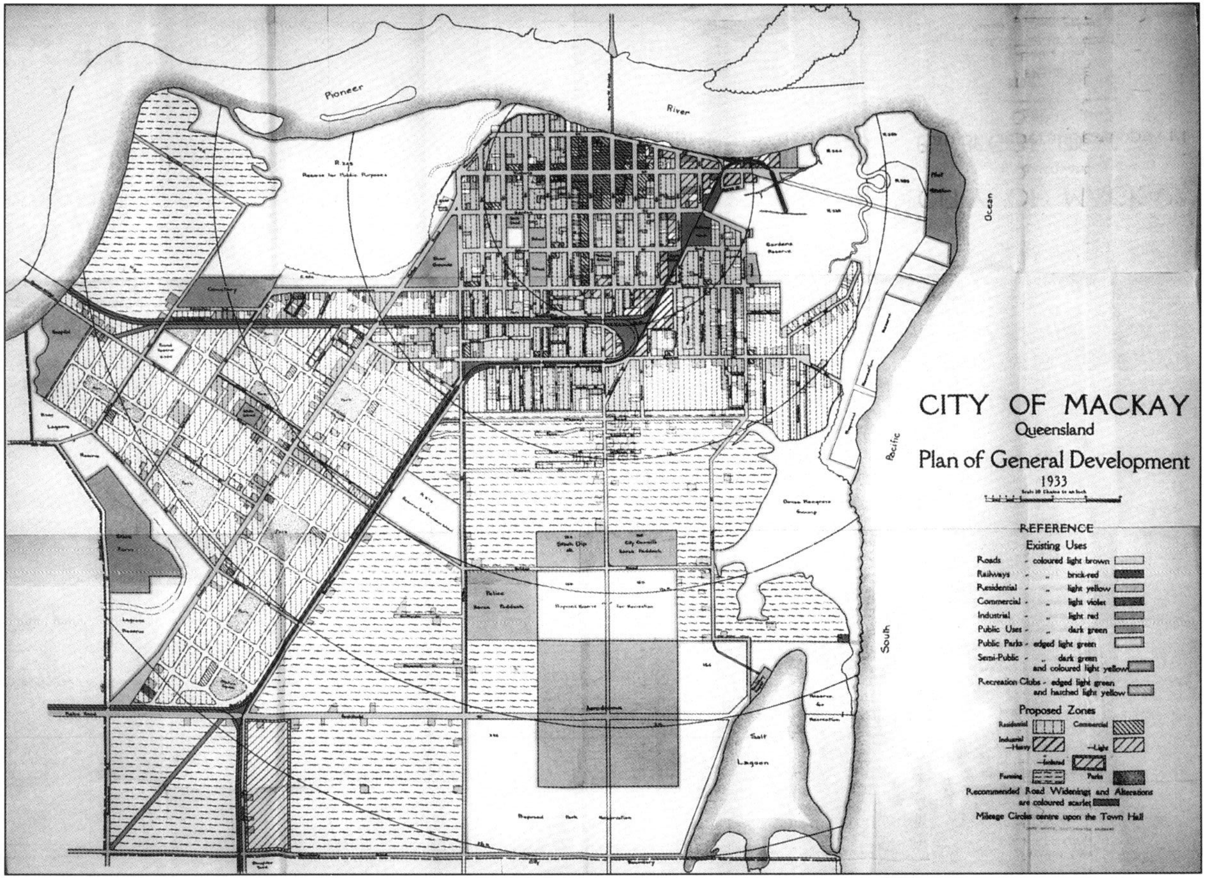

Figure 4.2 *Plan of General Development* for the City of Mackay (1933)

Source: The City of Mackay and Other Town Planning Schemes Act 1934, Schedule 3. Courtesy Queensland Government Printer.

planning schemes and zoning regulations that have featured throughout the states and territories of the nation since then.

The late 1930s saw some revival of interest in other states. In New South Wales, for example, there were a number of bills prepared both for the state generally and Sydney in particular. But nothing came of them.[39] Notwithstanding, they set the scene for the initiatives taken by the Labor Government of William McKell that culminated in the general planning legislation of 1945 and the County of Cumberland scheme three years later.

Conclusion

What can be said about the inter-war period? Freestone refers to 'the grand goals and limited achievements of urban planning in the early twentieth century'[40]—a fair summary, but the same could be said of many innovations in public administration during the period. In any field of human endeavour there are high points where its protagonists come together, where ideals are burnished, where concepts are clarified, and when the excitement of invention and creativity advance endeavour into a new phase. Such were the conferences of 1917 and 1918. However, it is perhaps too much to ask that the intensity of such high points be maintained indefinitely. Day-to-day reality sets in and it is enough that some commit themselves to the hard grind of implementation. After 1918, new challenges had to be met in administration, legislation and policy.

Probably the greatest challenge was resolving the tensions between the 'centre' and local government. Debate about their respective roles pervaded the national conferences and it was local government pressure as much as anything that brought Reade down in South Australia. Whether one sees the 'centre' as the state government, a metropolitan-wide authority or a combination of both, a workable balance between it and local government was rarely struck during the period, except perhaps in Brisbane. There again, it is still a challenge that remains today in most parts of the nation.

Driving both this challenge and that of formulating workable administrative arrangements was the search for coordination. Whether motivated by social reform, functional effectiveness, improving amenity or all three, the pioneers clearly saw that the coordination principle was crucial. From Reade's central planning board in South Australia to the metropolitan commissions in Melbourne and Perth and the coordinator general in Queensland, there were experiments in ways and means to get public authorities to pull together. While most failed, they nevertheless became the forerunners of the state planning authorities, advisory boards and inter-ministry committees of the era since 1945.

Sandercock has said that during the inter-war years the translation of the planning movement's ideals into a legislative basis led to a narrowing of focus.[41] But in a parliamentary democracy that misses the point—legislation is often required to translate ideals into practice. It is true that nothing in the period was as all-embracing as the 1916 South Australian Bill, but that state's subsequent 1920 Act, those for the commissions in Melbourne and Perth, the general planning legislation of 1928 in Western Australia and, to a lesser extent, in Queensland in 1934, were all reasonable attempts to address the difficult task of establishing coordination arrangements so that a joint central–local government system could put into effect some form of long-term metropolitan plan and, additionally, regulate individual land uses. Indeed, the Western Australian statute was robust enough to essentially survive until the present day. Also, in most of these statutes there were provisions—albeit weak and clumsy—to deal with public objections to draft policies. Whatever the motives for their introduction, they were the forerunners of the complex systems of citizen participation, comment and appeal that now characterise all modern planning legislation (Table 4.1). In this as well as in the areas of policy formulation and implementation, the legislation of the period forms one foundation for what has followed since.

What though of the plans? Administration, legislation and governance are all very well but a process without products is pointless. Very few plans were prepared during the period. Surveys were done, reports written, and major urban functions identified and evaluated but, except for Melbourne, no truly comprehensive products resulted. Nevertheless, it could be said the 1929 Melbourne plan illustrates key concerns of the period. From the earliest days of comprehensive town planning there has

Table 4.1 Town planning and related legislation, 1918–40

Legislation	*WA*	*SA*	*VIC*	*ACT*	*NSW*	*QLD*
State-wide general planning	1928	1920		1921		1936
State-wide coordination only						1938
Metropolitan comprehensive planning	1928		1922			
Metropolitan coordination only						1924
Minimal zoning and subdivision control		1929	1921		1919	1923
Public housing		1936	1938		1941	

been tension as well as cooperation between social and amenity (now environmental) ideals, and this plan, structured as it was by a park system, leans towards the latter. With its highly detailed zoning and road classification, a framework was also established for functional effectiveness which, we must remind ourselves, can be as much a tool for social reform and environmental improvement as it can be for business efficiency. This point was not lost on those drafting public housing legislation.

Finally, who would administer the coordinated systems, organise the strategic plans and regulate the uses? Uffindel and Fitzgerald expressed the early realisation that these tasks could not be left to the existing land and design professions, to dilettantes, nor to administrators with, perhaps, an innate flair. Thus the period ended with the establishment of organisations such as the Town Planning Institute of New South Wales. Again, the significance of the period in crystallising the practices of the modern era is underlined.

5 A new paradigm: planning and reconstruction in the 1940s

Renate Howe

The post-war reconstruction period is exceptional in Australian metropolitan planning history for the integration of economic and social policy with housing and planning strategies. The construction of planning as an all-encompassing concept was fundamental to international debates on the need for a new world order of peace and equality, reflected in the mid-century shift towards more government control of the urban development process. For the first time the Commonwealth had the opportunity to assume a strategic financial role in housing and urban policy due to wartime conditions, the transfer of taxing powers from the states and the establishment in 1942 of the Department of Post-War Reconstruction (DPWR) by the Curtin Labor Government. At the state level, infrastructure agencies and local government increasingly regulated land use in the fast-growing and industrialising cities culminating in steps to develop comprehensive metropolitan plans. The Cumberland County Council plan for Sydney (1948) was the first of the post-war metropolitan plans. It drew on increasingly sophisticated planning expertise and marked a transition from the planning frameworks of social reformers in the 1930s to those of the technical professions in the 1950s. Although the consensus around the new paradigm of integrated planning focused on national development had unravelled by the end of the 1940s, the advances in legislation, administration and professional development provided the main framework for post-war metropolitan planning.

The new paradigm

The reconstructionist push for comprehensive physical and policy planning had its roots in the pre-war period. Minimal investment in urban infrastructure during the Depression of the 1930s was exacerbated by the social and economic disruption of the war years. Deterioration of housing, high rents, exploitation by landlords and the unregulated expansion of industry, had taken their toll on the inner areas of Melbourne and Sydney, where most Australians lived. The response of the states in establishing the South Australian Housing Trust (SAHT), the Housing Commission of Victoria (HCV) and the Housing Improvement Board in Sydney in the 1930s, has been noted in Chapter 4.[1] Government regulation was extended when wartime shortages of labour and building materials and stringent controls on non-essential construction brought residential development to a virtual halt after 1941. As the Pacific war intensified, it was widely accepted that national development should be the responsibility of government, not private enterprise, and that public sector investment and initiatives would set the pace and form of urban development in the post-war economy.[2]

In this more cynical age, it is difficult to imagine the intensity and excitement of the international debate around planning and urban development. HCV Commissioner Oswald Barnett described the 1940s as 'the most mouldable time in the history of the world'.[3] Barnett had been a major force in the Victorian reform consortium responsible for establishing the Housing Commission. His newspaper articles and books were widely read, especially *Housing the Australian Nation* (1942), which set out the achievements of the HCV and promoted it as a model for other states, and *We Must Go On* (1944), a call for centralised planning of economic development, urban infrastructure and housing to ensure a more fair and equal society.[4] Barnett's books were part of an avalanche of publications envisioning the possibilities for a new social order. As Australia did not face the rebuilding problems of war-devastated Europe, the discourse of 'reconstruction' developed around building a strong post-war economy rather than recovering from war damage. Reconstruction was defined as ensuring an equitable standard of living based on secure male employment, adequate housing and well-planned communities.[5]

A Keynesian economic strategy to achieve these aims was spelt out in the Commonwealth Government *White Paper on Employment* (1945). Employment was to be created by regional development, the building of large infrastructure projects and the growth of manufacturing industry. Immigration would meet labour shortages and populate regional areas. National urban and regional development policy would be focused on full employment, housing, immigration and industrial development. A reconstructed Australia 'would be based on proper planning principles, with a government committed to full employment and armed with enhanced Commonwealth powers'.[6] This was the task of the DPWR, established with Ben Chifley as minister and H.C. Coombs as secretary.

As Coombs recalled, 'it is difficult in retrospect to recapture the intellectual excitement which these ideas generated'. He went on,

> From the outset, those involved in the Ministry had emphasised that the government's commitment to a better life after the war, especially for those who had been denied it by unemployment and poverty, would make it important to ensure a physical and social environment in which an adequate and fulfilling life would be possible. The task of creating such an environment extended beyond the scope of the market economy. Decisions about its form, and about the resources to be allocated to it, would have to be made through social and political means.[7]

Full employment and adequate housing were the cornerstones of post-war reconstruction and for the first time housing was seen as a national issue requiring national strategies. One of the early actions of the DPWR was the appointment of a Commonwealth Housing Commission (CHC) to report on housing requirements in the post-war period. The Commission travelled around Australia for hearings and produced an interim report in October 1943 and a final report in April 1944. The outcomes reflected the inputs of CHC members, especially Victorian architect–planner John Gawler, and the expertise of the young supporting staff, Sydney architect Walter Bunning and secretary Mary Phillips. The recommendations went far beyond housing design, administration and policy, and assumed acceptance of the necessity for centralised government intervention and control. The CHC recommended a Commonwealth planning authority to develop a national plan to direct development and coordinate Commonwealth and state government departments. The authority would be responsible for determining the planning implications of proposed large-scale industrial development in the post-war period and would have a research capacity.[8]

The CHC report also had recommendations on regional and town planning covering decentralisation of industry, satellite towns, neighbourhood units, land nationalisation, infrastructure development and slum clearance. Model legislation on housing and planning was included for the guidance of the states. Overall, the report projected an image of rationally planned and zoned cities designed to stimulate economic growth. Given the pressures of time and politics, Leonie Sandercock is right to describe the CHC report 'as a remarkable document, perhaps the most comprehensive and imaginative ever presented to a national government in Australia'.[9]

Yet according to Gawler, 'after the frenetic effort to produce such a comprehensive report in such a short time, it was left to gather dust'. He recalled with some bitterness the dichotomy between the 'sheaf of congratulations' and the international praise for the report, compared with the recommendations 'falling to the ground like autumn leaves, silently and gently, never to be heard of again'.[10] Implementation of the CHC report became a test of strength over housing and planning powers within the federal system as the Commonwealth, with its new financial and administrative strength, positioned itself for a national policy and administrative role. State governments, however, were determined to retain control over housing. Barnett, for example, refused an invitation from Coombs to be on the CHC as he judged the Commonwealth would have little influence on the housing programs of the states. In January 1944, after tense meetings between the DPWR and the states on the interim CHC report, Coombs noted that 'it quickly emerged that States would not welcome so direct an intrusion into what had in the past been an area of exclusive State concern'.[11]

State and local government planning

The weakness of the CHC report was that its recommendations had not taken seriously the existing piecemeal, yet significant, planning powers of the states and local government. The large states did not have planning legislation and the planning implications of the housing authorities had not been considered at the time of their establishment when state governments had put the 'housing cart before the planning horse'.[12]

In Victoria and South Australia, the housing authorities soon filled the planning void. Although the HCV had been given only rudimentary zoning powers by legislation, it moved under Barnett's leadership from a slum clearance to a major urban planning and housing development authority (Figure 5.1), buying sites in the Melbourne metropolitan area in readiness for the easing of post-war building restrictions.[13] The HCV was also preparing a master plan for Melbourne under the supervision of architect–planner Frank Heath, who had been recruited to oversee the HCV's estate design and planning responsibilities. In South Australia, the Liberal and Country Party premier, Thomas Playford, used government departments and the SAHT to push housing and industrial development in Adelaide. Susan Marsden has argued that the SAHT was a de facto planning authority for metropolitan Adelaide, crucial to the premier's determination to transform 'a big country town' into a metropolitan city through migration and industrial development.[14] After the 1941 election of the McKell Labor Government, the New South Wales Housing Commission (NSWHC) was established to drive the government's housing reform program in Sydney.[15]

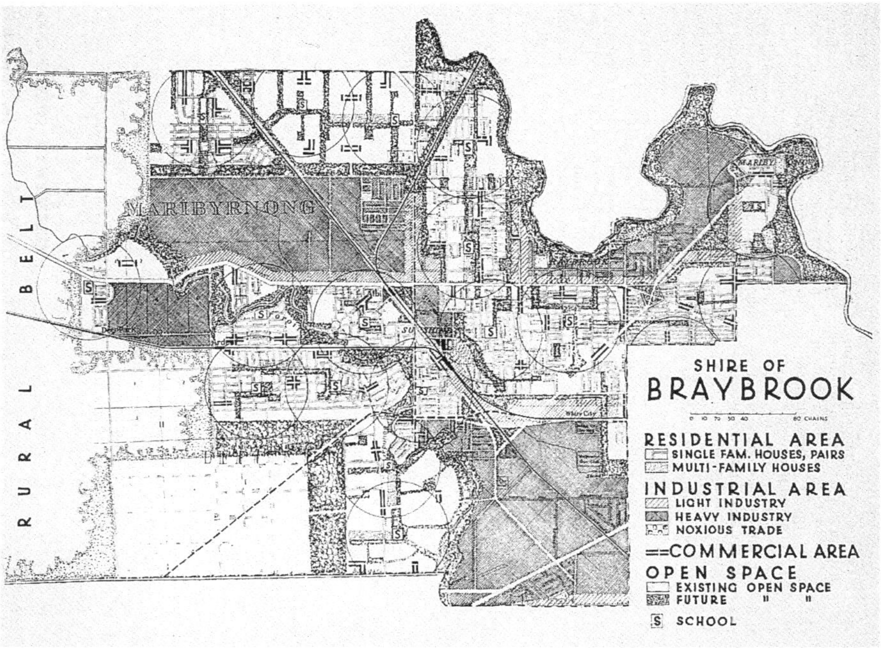

Figure 5.1 The ideal suburb: the Victorian Housing Commission's plan for the western Melbourne suburb of Braybrook (c1942)

Source: F.O. Barnett, W.O. Burt and F. Heath, *We Must Go On*, The Book Depot, Melbourne, 1944.

The CHC report also did not consider the role of local government in planning. Capital city municipal councils inspired by the spirit of post-war reconstruction had moved to initiate city plans. The City of Sydney—under the city engineer, A.H. Garnsey—was preparing a comprehensive plan, although little progress had been made by 1942.[16] The Labor majority on the Greater Brisbane Council (GBC), the only council which had successfully expanded its coverage of the metropolitan area in the 1920s, had also begun preparations for a city plan. Following the passing of the *City of Mackay and Other Town Planning Schemes Act* by the Queensland Government in 1934 (see Chapter 4), Ronald McInnis was appointed by the GBC to work on a master plan for Brisbane. By 1944, McInnis had completed a comprehensive zoning ordinance to guide Brisbane's transformation from frontier town to regional city. The Brisbane plan was not given statutory authority because of the Queensland Government's determination to restrict the power of the GBC.[17] In 1943, the Town Planning Committee of the Hobart City Council engaged architect–planner Fred Cook as a consultant to prepare a plan for Hobart.[18] The plan was completed but, as in the case of Brisbane, the opposition of the state government prevented its being given statutory authority, although both plans were influential in determining the shape of their respective cities. These one-man master plans—by Heath in Melbourne, McInnis in Brisbane, Cook in Hobart and Garnsey in Sydney—were either left unfinished or not given statutory authority.

After the release of the CHC report in 1944, the Commonwealth pressed for comprehensive metropolitan and regional planning in the states as an essential part of the reconstruction strategy for social and economic development. Coombs writes that the first step towards achieving planning schemes was to secure appropriate legislation and an objective was to make such legislation a prerequisite for states to obtain federal housing funds.[19] In 1944–45, new town planning legislation was passed in three states—Tasmania, Victoria and New South Wales. The three Acts had different solutions to the crucial question of state and local government responsibilities.

The Tasmanian *Town and Country Planning Act 1944* provided for municipal councils to prepare and implement land use planning schemes under the general supervision of a commissioner for town and country planning. Ronald McInnis, perhaps disillusioned with the fate of his Brisbane plan, came to Hobart to take up the commissioner's position in 1945. According to Peter Harrison, 'the framers of the legislation originally intended to grant the State Government wide powers' but this was resisted by local councils and responsibility for planning devolved to local government.[20]

There was a similar tussle between state and local government over the Victorian legislation. The Victorian *Town and Country Planning Act 1944* empowered municipal governments to prepare planning schemes and set up a Town and Country Planning Board (TCPB) as the senior state planning authority to advise the minister for local government. Much to Barnett's chagrin, planning powers were removed from the HCV, largely due to criticisms of the Commission by local government. The TCPB was to be a small body with a full-time chair and three board members drawn from professional town planners, engineers and surveyors. Local government could submit zoning proposals to the TCPB for review, but the board had no determining powers in relation to these plans, only advisory powers to the minister for local government. There was no power for the TCPB to prepare a metropolitan plan. John Gawler was eventually appointed TCPB chair and later assessed the Act as 'a weak piece of legislation indeed', especially as local authorities were given the right but not the legal obligation to prepare plans.[21]

The New South Wales legislation differed from that in Tasmania and Victoria by providing the state government with the power to require municipalities to prepare plans. The *New South Wales Local Government (Town and Country Planning) Amendment Act 1945* provided for the preparation and implementation of local planning schemes by municipalities and shires. As in Victoria, a Town and Country Planning Advisory Committee was set up to advise the minister for local government; the difference was that councils could be directed by the minister to prepare a scheme. The New South Wales legislation provided for metropolitan-wide planning through the setting up of county councils for special purposes, thus paving the way for the preparation of a broad plan for the County of Cumberland which encompassed the Sydney metropolitan region. Local government also influenced the direction of the New South Wales legislation. The original Bill had provided for the preparation of a Sydney metropolitan plan to be the direct responsibility of the minister for local government and the minister's department, but the Local Government Association, representing local councils, insisted that the Bill be amended to provide for the establishment of a Cumberland County Council elected and financed by constituent local councils for a limited period of three years to prepare a plan.[22]

There was no new legislation in the other states. The Queensland Government made no change to its 1934 legislation. Barrie Mellote argues that although Western Australia had the advantage of being one of the few states with planning legislation (since 1929), it missed the opportunity to develop more modern legislation at this time and therefore did not provide adequately for post-war metropolitan and regional development.[23] The Liberal and Country Party Government in South Australia resisted the national Labor Government's pressure to introduce legislation, relying on planning and coordination by the Housing Trust and other instrumentalities concerned with urban development. Peter Harrison concludes that by 1945 'all states except South Australia had legislation which gave local government the authority to prepare and administer statutory land use plans, subject only to the overriding powers of the responsible state minister'.[24]

These acts were passed before planning and housing initiatives in post-war Britain began to exert their influence on Australian planning practice and legislation. The Victorian and Tasmanian legislation owed more to the British *Town and Country Planning Act 1932* in giving priority to local over state authorities, despite the very different and ambiguous position of local government in the Australian federal system. The legislation also reflected the resistance of local government to the direct involvement of state government departments and authorities in the planning process. The 1940s Acts did not adequately address the planning role of the state departments and statutory infrastructure authorities which were increasingly determining land use in this period. As Harrison argues, it was the 'multiplicity of plans' implemented by local government zoning and by-laws that continued to be the major and underestimated influence on Australian urban form.[25]

The 1940s legislation was an important response to the Commonwealth's demand for state planning legislation, but it was a far cry from the expectations of the CHC report. Frank Heath later assessed the Australian legislation as largely directed towards negative control, and 'much in need of powers such as those of national importance in England', a reference to the *New Towns Act 1946* and *Town and Country Planning Act 1947* passed by the British Labour Government.[26]

Vision and reality

The rhetoric and idealism of post-war reconstruction created unrealistic expectations about the ability of planning to achieve radical change, and much of the analysis of this period develops a vision (early 1940s) and reality (late 1940s) duality.[27] An important factor in this perceived gap was that reconstruction strategies were based on preventing a return to the social and economic distress of the 1930s Depression and did not anticipate the post-war economic boom. Coombs acknowledges in his biography that:

> [I]t cannot be claimed that the planned scenario was closely followed. The feared unemployment following close on the transition did not eventuate, and we were soon wrestling with pressure on the construction industries almost as acute as that generated by the war itself.[28]

A return to the unemployment and stagnation of the 1930s had been anticipated, not labour shortages and explosive growth. With demobilisation of service personnel, a rising birth rate, settlement of refugees and then the first waves of the post-war migration program, the housing shortage in the capital cities moved from acute to desperate, especially in Sydney. On the eve of World War Two, there was an estimated national housing shortage of 120 000 units; by as early as 1945, the shortfall was estimated at 300 000 units, exacerbated by the Commonwealth's draconian wartime restriction on residential construction.[29] Images of protest meetings on housing shortages in Sydney, emotional crowds at the Lower Melbourne Town Hall awaiting the result of the HCV housing ballot, evictions of squatters and the mushrooming of temporary housing settlements underlined the seriousness of the situation in these two cities.

The population growth rate of the capital cities in the period 1947–54 surpassed any in their history. The annual growth rate of all the capital cities increased by 40–50 per cent between 1947 and 1954. In 1945–49, over half a million migrants settled mainly in Melbourne, Adelaide and Sydney. Despite all the rhetoric about integrated planning, the Commonwealth-initiated post-war migration program was poorly coordinated with states and local government in relation to planning and housing. By the late 1940s, the extent of the impact of immigration on the demand for housing and services in Melbourne and Sydney was emerging.

The post-war reconstructionists had underestimated not only population growth but also the growth of cities through new residential suburbs. Anti-urbanism was basic to reconstruction strategies which aimed to reduce the size of large cities. Barnett, for example, advocated regional development strategies in Victoria to attract population away from Melbourne, although large-scale developments in the Latrobe Valley and Geelong did nothing to quell the demand for Melbourne suburban housing. In Adelaide, the SAHT failed to anticipate the demand for suburban housing, especially the pressure from new household formation and moves by many inner suburban residents to the outer suburbs. Indeed, post-war reconstruction rhetoric contributed to this demand for suburban housing. The CHC report had prioritised the need to provide suburban family homes—well-serviced, located in neighbourhood units in reach of schools, by-passed by traffic on main traffic arteries, and with local shops and baby clinics within walking distance. The main breadwinner's place of employment would be located nearby and there would be outdoor recreation and open space for the family. This ideal post-war suburban life was also central to Barnett's *Housing the Australian Nation*, Gawler's *A Roof Over My Head*, and Walter Bunning's *Homes in the Sun*.[30]

The post-war public housing authorities in Melbourne, Sydney and Adelaide were leaders in outer suburban development. It had been anticipated in the early 1940s that the HCV and NSWHC would focus on inner city demolition and rebuilding after the war, yet their main focus in post-war Sydney and Melbourne was not the redevelopment of inner areas but house-building in the outer suburbs. Development in inner areas had a low priority in the 1940s with less than 100 acres (40 hectares) renewed by the New South Wales Housing Commission in its first six years before it began a clearance program in Redfern and Surry Hills under Clive Evatt, the minister for housing, in 1947.[31] In Melbourne, the HCV virtually stopped redevelopment work in the inner city after 1941 and in Adelaide the SAHT made little use of its demolition powers.

Perhaps the most significant difference between vision and reality was in the post-war role of the Commonwealth in housing and planning. The Commonwealth–State Housing Agreement (CSHA) of 1945 was a far cry from the recommendations for a central planning authority in the CHC's 1944 report. Accepting the political reality of resistance from the states and within his own party, John Dedman, who had replaced Chifley as minister for post-war reconstruction, reduced the Commonwealth role in housing to assisting states through grants and low-interest loans to build rental housing for those in most need.[32] The Agreement still met with opposition from the states and South Australia shunned the CSHA loans because of the strings attached.

Vision and reality came closest to convergence in the achievement of a coordinated approach to planning by the state statutory authorities in the development of working class housing and manufacturing industry in Melbourne and Adelaide. Both the HCV and SAHT bought sites in the early to mid-1940s before the real estate boom. In Melbourne, the HCV directed its estate building in proximity to industrial development in the north and west of the city where land was cheap and local councils were compliant. Preston, Heidelberg, Maidstone and Sunshine were suburbs with mass-produced rental housing, locating workers and industries in new settlements on the fringe. By the late 1940s, the HCV was the largest housing developer in Melbourne.[33] The SAHT was even more influential in determining the development of Adelaide. The control of commercial and industrial development exerted by premier and treasurer Thomas Playford was such that Susan Marsden named post-war Adelaide 'Playford's City'.[34] The SAHT coordinated Playford's promotion of manufacturing industry and public housing, providing suburban middle-range housing at low cost for a largely migrant industrial workforce. Hugh Stretton has described the South Australian Government's post-war industry and housing program as reshaping Adelaide 'in a way that demonstrated a practical and powerful method of metropolitan planning'.[35] As in Melbourne, it was the cost and availability of land that largely determined the development of the north-west area as an industrial and working class housing sector. The NSWHC was not as influential in the 1940s, but its large estates built in proximity to munitions factories at Villawood and St Mary's were precursors of the 1950s suburban working class public housing estates in Sydney's west (Figure 5.2).

As post-war recovery proceeded, there was an increasing push from the private sector into suburban estate development. An example was the residential construction firm led by A.V. Jennings. Jennings had gained experience in estate development as a contractor for the HCV and began building large suburban estates in Melbourne's eastern suburbs in the 1940s.[36] As developer interests increasingly influenced local and

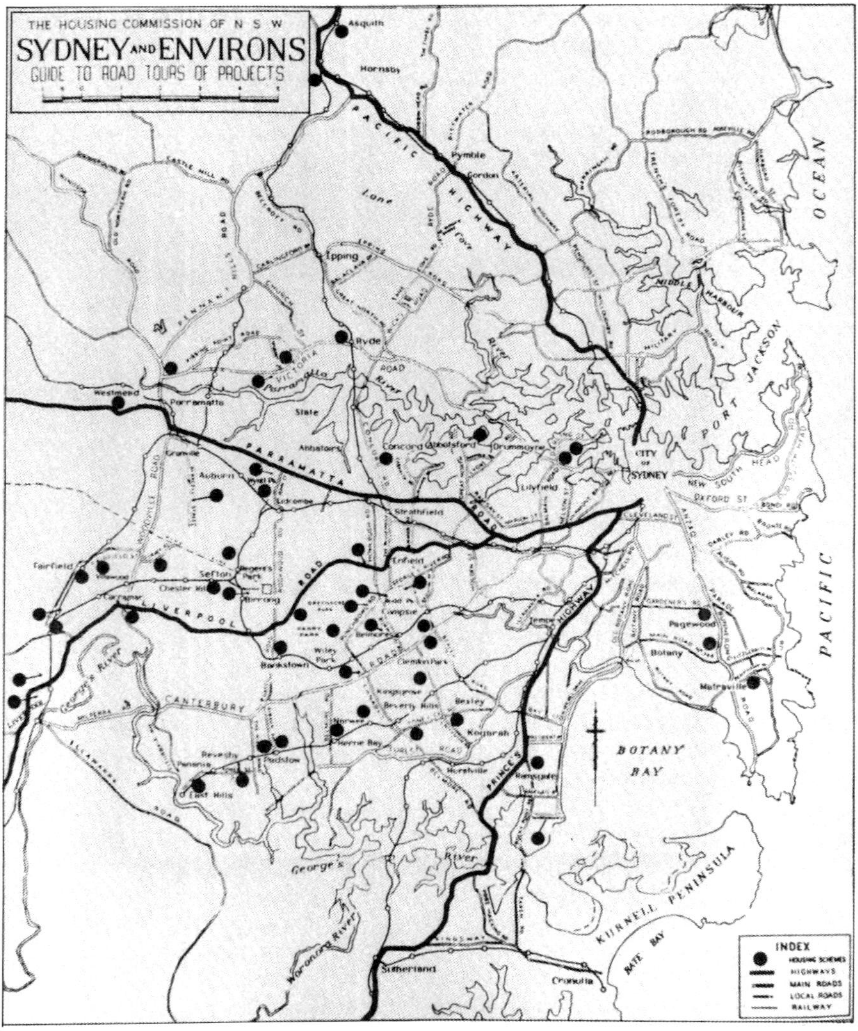

Figure 5.2 Divided by class: early New South Wales Housing Commission estates in Sydney's west and south-western suburbs

Source: NSW Housing Commission, *Homes for the People*, Government of New South Wales, Sydney, 1950.

state governments, the efforts of the HCV to exert control over the private market were eroded, although the SAHT continued to successfully influence housing costs in the smaller city of Adelaide. The implementation by these two state housing authorities of the post-war reconstruction agenda continued to be further eroded as the private sector recovered from wartime conditions and capital reasserted its influence on the economy and government.

Master plans and master planners

There was widespread recognition of the urgent need for metropolitan plans as suburban expansion impacted on cities. If the dominant concern in 1930s discourse on cities had been 'slums', in the 1940s it was 'sprawl', as housing spread to the cheaper land in the outer suburbs. Old and inappropriate subdivisions on the books of small outer suburban councils were activated and owner–builders were attracted by the lack of building controls. Blatant property and land speculation went hand-in-hand with development. The Sydney suburbs of Bankstown, Blacktown, Sutherland and Warringah were characterised by piecemeal development as speculative estates, owner–building and many fibro houses proliferated on the fringe.[37]

Problems associated with the powers of local government under the 1940s legislation were all too evident. Australian local authorities did not take a strategic metropolitan view. In Victoria, only six municipalities had availed themselves of the power to prepare plans for the TCPB and a frustrated Gawler called for local government to be overhauled 'to bring it into line with modern conditions', identifying problems in the small size of municipalities, poor staff, inadequate financial base, weak enforcement powers and opposition to regional organisations.[38] State authorities ignored local government planning requirements. The HCV and SAHT regularly overrode local councils. SAHT architect–planner Gavin Walkley recalled the ad hoc decisions made in the absence of an Adelaide metropolitan development plan, especially 'the unimaginative planning on lines that were current before the war' and the ad hoc siting of houses 'here, there and everywhere, without an overall plan to guide us'.[39] As Harrison concludes:

> It was eventually recognised that even if local government had undertaken the kind of planning made possible by the legislation, an assembly of local plans would not add up to an effective metropolitan plan. Within the metropolitan region it was necessary to have comprehensive plans.[40]

The Australian response was influenced by an international exchange of planning ideas on the need for urban restructuring, with the ideas of British and American planners especially influential.[41] Ronald McInnis, for example, felt part of an international planning 'brotherhood' for whom 'the problems differ in intensity and the methods of approach to them are not always the same, but there is basically little difference in their objectives'.[42] Cities were regarded as too large, in both population and area, and needed regional towns, satellite cities and green belts to limit their size. Inner city renewal by demolition and the construction of flats, spatial restructuring around distinct zones, ring roads and communities designed as neighbourhood units (Figure 5.3) were all part of the post-war planning consensus in Australia and overseas.

The influential icon of this international consensus was Patrick Abercrombie's *Greater London Plan* of 1944 with its emphasis on controlling the size and lowering the density of the city with a green belt around London, and proposals for satellite new towns, inner city clearance and modern flats. The *Greater London Plan* and general British legislation of the later 1940s were publicised during a five-week lecture tour by Abercrombie in 1948, concurrent with a travelling exhibition on British town and country planning. Not surprisingly, the Cumberland County Council (CCC) planning scheme report completed in 1948 was described as 'a planning scheme . . . for the second white city of the British empire' and echoed the *Greater London Plan* in language and style.[43] Although the *Cumberland County Plan* owed much to the *Greater London Plan*, it was focused on Australian issues of controlling suburban development and zoning industrial, residential and commercial uses (Figure 5.4). A green belt zone in a semi-circle around Sydney was used to prescribe the size of the city rather than satellite cities or new towns. Other main provisions were:

- proper servicing of rural land prior to development
- reserved land for open space and highways
- zoned areas for industrial expansion in middle and outer suburbs
- zoning of living areas which excluded substantial manufacturing and commercial uses
- slum clearance and redevelopment.

The political support of J.J. Cahill, the Labor minister for local government, was crucial to the completion of the plan, as was the involvement of local municipal councils through the ten members elected by the 69 constituent councils of the Sydney region. According to Barbara Norman, it spelt out principles which would underpin future metropolitan planning in Australia and was preceded in its strategic approach only by the Griffins' plan for Canberra and the 1929 plan for Melbourne.[44]

The release of the Sydney plan highlighted Melbourne's failure to make progress on a metropolitan plan. Responding to calls for action from architects and planners, local government through the Municipal Association of Victoria, the Town and Country Planning Association and other lobby groups, the Victorian Government had another attempt at legislation for metropolitan planning, this time turning to yet another state statutory authority, the Melbourne and Metropolitan Board of Works (MMBW). In the *Town and Country Planning (Metropolitan Area) Act 1949*,

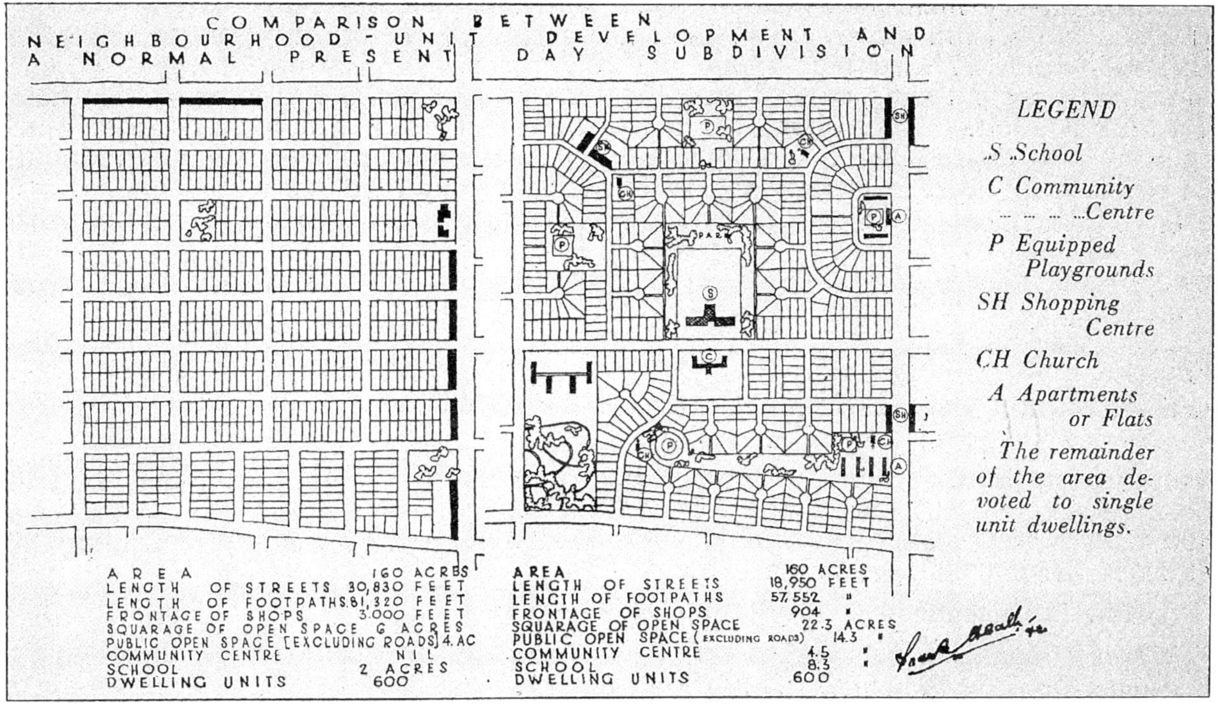

Figure 5.3 Frank Heath's concept of the neighbourhood unit

Source: F.O. Barnett, W.O. Burt and F. Heath, *We Must Go On*, The Book Depot, Melbourne, 1944.

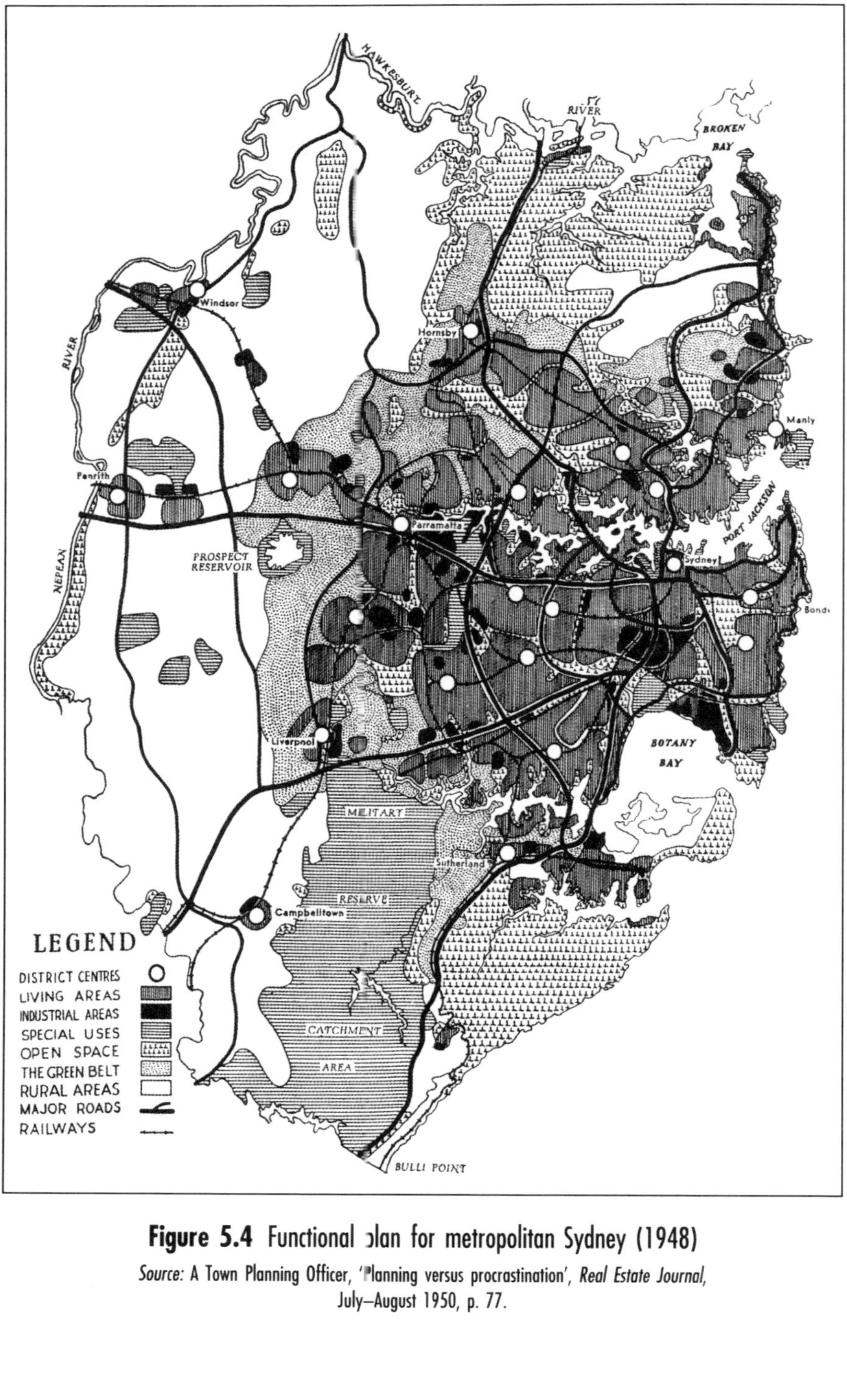

Figure 5.4 Functional plan for metropolitan Sydney (1948)

Source: A Town Planning Officer, 'Planning versus procrastination', *Real Estate Journal*, July–August 1950, p. 77.

the state water and sewerage authority was given the responsibility of preparing a metropolitan plan. In Melbourne, as in Sydney, some accommodation between state and local government was essential to get metropolitan planning off the ground. The MMBW—the 'Parliament of Local Government'—was made up of 53 members selected by metropolitan councils, including those of the fast-growing fringe municipalities. The 1949 legislation was supported by Gawler who believed that, unlike the TCPB, the MMBW had the technical expertise to undertake metropolitan planning and solve the political problem of the support of local government.[45] Brian McLoughlin's history of Melbourne planning is critical of the allocation of town planning functions to an 'engineer culture' in the MMBW and the subsequent influence of this culture on the 1954 plan for Melbourne,[46] a view also shared by many architects and planners at the time.

This development of metropolitan strategic planning stimulated professional training. In 1949, the inaugural meeting of the heads of schools of architecture recommended that architectural courses offer units that addressed town and country planning. Architecture courses at Sydney Technical College, Perth Technical College, the Melbourne Working Men's College and Hobart Technical College subsequently introduced planning subjects. In 1949, an Adelaide course sponsored by the Town Planning Institute of South Australia—and taught by Gavin Walkley—commenced, and Denis Winston—a former student of Sir Patrick Abercrombie—arrived to take up a position as the first professor of town and country planning at the University of Sydney. Gawler taught planning subjects in the Melbourne University architecture course in the 1940s before Professor Fred Ledgar arrived from Britain for the commencement of the first planning diploma course in 1952.[47]

The expertise of post-war planners in Australia, and the extent of their national and international experience, have been unappreciated. Gawler was widely travelled, had worked as an architect in Chicago before World War One, and was also a local councillor in suburban Box Hill in Melbourne. Ronald McInnis had prepared plans for Mackay and Brisbane in Queensland, and also for Darwin, following its destruction by wartime bombing, before moving to Tasmania. Frank Heath had studied planning in Britain and the United States and visited Russia to investigate the implementation of the Moscow plan of 1935. He co-authored with Barnett the 1944 book on reconstruction, *We Must Go On*. Margaret Pitt Morison, one of the few women involved in planning education, had studied architecture and design in Britain before teaching in Perth. The experience of working on the Cumberland County Council plan under chief planner Sidney Luker was crucial for younger planners such as Peter

Harrison, who was a graduate of Sydney Technical College and later influential in the planning of Canberra (see Chapter 7). Australia's developing planning profession in the 1940s fused a range of influences and experience; neither the planners nor their plans were as derivative as 'cultural cringe' interpretations suggest.[48]

Planning was finally establishing itself as a profession in the 1940s, with professional planning institutes formed in New South Wales, South Australia and Victoria. The professional planners were drawn largely from the technical professions—architecture, surveying and engineering—not the economists, social scientists and reformers who, for instance, had driven Melbourne's housing reform in the 1930s. But there was no clear-cut division and the planners of the 1940s were notable for their public spirit and dedication. McInnis wrote in 1949 'that it had been a long, and at times, heart-breaking job to pioneer planning in Australia' and that the task had required the commitment of all reformers.[49] Geoffrey Faithfull, who served as deputy chief planner of the Cumberland County Council, recalled that:

> In the early days it was a bit of brave new world stuff; we were all learning and there was a feeling, a spirit, that you were trying to do something to improve the situation, and in fact doing it in spite of adversity.[50]

Conclusion

The 1940s were essentially years of transition from cities rooted in the colonial period and scarred by depression and war to modern complex cities central to national development and pioneering metropolitan planning. The tensions between levels of government reflected the immaturity of the post-war federal system and frustrated many of the positive initiatives of the period. The new paradigm of a planned society, with the government a vanguard for social change, increasingly came under challenge in the Cold War period. As the threat of war faded and the authority of the Chifley Labor Government declined, the political and ideological tide swung against the reconstructionists.

The reconstruction period has been extensively criticised in studies of Australian metropolitan planning published since the 1970s—during an era that has emphasised participation in the planning process. The advocacy of centralised planning departments and 'master plans' strikes most present-day planners as 'hopelessly outmoded, naive and undemocratic'.[51] Carolyn Allport underlined the paternalism and political naivety of planners in her analysis of Bunning's *Homes in the Sun*:

> Like many plans for the period, Bunning uses a simple dichotomy between good and bad, between before and after. There was little realisation that the political structure would probably accept piecemeal recommendations and shelve those that were too expensive or likely to create political antipathy in the electorate.[52]

The 1940s have been seen as a lost opportunity for the Commonwealth to have developed a national role in housing and urban development policy.[53] Others have deplored the failure of the state housing authorities to consolidate their position and to supply affordable rental accommodation as in Britain.[54] Political economists have seen the period as one of 'state capitalism' through planning and housing initiatives serving the interests of industrial capitalists and urban developers, and leaving a legacy of cities segregated by class.[55] The simplistic approach to gender roles implicit and explicit in the dominant planning paradigms of the 1940s, and the failure to acknowledge the increasing workforce participation of women, have been criticised by feminist writers.[56] The period has also been criticised for neglecting the rejuvenation of inner and central city areas and ignoring those in most housing need, especially newly arrived migrants.[57]

Hugh Stretton, however, took a more positive view of the contribution of the 1940s in his influential book *Ideas for Australian Cities*, especially the contribution of the post-war suburbs as creative family living environments and the leadership of the public sector in coordinated and equitable urban development at a time of unprecedented urban expansion. As well, this chapter has demonstrated the legislative and administrative frameworks for essential metropolitan strategic planning which were set in place in the 1940s. Sydney, the largest city, had completed a comprehensive plan of international standard and the development of a Melbourne plan had commenced. The founding of state planning institutes and of planning courses at universities and colleges provided the infrastructure for a developing and more sophisticated profession. Ironically, the expectations and rhetoric around the 'new paradigm', which the post-war reconstructionists created, have perhaps served to obscure the achievements of the post-war period in determining the direction for Australian metropolitan planning for the next 30 years.

6 The post-war city

Ian Alexander

From a vantage point on the eve of the millennium and faced with acute global economic and environmental problems, the 1950s do indeed seem to be a 'golden (economic) age'. This was a time in the history of global capitalism when optimism and economic growth were both high. What is more, with the conspicuous exception of the Aboriginal population, Australia retained its relatively egalitarian distribution of income and wealth through the decade. This offset, to some extent, the uneven nature of development that is endemic to capitalism. But the failings of the capitalist system were not a focus of public attention in the 1950s. While the Australian Government's efforts to outlaw communism in 1951 were unsuccessful, the 1950s saw the start of a long stretch of conservative political dominance which lasted in Canberra until 1972. It was also a period of general social conformity.

Australia continued to be ruled by a hegemony of interests, of which land and urban development, including real estate and valuation, building and construction, road building, car manufacture, sales and repairs, were (and still are) key parts.[1] This constellation of interests had close connections to the state plans devised in the 1950s that are the focus of this chapter. But on occasion the influence of these vested interests was modified for collective gain by land use planners, backed by alliances of progressive community interests. While some have argued that planning always acts to the advantage of private interests, there are circumstances in which planning contributes to public gain.[2]

As a part of the developed capitalist world, the Australian nation state and many of its people did share in the prosperity of the long boom: between 1950 and 1960, growth rates in gross national product averaged between 2 and 4 per cent.[3] As a child growing up in the 1950s in Guildford, an outer suburb of Perth, and coming from a middle class family, I was lucky enough to be in a household that had a manageable mortgage on the family home, a car and a fair provision of consumer goods. But living and economic conditions for many others were not so comfortable, as Tim Winton illustrates so well in *Cloudstreet*.[4]

High economic growth meant expansion in the cities. Max Neutze points out that Australia's 'third main period of urban expansion began in the early 1950s'.[5] Another feature of the 1950s pattern of urban growth was a continuation of the long-standing trend of increase in the proportion of population living in the capital cities.[6] Part of these growth patterns was attributable to immigration. Levels were high, at least from traditional British and new European sources, as the ambitious post-war immigration program was implemented.[7] Most migrants ended up in the cities, which boosted their growth considerably. A large proportion (between 45 and 59 per cent) of the 1947–66 population increase in Perth, Adelaide, Sydney and Melbourne resulted from overseas migration.[8]

Australia was still under the strong influence of its Anglo-Saxon heritage. On the other hand, as Lees and Senyard graphically point out, Australia willingly adopted the United States as its new cultural model.[9] After the dark days and the 'American rescue' of World War Two, by 1950 the Australian nation seemed on the brink of 'big things'. In the cities, this translated into enthusiastic support for government policies which encouraged consumerism via home ownership and mobility via car ownership. This was the new path to riches promised by the US version of modernism. A typical example of the new consumer products on offer was television, which arrived in a few lucky Australian households just in time for Melbourne's hosting of the Olympic Games in 1956, and then spread like wildfire.

Given the ascendancy of modernism, with its accent on scientific method and rationality, optimism and faith in technology were other aspects of the 1950s. They were typified by the advent of schemes of 'national reconstruction', such as the massive Snowy Mountains Scheme which involved diverting the waters of the Snowy River into the Murray–Darling system over the Great Dividing Range. The scheme promised benefits from irrigation and hydro-electric power but also borrowed from US expertise and technology. In the cities, freeways were a prominent example of another idea welcomed from the United States and indiscriminately applied. Little or no thought was given to what has recently been described as the 'environmental footprint' of these engineering projects, which do not tread lightly on people or on the earth.[10]

There was little or no questioning of the growth that was to fuel the expansion of urban Australia during this time. Post-war social mores saw many women return to domestic duties after a brief period of 'men's work' during the war; 'old ideas of male dominance were re-stated: the Australian was male and master of the physical world. This figure was so frequently encountered it was proffered as the truth'.[11]

Make no small plans

Given the growth paradigm of the 1950s, it is not surprising that the decade saw the launch of several large and ambitious plans to cater for the future growth of the capital cities. The first generation of metropolitan plans were either published or in the first stages of implementation in Sydney, Melbourne and Perth (Table 6.1). As pointed out in Chapter 5, these 'Mark One' plans came into being in a period when 'post-war reconstruction' ideals loomed large. These ideals were translated into plans which contained ideas imported from the United Kingdom. Many prominent British planners were among the wave of post-war migrants. They included Alistair Hepburn, who worked on metropolitan plans in both Melbourne and Perth, and Gordon Stephenson.

Planning in the 1950s was not primarily concerned with social issues, but there is some evidence of priority being accorded to equity where state governments of the day had it high on their priority list. This happened in New South Wales, which had a Labor Government throughout the 1950s, and Western Australia, which had one from 1956 to 1959. This was modernism tinged with a 'sense of compassion', as Stephenson put it.[12] In Victoria, on the other hand, economic efficiency was much more towards the top of the Bolte Liberal Government's (1955–72) agenda than was equity.

Typically, the plans comprised comprehensive reports and recommendations for zoning plans which would enable their implementation. The zoning approach was in line with previous local government planning: development control at a metropolitan scale.[13] The reports were based

Table 6.1 Metropolitan plans of the 1950s

City	*Plan*	*Date published*	*Date adopted*	*Planning body*	*Initial planners*
Sydney	*Cumberland County Plan*	1948	1951	Cumberland County Council	S. Luker
Melbourne	*Metropolitan Planning Scheme*	1954	1968	Melbourne and Metropolitan Board of Works	E. Borrie
Perth	*Plan for the Metropolitan Region, Perth and Fremantle*	1955	1963	Metropolitan Regional Planning Authority	G. Stephenson and J. Hepburn

on the survey–analysis–plan formula, popularly attributed to Patrick Geddes and fashionable at the time. The zoning plan for Sydney's County of Cumberland plan was approved by the New South Wales Parliament in 1951 in what Harrison describes as 'the most definitive expression of public policy on the form and content of an Australian metropolitan area ever attempted'.[14] Perth and Melbourne had to wait until the decade was over before their plans were given the official stamp of approval. In the later years of the 1950s, however, the plans became guides to major metropolitan land use decisions. In Perth, interim development controls, based on the Stephenson plan were introduced in 1956,[15] while in Melbourne a similar situation prevailed throughout the 1950s.[16]

Bureaucracies charged with implementation had been established in each city more or less coincident with the publication of the plans. These bureaucracies took varying form, with Sydney perhaps 'closest to the people'.[17] Here local government successfully lobbied for the establishment of a metropolitan body elected and financed by constituent councils.[18] However, as Sandercock points out, this arrangement also set up or heightened tensions between state and local interests.[19] A somewhat similar situation prevailed in Melbourne, where plan implementation was handed to the already-established Melbourne and Metropolitan Board of Works, which consisted of over 50 members elected by metropolitan councils. The Board had been empowered by an Act of parliament from 1949 to undertake such duties.[20] In Perth, the Metropolitan Regional Planning Authority (MRPA) was set up following legislation in 1958; while it was a state body, it did have local government representation on its committees.

Adelaide could not complete a metropolitan plan during the 1950s, although the committee responsible for drawing it up was appointed in 1955.[21] In Brisbane, enabling legislation was passed in 1959, but delays meant that a planning scheme for the city, which covered most of the then metropolis, was not gazetted until 1965.[22] However, the absence of a gazetted metropolitan plan did not exclude planning by other means. For example, the South Australian Housing Trust had a huge influence in terms of developing a new town at Elizabeth, north-east of Adelaide. Peel labels this development 'an intervention perhaps unparalleled in Australian planning'.[23] Elizabeth was designed along garden city lines, with emphasis on concepts such as self-containment and social balance. Elizabeth's development, then, emphasises that some metropolitan planning in the 1950s did pay attention to issues of social equity. In Hobart, the late 1950s saw the establishment of a planning authority for southern Tasmania and work began on a master plan for Hobart in the late 1950s. A draft metropolitan plan was completed in the 1960s and adopted in the 1970s.[24]

Overall, 1950s plans in Australian cities were top-down documents, largely concerned with issues of facilitating development efficiently in the interests of the ruling hegemony of land-related interests. This was done by allocating land and providing good transport (particularly road) connections between developing suburbs and the older central areas. None of the plans was strong on public participation, although people in the community made their voices heard on specific planning issues such as the location of roads. It was not until later decades that the community reacted more widely against redevelopment plans and freeway extensions as their implementation accelerated (Chapter 8).

In the remaining discussion attention is focused on the 1948 Cumberland plan for Sydney, the 1955 Stephenson–Hepburn plan for metropolitan Perth, and the 1954 Melbourne metropolitan plan. The land use and transport aspirations of the plans are analysed and the outcomes evaluated. Two of the plans underestimated the growth of metropolitan population, while all the plans underestimated the space required for increasing living standards and new consumer goods such as cars. As Rickard puts it, 'the prosperity of the 1950s took shape in the multiplying vistas of suburbia'.[25]

In the metropolitan plans of the 1950s, classic town planning was evident in the emphasis placed on the orderly development of residential, industrial and commercial land use. Transport recommendations were also included, but they came from other sources. The plans emphasised the importance of the traditional central business district (CBD) and were happy to promote redevelopment as necessary or inevitable, regardless of its toll on the heritage of late Victorian and Federation buildings, which at the time dominated many CBD office areas (Figure 6.1). What Marsden calls 'the transformation' of the built environment of the capital city centres started in the mid-1950s with the upturn in the availability of materials following years of post-war shortages.[26]

But beyond the CBDs, the metropolitan land use plans of the 1950s supported the controlled expansion of suburban industrial areas and retail centres. This was one way in which the planners sought to guide and modify the Australian suburban dream, although they met with mixed success. A further important objective was to reduce the amount of scattered subdivision and land speculation which was evident on the urban fringe.[27] This objective was to be implemented by greater controls on the conversion of rural land to urban use.[28]

A particular feature of the pioneering *Cumberland County Plan* for Sydney was the provision of an encircling green belt, a concept drawn from the innovative *Greater London Plan* of 1944. It was designed to secure ready access to rural areas for the burgeoning suburban population.[29]

Figure 6.1 'The main street of Perth in the heart of the office area' (1955)

Source: Plan for the Metropolitan Region, Perth and Fremantle, 1955, Report, WA Government Printer, Perth, 1955. Photo of St Georges Terrace by F. Hurley.

The green belt is a classic planning idea, which has its roots in the ecological approach to planning urged by luminaries such as Raymond Unwin, Lewis Mumford[30] and their Australian counterparts earlier in the century (Chapter 3). Classic it may have been, but the green belt was also to be the undoing of the Cumberland County Council (Chapter 7). The theory was for 'overspill' growth to be accommodated in discrete satellite towns located beyond the green belt. Elizabeth, on Adelaide's fringe, embodied the same thinking. In Perth, Kwinana was built in the early 1950s to accommodate the growth of new industrial enterprises and their workforce. While the plans for metropolitan Melbourne and Perth did not designate green belts as such, both plans were concerned to limit suburban growth. In Melbourne's case, the 'intention was to limit urban sprawl by surrounding the built-up area with a rural zone which specified minimum allotment sizes of 2.5 acres (about 1 hectare)'.[31] In the 1955 Perth plan, the areas designated for suburban expansion (shown in Figure 6.2) were—with the exception of Kwinana New Town—of a much more compact form than subsequently came into being.[32] The power of the land market and the mass appeal of the suburban dream were both underestimated by planners of the 1950s.

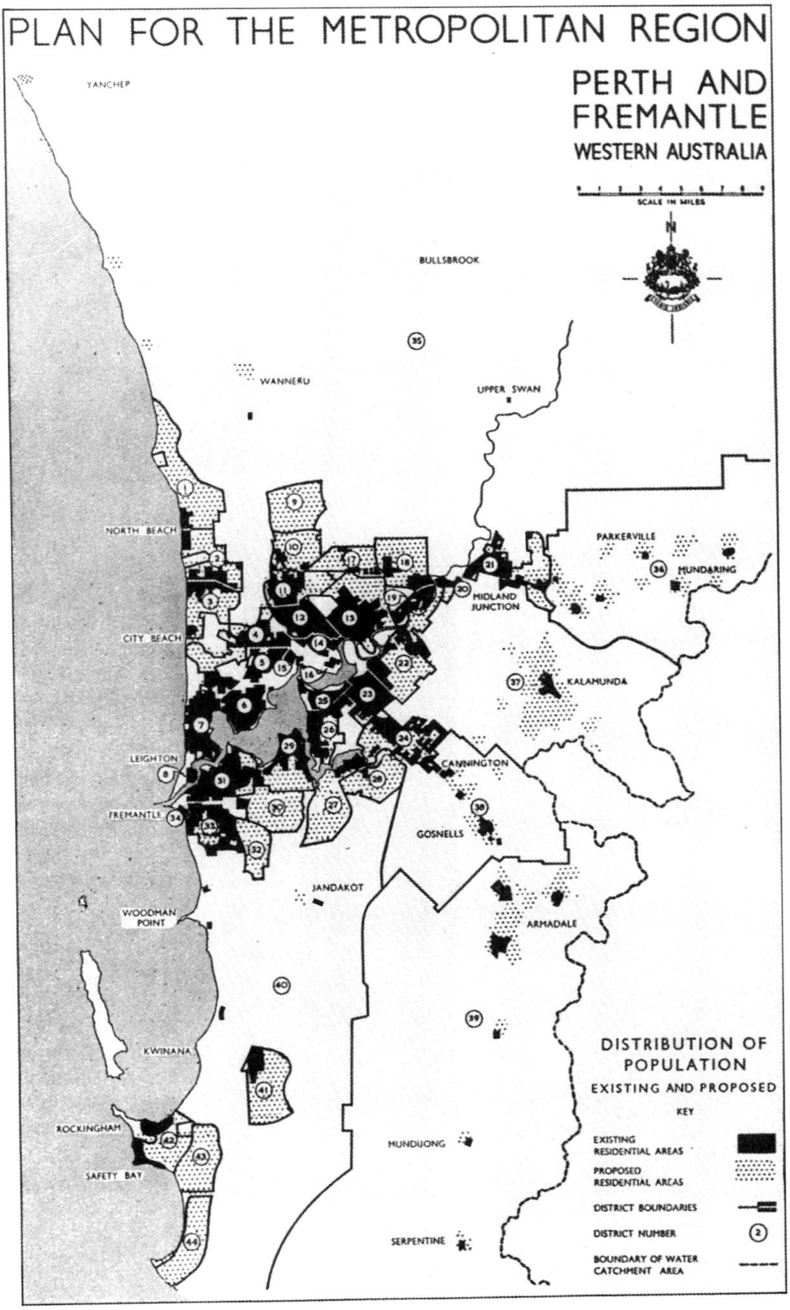

Figure 6.2 Proposed residential development pattern for Perth (1955)

Source: Plan for the Metropolitan Region, Perth and Fremantle, 1955, Report, WA Government Printer, Perth, 1955.

Housing issues

The suburban mosaic of the 1950s, which came to be dominated by single-family housing, opened up potential solutions for planning problems in the inner city. Many people were to be shifted from what was generally regarded as crowded and inadequate inner city housing to more spacious and presumably healthier suburban housing. This decentralisation was accompanied by restrictions on further industrial growth in inner city areas. Integral to the program, particularly in Sydney and Melbourne, were 'slum clearance' projects in the modernist paradigm.

These projects, undertaken by the relevant state housing authorities, had begun in the 1940s following the Commonwealth–State Housing Agreement of 1945. Continuing into the 1950s, they involved demolition of vast areas of terrace and row housing, and their replacement by tower or slab blocks of flats. These were supplemented by new estates in suburban areas. The plans went back to the Great Depression years, and were inspired by a genuine desire to improve housing standards and tackle problems of overcrowding and poverty in the inner city, featured in many novels such as Ruth Park's *Poor Man's Orange*.

There is little doubt that, for many people, a move from a crowded inner city location to the more spacious suburban realm meant an improvement in housing standards. And yet the plans ignored the harsh impact that such redevelopment and relocation programs had on families and social networks as people were re-housed, often in new estates miles from their original neighbourhoods. They also failed to anticipate the difficulties that living in high-rise flats posed for families with young children; the flats were said to 'irritate and impoverish family life'.[33] Such problems created by the redevelopment programs eventually—but not during the 1950s—forced the housing commissions to review their plans.

But the inner city housing market itself provided an even greater barrier to redevelopment. The planners failed to recognise that many people—particularly migrants coming from overseas—were prepared to invest substantial sums in buying and renovating so-called slum housing. It was not long before this was reflected in increased home ownership rates and rising property values in inner city housing areas. More than any other trend, this one, coupled with the later rise of gentrification, prevented the completion of comprehensive redevelopment programs in both inner Sydney and Melbourne.[34] But this was not before much damage had been done to social networks, and to the ambience and human scale of many inner city suburbs.

Equity: Improvements for some

Social priorities, however, were not ignored in all aspects of metropolitan planning in the 1950s. One of the features of the plans was to encourage the dispersal of industrial jobs from central concentrations to suburban industrial areas. One reason for this, especially in the case of Sydney, was that suburban jobs could be more easily accessed by the growing suburban workforce. An analysis undertaken in the early 1980s showed that the Cumberland plan succeeded in producing a more equitable degree of balance between jobs and resident workforce in Sydney during the 1950s than was the case in Melbourne, Perth or Adelaide.[35]

The trend for industrial jobs to be located in suburban rather than central city areas was favoured by industrial capital in any case. Indeed, in Perth, the demands of industrial development at Kwinana was one of the driving forces behind the commissioning of a metropolitan plan. Gordon Stephenson, in an interview recorded late in 1995 (just eighteen months before his death), recalled: 'BP saw they needed a new town, and then there was the question of water supply, the pipeline, and the roads, and so Russell Dumas [Western Australian Director for Works] saw that a regional plan was required and that is how regional planning came into being.'[36]

This is a clear illustration of the power of capital in relation to state planning of the time. The states took a leading role in attracting investment capital to their shores, and the Federal Government was keen to encourage industrial growth in the cities. Between them, the various arms of the state provided plenty of lures in the form of land, infrastructure and housing for workers. Indeed, incoming industries were able to play the states off against each other, with the result of increased assistance. The formalisation of metropolitan planning gave the state planning machinery a key role in determining the location and speed of urban growth associated with the new industries.

But whatever the forces behind industrial job dispersal, Sydney's Cumberland plan affected the location of jobs to the greatest degree. This was recognised in the 1950s by Denis Winston when he noted that 'quite dramatic progress has been made with the improvement of the relationship between home and work'.[37] However, as demonstrated subsequently by Allport,[38] this trend benefited men in the workforce to a far greater extent than women. This is because men had greater access to cars for work journeys which became increasingly car-oriented as jobs and housing suburbanised. In this case, therefore, overall equity gains afforded by the Cumberland plan were undermined by gender-based disadvantages. This is an important caveat qualifying the relative success of the Cumberland plan in improving accessibility to jobs. According to Allport, the trend compounded the 'immense difficulties' faced by women who were part of families relocated from central to distant suburban areas. However poor the conditions from which they moved, one clear advantage the inner city had offered was ready access to employment.

While unfortunate, this trend is predictable given the previously noted mores of the era. The plans were largely written by men who accepted the dominant patriarchal paradigm. This placed 'men's business' (the world of work and strategic planning) before 'women's business' (the world of home and bringing up the kids). And quite apart from such inequitable spin-offs, the drift of jobs from central city to suburban locations created suburban traffic problems and contributed to subsequent environmental degradation associated with excessive car use in Australian cities.

The question of access is also relevant to the planned provision of retailing facilities in suburban areas. The plans in general underestimated the demand for another American-inspired commercial invention—free-standing suburban retail centres or 'malls' surrounded by acres of bitumen and concrete car parks. They were proffered as a desirable model in plans of the early 1950s (Figure 6.3). However, somewhat narrowly, the planners focused not on the design of these centres, but rather on their location. The question was how to steer developers to the designated 'district centres' which were nominated in all the 1950s plans and which were generally located in areas accessible to both public and private transport.

Again, a previous analysis shows that this objective was achieved to the greatest degree in Sydney where several designated district centres contained regional suburban retailing facilities including department stores by the early 1960s.[39] In Melbourne, free-standing centres outside of designated areas were more common, while Perth only got its first free-standing suburban centre in 1958. Marsh notes that Perth had a very centralised retail pattern until the 1960s, with a few suburban ribbon and strip centres evident in inner and middle suburbs.[40] In this instance, therefore, women and other suburban residents without access to cars would have been better off in Sydney than in Melbourne. However, at the same time, commercial office construction was booming in central city areas which meant lengthening commuting trips for office workers—many of whom were female—living in the expanding fringe suburbs.

Metropolitan transport systems

The appearance of 'Australia's own car', the FX Holden of 1948, set the scene for the strong and continuing love affair which Australians have

Figure 6.3 The American dream: a 1950s vision for Australian cities

Source: Stonestown Mall, San Francisco, featured in the *Plan for the Metropolitan Region, Perth and Fremantle, 1955, Report*, WA Government Printer, Perth, 1955.

indulged in ever since. The metropolitan plans of the 1950s each included a comprehensive system of major highways and freeways designed to cater for this trend. These systems, however, were not a result of any comprehensive land use–transport planning, but rather were the creatures of road construction authorities incorporated by rather naive land use planners.

Thus, in Sydney, the Cumberland plan incorporated a 1945 expressway master plan devised by the powerful Department of Main Roads,[41] while in Perth and Melbourne, ambitious road-building plans were also incorporated. One of the aims of these proposed road systems was to provide better access for planned suburbanisation of employment, 'to ease congestion at the centre by dispersing the destination points'.[42] Circumferential road routes were also added to encourage traffic to by-pass the increasingly congested central city areas, although these often appeared to be at odds with plans for a relatively compact metropolitan land use pattern.

At the same time, the plans also laid down new routes for passenger and freight railway lines to serve parts of the metropolitan areas not covered at the time. In Sydney, this translated into plans for the completion of the City Circle line in the CBD and the building of the Eastern Suburbs railway and new circumferential links in outer suburban areas. Similar proposals were made for Melbourne. In Perth, two new lines to designated suburban areas to the north-west and north-east of the city centre were proposed.

However, in the 1950s these plans underwent some dramatic changes. For a start, land needed to be acquired, which was time-consuming and expensive. Second, construction capital needed to be raised. When it came to the crunch, the highway networks received easily the highest priority on both counts. In addition, under the growing influence of American traffic engineering consultants, and in line with the technological imperatives of the day, the planned highways were gradually upgraded to freeway status.[43] Construction started on glamorous parts of the networks, such as the Cahill Expressway in central Sydney, completed in 1962, and the Narrows Bridge from South to Central Perth, which opened in 1959.

Meanwhile, as a symbol of the diminishing role of public transport, trams began to be phased out in both Sydney and Perth (as they were in all capital cities except Melbourne) during the 1950s, primarily on the grounds that they held up road traffic and that buses were more in line with the mood of the decade. Suburban rail systems were operative but not that efficient. In Perth in the 1950s, I can vividly recall travelling by rail to the city on trains powered by dirty steam-powered locomotives or, towards the end of the decade, inefficient diesel cars. The rail systems were being allowed to run down while more funds were allocated to road building.

This was a sign of things to come, for, in the latter years of the decade, the plans for suburban passenger rail extensions were either deferred or dropped. In Sydney, the City Circle train line was completed in 1956, but it was the only rail line built in the metropolis during the decade and had in fact been planned 40 years earlier. While the Cumberland County Council itself was giving warnings of the high environmental and financial costs of the proposed freeways, the next few years saw the deletion of proposed outer suburban rail routes from its own master plan.[44]

Similarly, the proposals for new suburban rail lines in the Stephenson–Hepburn plan for Perth were also scrapped in the late 1950s, and hence did not appear in the 1963 Metropolitan Region Scheme. On the other hand, a massive proposed freeway network did. Governments of the 1950s had apparently been persuaded by the main roads departments that freeways could do a far better and more efficient job. Departmental engineer Stafford argued that the additional railways proposed in the Stephenson–Hepburn plan 'would be most unlikely to attract the patronage required to justify their construction'.[45] Ironically, when a Northern Suburbs railway—built in a freeway reserve—was finally opened in Perth in 1993, its patronage exceeded year 2000 forecasts within months of its opening.[46]

But, in the 1950s, road and freeway plans dominated, and the metropolitan areas were clearly in the grip of 'auto-mania'. This helped to accelerate not just road building but also the planned dispersal of industrial and commercial activities from central city locations. The result was an increase in commuting and travel to locations other than the city centre. This may have been to the immediate benefit of resident suburban workers with access to cars, but the emphasis on road traffic and building which was endorsed in the 1950s led in the long run to social and environmental costs, ranging from the cutting up and dislocation of communities to pollution.

Overall, it can be concluded that the 1950s saw the start of a long period in Australian urban history during which the road lobby, backed by powerful statutory authorities in the form of main roads departments and their equivalents, took over the transport planning agenda of the capital cities. The land use planners may have initially put up some token resistance to these forces, but it was not long before they adopted the philosophy of 'if you can't beat them, join them'.

Population growth: the market rules

This emphasis on suburban growth ensured the continued outward spread of the metropolitan areas. In Sydney, the first census of the 1950s (1954) showed that the rate of population growth was about twice that forecast in 1948.[47] Proposals to establish a new town beyond the green belt at Minto (in south-western Sydney) were put forward by the state Housing Commission in accordance with the strategy of the Cumberland plan. Even so, the Cumberland County Council opposed the plan on the grounds that there was still sufficient undeveloped land in existing housing areas.

A protracted argument between the council and the state government followed and, by 1959, the government had announced the suspension of 46 square miles (119 square kilometres) of the belt. The abolition of the green belt was regarded by many pro-development interests and land development companies as essential to the protection and expansion of their land investments. While considerable public debate followed, as shown in Chapter 7, it was only a matter of time before the Cumberland County Council was abolished. Clearly development interests held sway in this debate.

In Melbourne, the metropolitan plan of 1954 had been based on an assumption of a continuation of the relatively low population growth rates which had prevailed in previous decades. As in the case of Sydney, this meant that the planners underestimated the subsequent growth and physical spread of suburban development. Logan and McLoughlin have demonstrated how population growth translated into far greater extensions of the physical fabric of the metropolis to both the east and the north of the CBD than allowed for by the plan.[48] In Perth, while the population growth forecast by the Stephenson–Hepburn plan was closer to the actual mark than in either Sydney or Melbourne, the degree of urban spread was nonetheless far beyond the plan's expectations. This was due to the land development market combining with rapid expansion of car ownership and use to produce a much lower density of urban development than anticipated.[49]

Conclusion

The 1950s were years of great initiative and energy in Australian metropolitan planning in at least three Australian cities in a formal sense, and in others on an informal basis. Plans were drawn up under the strong influence of international movements such as modernism, and British planning ideas and personalities played an important part. In turn these planners, and Australians in general, were increasingly influenced by American cultural values. The plans were being implemented in a society governed by conservatives and heavily influenced by the power of capital. Increasingly, the cities were imbued with values of patriarchy and consumerism.

Metropolitan plans of the decade nonetheless sought to restrain and order the outward growth of the cities. But the ideals of compact development and green belts were soon to fall victim to demographic, developmental, transport and political priorities. It is clear that industrial and land development capital, combined with the powerful car lobby, played a much larger part in determining the overall disposition of metropolitan expansion than did planning ideals of environmental protection or equity.

The plans for redevelopment of inner 'slum' areas in the cities, and accommodating overspill development in planned suburban estates, led—as they had in so many British cities where similar plans were being implemented during the decade—to the breaking of social bonds among poorer inner city communities displaced by redevelopment. They also made incoming families more car dependent as they were reresettled in newer suburban developments. Inner city housing redevelopment slowed in later years of the decade due to political reaction and to the infusion of capital into house renovations among immigrant families moving into these areas, combined with increasing gentrification.

The metropolitan plans also aimed to provide a better measure of jobs and facilities in rapidly expanding suburban areas. A small measure of progress was made towards meeting these objectives in the decade, as the dispersal of industry allowed some improvement in the balance of jobs to workers resident in suburban areas, particularly in Sydney. This outcome can be regarded as more equitable in an overall sense, but given greater access to expanding car ownership among male workers, the greatest accessibility improvements accrued to men rather than women.

These inequities were heightened by the way in which governments failed to adopt improvements to the public transport systems recommended in the 1950s plans and in fact ran down the systems in many regards. Instead, the priorities of the road-building authorities took over, fed by the activities of the car builders. They promised to provide suburban families with the ideal means of transport—the 'family car'. This was made more attractive by generous freeway and highway systems built into the plans, construction of which was getting into full swing by 1960.

So the 1950s was a decade in which planning virtually institutionalised the suburban mosaic which is still expanding rapidly half a century later. This expansion is helping to create metropolitan areas which are increasingly regarded as unsustainable for the new millennium.

7 The corridor city: planning for growth in the 1960s

Ian Morison

After one and a half decades of assisted European migration, expansion of tariff-protected manufacturing and continuing movement from the bush due to farm mechanisation, the population of Australia's major cities by 1961 had grown by over two million from their immediate post-war base of under four million people. The mainland capitals would grow by another two million in the 1960s, having absorbed 80 per cent of the national post-war population increase. They would take in nearly a half million more before world oil price rises and economic recession, plus tariff cuts and inflation in the early 1970s ended 25 years of continuous growth. By the early 1960s, planners were making drastic revisions to earlier forecasts of city growth, preparing for populations to double in 30 years. Less demanding circumstances faced them after 1975.[1]

By 1960, the metropolitan regions, especially the largest, were experiencing serious supply problems with urban land and infrastructure. Sydney and Melbourne would each continue to grow by about 50 000 people a year until the out-migration of the 1970s, due to unemployment plus the effects of a gradual decline in the national birth rate, halved their annual increase. About 20 000 people a year would be added to the other mainland capitals: Adelaide's numbers dropped after mid-decade but Perth's and Brisbane's increased as markets for their states' natural resources strengthened.

Pressure on the cities was not simply because of population growth. They also had to absorb the effects of increased consumption by a society enjoying a higher standard of living. Rates of car ownership had doubled in the 1950s and would rise another 50 per cent in the 1960s. Increased mobility for shopping, social and recreational purposes would in this decade double the kilometres travelled on metropolitan roads. The cities would acquire important new reference points as retailing, manufacturing and goods handling centres moved away from the inner city areas to larger and more accessible sites. High levels of family formation and full employment fostered expectations of home ownership with convenient access to schools, shops and recreation. For some, this dream would later be realised in the form of gentrified inner city housing and ex-urban hobby farms, but for the vast majority of new households, plus those that moved out of rented accommodation in the inner city, the route would be affordable housing in new suburbs.

Metropolitan planning in the 1960s was primarily about meeting the needs of population growth, which in practice meant development at the urban fringe. Without the cooperation of local councils, metropolitan planning had limited influence over developments in already built-up suburbs, such as the relocation of inner city activities to sites not well served by public transport. Local government had direct contact with the social and environmental aspects of urban change—manifested by increasing public interest in planning decisions, skilful use of media and organised protest, and calls for public participation. Pressures to be more effective in meeting the demand for new housing wrought fundamental changes to metropolitan planning and organisation: the emergence of a real urban development industry, replacement of more or less concentric growth by the concept of growth corridors, and the introduction of simpler and more flexible strategic plans.

Taken together, these changes raised the quality of metropolitan planning and development. The tradition of unserviced land subdivision, which led to uncontrollable public costs and urban sprawl, was not replaced by a packaged land development process until the early 1970s. Early in the 1960s, it was thought that better knowledge of urban dynamics would lead to new concepts of metropolitan form and structure, but serious exploration was delayed when state governments gave priority to dealing with urban transport problems. It was not until the latter half of the decade, when an open-ended framework for metropolitan growth and change was adopted for Canberra, that growth corridors began to be considered for other Australian cities. By the early 1970s, in parallel with the statutory system of land use schemes, explanatory documents at local, metropolitan and state level would prove more useful to the many public and private agencies that needed to negotiate and plan ahead.

This chapter traces these changes—organisational, conceptual and administrative—brought about by the pressures of growth and higher living standards. Events in Canberra, Sydney, Melbourne, Adelaide and Perth illustrate perceptions of the corridor city and the changing nature of metropolitan planning in Australia.

The land development process

By the early 1960s, it was evident that post-war metropolitan plans for Sydney and Melbourne had not only underestimated their rates of growth, but that some of the ways in which the cities had been expected to absorb the added population were proving almost totally ineffective. Run-down inner areas were not being redeveloped at higher density, but instead were proving popular with European migrants (Chapter 6). Decentralisation policies were not working, with most satellite towns either too small or too distant. The only effective avenue for raising the stock of housing was the one sought almost universally by homeseekers: new housing on the metropolitan fringe. The necessary land had to be made available for subdivision, an action which had to be initiated by individual landholders in areas zoned for conversion from rural to urban purposes.

Post-war metropolitan plans sought to contain outward expansion within a defined envelope to avoid premature land subdivision and its legacy of scattered suburban lots—largely vacant and without urban amenities or services. But within that envelope the traditional way of extending Australian cities was still producing poor-quality and scattered urban sprawl. The subdivision and sale of rural land was followed at varying intervals by the provision of utility services and the sporadic development of houses, schools and shops. Huge tracts of land were being consumed to meet sustained demands for housing by a process which could take several decades to complete.

Few areas were still available within the statutory planning schemes. Melbourne's 1954 plan was just coping with rapid eastward expansion, but Sydney's green belt policy under the 1948 *Cumberland County Plan* was defeated late in 1959. The plan had helped to get more economic use of serviced vacant land in existing urban zones but county planners, recognising that further outward expansion was inevitable, recommended the excision of an initial 5000 acres (2000 hectares) of green belt land. However, the planning minister undermined the whole green belt concept by announcing that 46 square miles (12 000 hectares) would be made available for urban development. This dramatic move against the plan's control over rural subdivision encouraged lobbyists and demoralised evangelical planners, but subsequent public debate persuaded the minister to agree that subdivision plans in these release areas would not be approved unless the developer provided local water and sewerage services and contributed to trunk service costs. That would prove to be a significant step for coordinated development.[2]

The minister's decision applied only to the approved release areas but, because it relieved the public purse and made the developer rather than the landholder the key player, it would gradually apply to all of Sydney's land releases. This new nexus between land subdivision and provision of engineering services had parallels in the other capitals. Priority would also be given to releases of rural lands amenable to early servicing around Adelaide, the release of 'preferred areas' in Melbourne and the phased conversion of 'urban deferred' land around Perth. The result was a deepening of financial commitments by land developers. By the 1970s, land developers would be organised into a uniquely Australian form of development industry which, because its members had to outlay substantial funds on land and engineering services, had a strong interest in working with the planning authorities to safeguard their own forward planning of expenditures and sales to ensure returns on capital.[3]

State governments responded in different ways to the realisation that the financial burdens placed on public agencies by unserviced suburban growth could be better managed if they created an appropriate metropolitan planning body. Victoria had quarantined the problem within the local government arena via the Melbourne and Metropolitan Board of Works (MMBW), leaving it without effective state links until the 1980s. In Perth, where the seeds for cooperative city planning among state and local agencies had been sown in the 1950s by planner–educator Gordon Stephenson, the Metropolitan Region Planning Authority (MRPA) established in 1960 included five state infrastructure agencies, five representatives of local government and one from the private sector. A few years later, South Australia and New South Wales established state planning authorities on similar lines.[4] Queensland would not risk the creation of a political competitor even larger than Brisbane City Council.

The search for new approaches

The first *new* metropolitan plan of the 1960s was for Adelaide. After three decades of nothing more than subdivision control, the *Town Planning Act 1955* had provided for a metropolitan plan, and in 1962 state planner Stuart Hart presented the results of five years of systematic teamwork in his innovative *Report on the Metropolitan Area of Adelaide*. In response to recent population growth of 20 000 per year, the plan envisaged a number of metropolitan districts of 80 000–150 000 people with their own centres as 'the most economic form of expansion where most people prefer to live in detached single-storey dwellings',[5] spreading for 80 miles (128 kilometres) from Gawler in the north to Sellicks Beach in the south in the wedge of land between a protected Mt Lofty Range to the east and Gulf St Vincent to the west (Figure 7.1). This arrangement

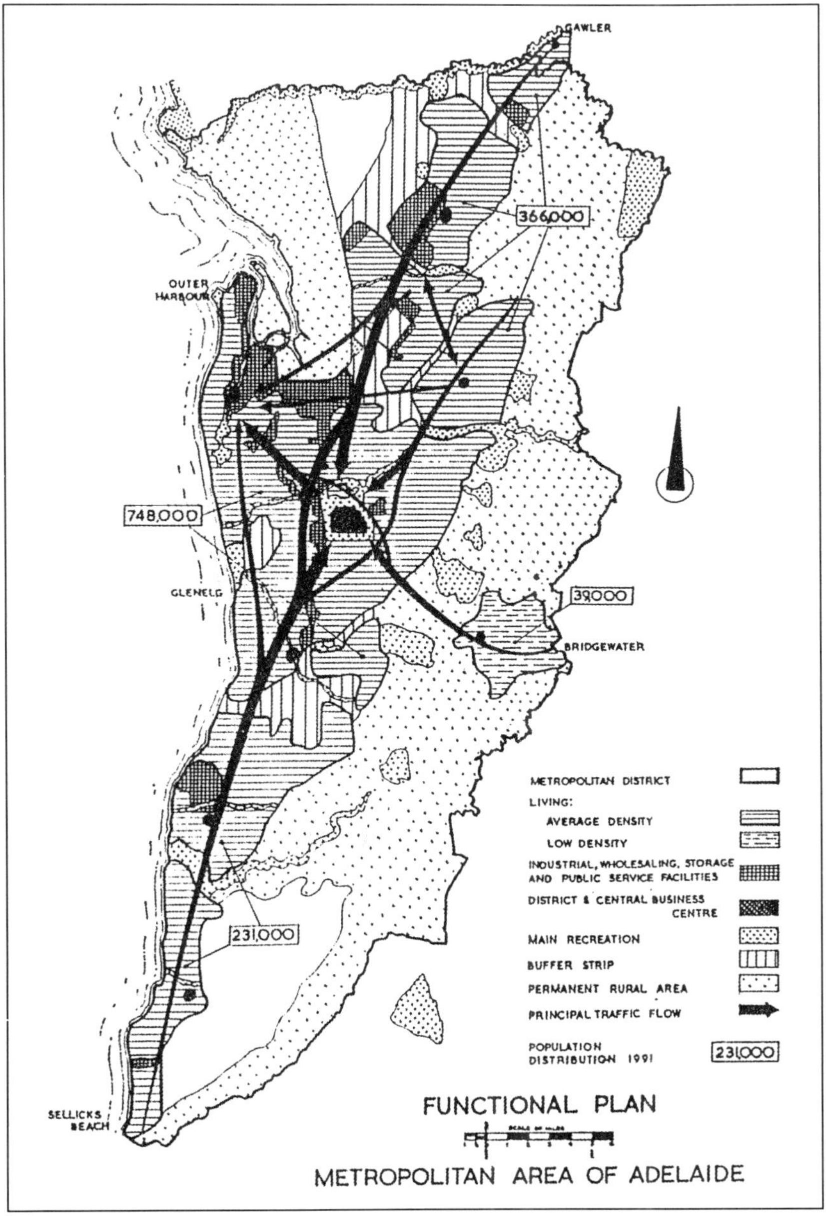

Figure 7.1 Functional plan for metropolitan Adelaide (1962)

Source: Australian Planning Institute Journal (APIJ), January 1963. Courtesy *Australian Planner.*

had much in common with later corridor plans but was not adopted as the *Metropolitan Development Plan* till 1967.

Meanwhile, urban planners were trying to understand where society in the space age, and the contradictions of structural changes in major cities, were leading them: movements of industry and services to the suburbs left an office monoculture at the centre; lifestyles needed cars which choked streets; there were fewer inner city workers despite ever-higher office buildings; and there were congested peaks yet growing deficits in public transport. The threat to the human scale posed by massive new roads and tall buildings was 'one of the central problems of urban design today'.[6] It was a time to look overseas for guidance. Colin Buchanan, author of the best-selling government report *Traffic in Towns* and invited to Melbourne in 1964 to explain his approach to planning and transport systems, declared that the car had killed the street.[7] Canada's Humphrey Carver saw new opportunities for 'cities in the suburbs', but the first crop of free-standing regional shopping centres built by department stores in Australia fell short of what he had in mind.[8] The flight of formerly centralised functions to the suburbs was shifting the emphasis away from the historic centre, but toward what kind of metropolitan form and structure?

Plans for land use in conjunction with an expanding arterial road network were strengthening Perth's metropolitan structure in the early 1960s, despite controversial changes to the city landscape wrought by the Mitchell Freeway which had long been accepted in the public mind as a necessary spine to planned urban expansion. Adelaide and Melbourne were less fortunate in the late 1960s. Their transportation studies under the control of ministers for highways sought to improve access to the inner city area rather than try to resolve questions of metropolitan form and structure. Highway engineers had acquired control of the influential transport component of metropolitan planning, but would lose it in the early 1970s when inner city residents demonstrated the political fallout from unwanted urban freeways and state governments arbitrarily scrapped them. Similar studies for Perth and Sydney, completed early in the 1970s, would pay more attention to metropolitan planning strategies but were still focused on improving city travel rather than improving the cities. Transport planning in the 1970s would shift to managing demand rather than catering for it, and to studies of transport-related social and environmental issues. The two-way relationship between metropolitan planning and transport would remain unexplored as an influence on metropolitan planning.[9]

The 1964 Congress of the Australian Planning Institute or API (soon to be the Royal API), in an effort to understand the processes of change in urban Australia, initiated moves to establish a small centrally placed research bureau, similar to those in Ottawa and Washington, to provide a clearing house for investigative work in Australian urban planning.[10] Later that year, the University of Sydney launched its Planning Research

Centre under Denis Winston. The Australian National University's Noel Butlin began a seminar series on urbanisation in Australia,[11] and in the spring of 1965 its Urban Research Unit began working on issues of urban administration and the links between housing, planning and transport.[12] The API's research centre initiative bore fruit soon afterwards as the Australian Institute of Urban Studies, with a small federal secretariat in Canberra attracting contributions from industry and the professions to early work on developmental issues in land and housing. By the late 1960s, urban protest, among the earliest movements being inner Sydney residents in January 1968 demanding participation in planning policy,[13] heightened academic interest in the politics of urban growth and change in Australian cities.

In March 1965, Gough Whitlam, soon to be leader of the Federal Opposition, started to campaign on behalf of the growing numbers of people who were either suffering neglect in the new outer suburbs or destructive change in the inner city, by telling the Australian Parliament of the bipartisan support for national land and housing programs in Britain, Europe and North America.[14] He gathered information for later speeches about conditions in Australian cities from many sources, including studies by the new research centres and the National Capital Development Commission (NCDC). With its different discussion venues, and warming political interest at federal level, Canberra over the next ten years became a hotbed of opportunities for exposure and contact between players from all areas of Australian society with an interest in metropolitan issues.

National capital new towns and corridors

In the Griffin plan, gazetted by parliament in 1925, provision for a Canberra of 75 000 people seemed at the time to be grossly excessive. The plan remained a skeleton in the government closet until late in 1957 when, as a critical element of his task, the astute John Overall demanded, and was given, responsibility for all government works, free of any departmental control, for the National Capital Development Commission to plan, construct and develop Canberra. With 36 000 people in a scattering of suburbs (but no land ready for house building) and the Molonglo River flood plain devoted to farm paddocks, a racecourse and a golf course, he had to initiate action on three fronts: to reinstate the Griffin city beautiful plan for a lake and parliamentary triangle (Chapter 2); to organise programs for defence personnel to move from Melbourne with a guarantee that they would have adequate housing, schools and community services on arrival; and to rework the gazetted plan for a much larger population.[15]

Under a spotlight, the NCDC had to deliver a quality product quickly on the first two fronts. Guided by Sir William Holford's recommendations to the Commonwealth Government,[16] an immediate start was made on the lake, bridges and a new defence department complex. New neighbourhoods were designed and developed as complete and fully serviced living environments under a works program that covered all of the urban capital expenditures which elsewhere in Australia were spread over decades among local councils and several government departments. Five-year development plans allowed continuity of operations, with productivity increases through long-term construction contracts, and encouraged business investment.[17] Sound financial returns accrued to the Commonwealth from this approach, confirmed by the audits of British experts.[18] No government forecast was ventured as to Canberra's ultimate size, so work on the third front was kept in-house until urban land servicing had to move beyond the area of the Griffin plan. In 1964, a scheme with separate residential districts for a city of 250 000 people was presented to government, but not made public.

Lake Burley Griffin, 'inaugurated' by Prime Minister Menzies in October 1964, brought the National Capital Triangle to life. The monumental National Library and Anzac Parade were under construction, as was the development of Commonwealth Park to Sylvia Crowe's design. Earthworks and plantations were bringing Griffin's composition into sharper focus, in spite of many vacant sites for future buildings. The impressions of future visitors, in particular the approving analysis of eminent experts such as US planner Edmund Bacon, would bring forth national appreciation of a vast urban landscape, and of Canberra 'as a statement of world culture'.[19] It was time for the Australian public to contemplate a metropolitan future for the bush capital. *The Future Canberra* (1965) laid out the NCDC's approach to planning for a city of at least 250 000 'by the development of clearly defined districts occupying the valleys . . . in the vicinity of the existing city', with hills and ridges forming part of a permanent parkland system providing corridors for future transport services.[20] By then even longer term horizons were being examined.

The recommendations of a 1963 transportation study for major new roads and interchanges to serve the city of 250 000 were not compatible with the symbolism of the national centre, so the NCDC set most of them aside. However, it still needed to find a strategy for the long-term future: the 250 000 horizon was only 20 to 25 years away. At a convention on this subject, organised by the new Canberra Branch of the API's Sydney Division in November 1963, Gordon Stephenson and NCDC chief planner Peter Harrison recommended the examination of an approach which would allow for continuous growth:

> Such an exploration moves beyond the realm of planning as generally understood . . . the main aim being to establish a principle of growth rather than a precise plan . . . a background against which current land use decisions and land reservations can be made . . . [for] airports, power transmission routes, cemeteries, treatment works and many institutions requiring broad acres . . . [and] a variety of entirely unpredictable demands . . . The notional pattern . . . is a series of districts of the order of 100,000 population . . . linked by a web of transportation corridors . . . The similarity in principle to Ebenezer Howard's ideas of orderly urban growth will be apparent. The important differences are in the enlarged scale . . . the principle of continued growth in a guided but restricted sequence rather than by aggregation appears to offer a rational framework.[21]

Here were two respected educator–planners soberly asserting that the NCDC needed to look beyond the limits of the Australian Capital Territory (ACT) to prepare for the prospect of a substantial metropolitan region if it was to find a means of dealing with a universal problem: the tendency of cities to become over-centralised.

The framework they envisaged would provide for unbounded metropolitan growth, an idea similar to that of Howard's disciple Thomas Adams in the 1920s to ameliorate the congestion of New York. But where Adams relied on the intersection points of planned regional highways to form growth nodes, the less accessible land being reserved for regional parks, the idea for Canberra was the reverse: roads would not be built in suggested non-urban corridors until they were needed to serve the growing urban districts. The Adams plan had been attacked for naively relying on private enterprise to achieve social ends, and he was criticised in planning circles despite his eminent standing as founding president of the British and Canadian town planning institutes and his prominence in the US equivalent.[22] But his strategy of using the power of highways to influence patterns of urban growth retained its currency as a planning tool in the United States. The 1961 corridor plan for Washington DC was a recent example familiar to visiting NCDC planners.[23] Much of the expansion into Virginia and Maryland was fairly chaotic and patchy because of land speculation and lack of coordination, but two planned communities along similar lines to Canberra's new districts were of particular interest. These were Robert Simon's Reston for 75 000 people near Dulles airport and James Rouse's Columbia for 120 000 people beside the highway to Baltimore. Both were designed to grow as satellite villages around a town centre, the developers having made sure that they controlled enough land to comprehensively program, coordinate and market the towns. With the right kind of organisation, nominated corridors could concentrate and direct urban development.

Before it could justifiably spend public funds on new districts, the NCDC needed to know more about the arrangement and design of urban growth corridors, to see how they might best be used to serve the interests of Canberra in the short and long terms. Prompted by Gordon Stephenson's question, 'Where's your plan for a million?', planners Tom McKenna, Keith Storey and Ian Morison prepared material on possible long-term urban forms and structures for a study which would look for a suitable combination of land use and transport characteristics. Contact with urban researchers and planners in Washington led in May 1966 to the acceptance by Alan Voorhees of 'a brief to devise a plan which will provide a physical symbol to the rest of the country and the world of the strength and character of Australia'[24] by developing a simple structural framework around which the city could renew itself over generations, while avoiding a chaotic environment of continual destruction and reconstruction, and by allowing individual towns to be built quickly and remain stable thereafter.

Voorhees' operational task was to find an urban form and development program able to accommodate increasing levels of activity without developing transportation bottlenecks. He answered the brief by comparing the transport characteristics of urban forms for a future region of a half million people and upward to one million. This provided evidence of likely pressures on the metropolitan centre, the viability of different locations and sizes for district centres, and the potential for rapid public transport by rail. The *General Plan Concept* derived from this analysis aimed for long-term efficiency and stability through interdependent metropolitan systems of land use and transport fitted to the region's topography, with towns of 80 000–100 000 people around strong multi-purpose centres, linked by a public transport spine (on its own right-of-way) along three growth corridors, and flanked by freeways to be developed when needed.[25]

In draft form the concept was endorsed in October 1966 by the NCDC's professional watchdog, the National Capital Planning Committee, and from early 1967 the *General Plan Concept* guided important NCDC decisions on the location and sequence of what would henceforth be called 'towns' instead of 'districts'. Lands reserved for unwanted urban expressways were deleted from the plan to free up community planning in the towns of Woden and Belconnen. Reserves for future north–south freeways were relocated away from inner Canberra to reduce future impacts on the central area. Programmed moves of public service departments, Canberra's basic industry, became an integral part of the employment pattern at town centres. The *General Plan Concept* (by now known as the

'Y Plan') was first made known to the public through a drawing in the professional press in August 1968[26] (Figure 7.2). Landholders, would-be developers and hobby farmers saw new opportunities over the border, causing a sharp rise in land prices and rural subdivisions until it became clear that piped water for small lots would not be supplied from the ACT. The NCDC had sought to initiate inter-governmental discussions about planning for possible urban development in nearby New South Wales, but was frustrated by prime ministerial changes.[27] Inter-governmental work on this wider metropolitan region began during the Whitlam administration, then ceased to be an issue for another fifteen years.

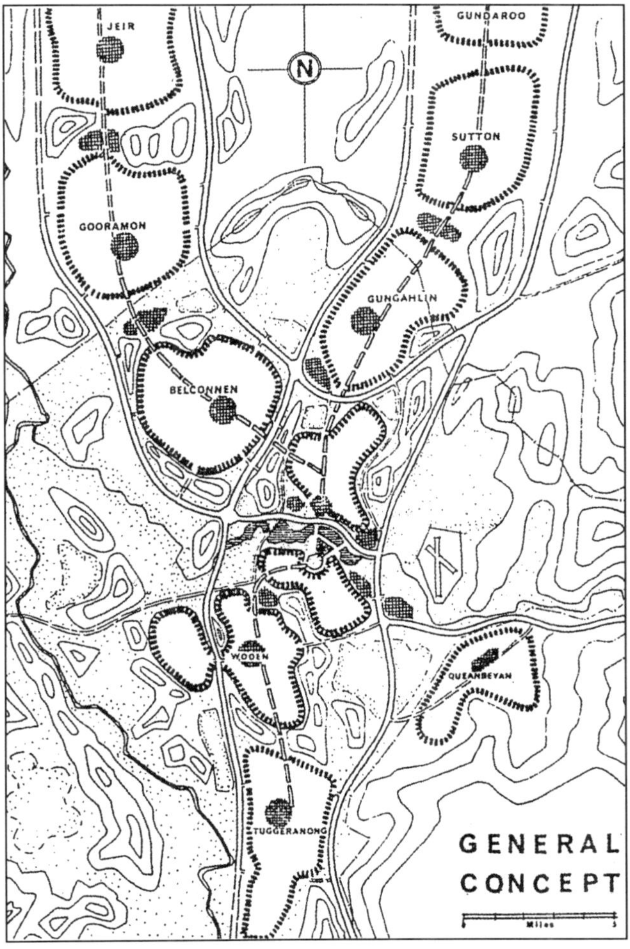

Figure 7.2 A 'General Concept' for metropolitan growth: Canberra's Y Plan by Peter Harrison

Source: Architecture in Australia, August 1968. Courtesy S. Harrison.

The NCDC's *Tomorrow's Canberra* of 1970 presented at length the rationale for its towns-in-corridors strategy, at the same time recognising that what has 'the force of logic today may not be valid tomorrow because the values of society may have changed'.[28] In the 1980s, city centre business interests started to campaign for a more centralised city and the NCDC published senior planner John Gilchrist's reworking of arguments for the Y Plan's balanced metropolitan structure.[29] In the 1990s, a self-governing and cash-strapped ACT would cut back expenditure on new urban infrastructure and promote residential redevelopment in older areas (Chapter 10). Proponents of urban consolidation and increased use of public transport claim Canberra encourages excessive travel by private transport.[30] In fact the people of Canberra localise their activity as much as, and travel no further than, other people in metropolitan Australia.[31] Despite 30 years of social and economic change, the interests of the Griffins' national capital landscape are still served by the Y Plan.

State capital corridors

The multidisciplinary NCDC had developed a scheme for unlimited growth by integrating transport planning and town planning. But, in the state capitals, different levels of government, competing authorities and a limited engagement in the processes of development, placed metropolitan planning in a lesser role. Railway lines had given Australian cities their early corridor structure, now being lost to a formless suburban spread that relied on road-based transport. American visions of corridor cities were, to Australian planners, of little more than academic interest because of their association with massive American highway programs. But as there seemed to be no alternative to growth at the suburban fringe, the question was: what *form* should it take?[32] Canberra's adaptation of the corridor concept gave impetus to directional growth as the answer to continuing metropolitan expansion in Australia.

What planners in some of the states tended to overlook, however, was the *structure* that planning had to embed in the corridor concept if it was to avoid a continuing raw deal for dwellers at the metropolitan fringe. Within the corridors there needed to be plans and programs for water and sewerage trunk lines, transport access, and health and education services. What some state governments had done occasionally in the past for purposes of industrial development—most notably at Elizabeth—ought now to be done in a routine manner to end the tradition of new suburbs that lacked services for as long as residents could be persuaded to travel elsewhere to reach them. By the mid-1960s, land developers in the states were beginning to contribute to public expenditure on water and sewerage for new suburbs but state governments faced huge backlogs of services elsewhere.

A more affluent population was looking for something better and Whitlam had started to draw this to the attention of the Federal Government and metropolitan electorates.[33] Liberal and Country Party governments of the more populous states wanted to avoid spending more money on the cities by attracting people to country regions. The practicalities of doing this in a planned manner were put forward by the NCDC's Bob Lansdown in 1966, using figures from Canberra to show that a program to quickly build a regional city would cost no more than adding the same population to the metropolis. But state governments had first to grasp a political nettle by deciding where to put the regional city.[34] They did not and the cities urgently needed to cope with expansion. Senior planners in Melbourne, Sydney and Perth, taking on board the scheme for Canberra's growth recently endorsed by their colleagues, commended the concept to their political masters. They had mixed success.

Melbourne

In May 1966, the Victorian minister for local government, Rupert Hamer, asked the state's two planning bodies, the Town and Country Planning Board (TCPB) and the MMBW, to report on Melbourne's future growth. Rod Fraser, Sydney's former chief planner recently appointed as chairman of the TCPB, advised him that Victoria lacked the appropriate organisation to implement a plan, and that among the three possible growth concepts for Melbourne, only corridors of 'metro-towns' could provide for the 'regulated growth of communities'. His report outlined a scheme for metro-towns of up to 100 000 developed from either new or expanded settlements to the east, and in corridors extending east and south of Dandenong. This pattern accorded with the preference people were expressing with their feet but was seen as a threat to business and government interests, shifting growth away from the City of Melbourne.[35]

The advice of the MMBW's chief planner, Alistair Hepburn, was that corridors were a compromise between satellite and fringe growth rather than solutions in their own right, growth should be redirected to less attractive areas north and west of Melbourne, the Melbourne Transportation Study should test alternatives and, finally, the MMBW's statutory scheme should be enlarged to cover the whole zone undergoing rural–urban conversion.[36] This battle was easily won by the MMBW, whose revised statutory scheme of 1971 included urban extensions along all rail lines, thus maintaining the tradition of locally controlled creeping suburbia

(Chapter 8). The attractions of areas south and east of Dandenong for farming, recreation and urban living would turn the region into a 1970s battleground between landholders, conservationists and land developers.[37] Fraser was right; Victoria did not possess the organisation to build metro-towns. Nor did it have the political commitment to create such an organisation.

Sydney

In Sydney the chief planner of the State Planning Authority (SPA), Peter Kacirek, with the leader of his metropolitan planning team, Tony Powell, proposed in 1967 to provide for Sydney's growth by planning for half a million more people in each of four corridors. The resulting scheme, published in March 1968, avoided precise boundaries but used existing transport routes as spines and existing towns as nodes of growth, taking in Campbelltown to the south-west, Mt Druitt and Penrith to the west, and the more distant towns of Gosford and Wyong to the north. The fourth corridor, to the north-west, would come later. Existing, proposed, future and possible urban areas were welded together in diagrams promoting aims and principles for staged development of balanced communities with a wide variety of employment to help offset pressures on the metropolitan city centre[38] (Figure 7.3).

Confident presentation of Sydney's economic future in an international setting, with a strategy for its physical growth and change, gave the *Sydney Region Outline Plan* a dynamic appeal, helping to restore respect for metropolitan planning.[39] Subsequent action by the SPA, using its power to acquire land, was directed primarily to these areas of new growth, with the purchase of 4000 hectares of land for key areas of Campbelltown. In the western corridor the Authority acquired 136 hectares for the commercial centre of Mt Druitt, enabling a level of entrepreneurial involvement without precedent in New South Wales.[40] Although Sydney's metropolitan growth would drop markedly in the 1970s, the high levels of growth assumed for new areas in the 1968 plan would be maintained because of the 'doughnut' effect of baby boomers moving out of households in older areas. This component of growth would be felt to varying degrees in other cities in the 1970s.[41]

Perth

The chief planner of Perth's MRPA, David Carr, gave a paper with Gordon Stephenson in May 1966 to a Royal Australian Institute of Architects convention, in which they said that in the 'new era of planning

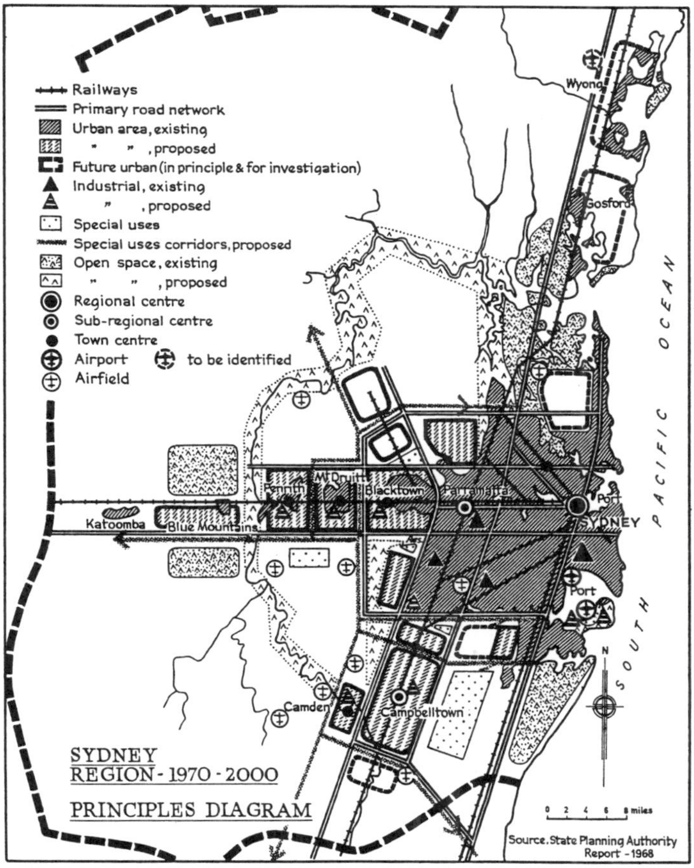

Figure 7.3 'Principles Diagram': *Sydney Region Outline Plan* (1968)

Source: Australian Planning Institute Journal (APIJ), April 1969. Courtesy *Australian Planner.*

ideas . . . corridor development must be positively planned and services closely programmed' to avoid haphazard development.[42] Mineral exports were fuelling a land boom around Perth, with demand being inflated by real estate promotion. To prick this balloon and bring down prices the MRPA released 15 000 acres (6000 hectares) to the north-west and south-east of Perth, bringing forward the need to define new areas for urban development. In August 1968, the MRPA's *Perth Region and People* canvassed two concepts for growth—corridors and clusters—commencing six months later to prepare strategic plans for extensions in four corridors. In November 1970, the structure, development strategy and measures for implementing them were explained in *The Corridor Plan for Perth* (Figure 7.4).

This carefully prepared sequence of moves almost came to naught in 1972 when the planning minister of a new Labor Government, who had

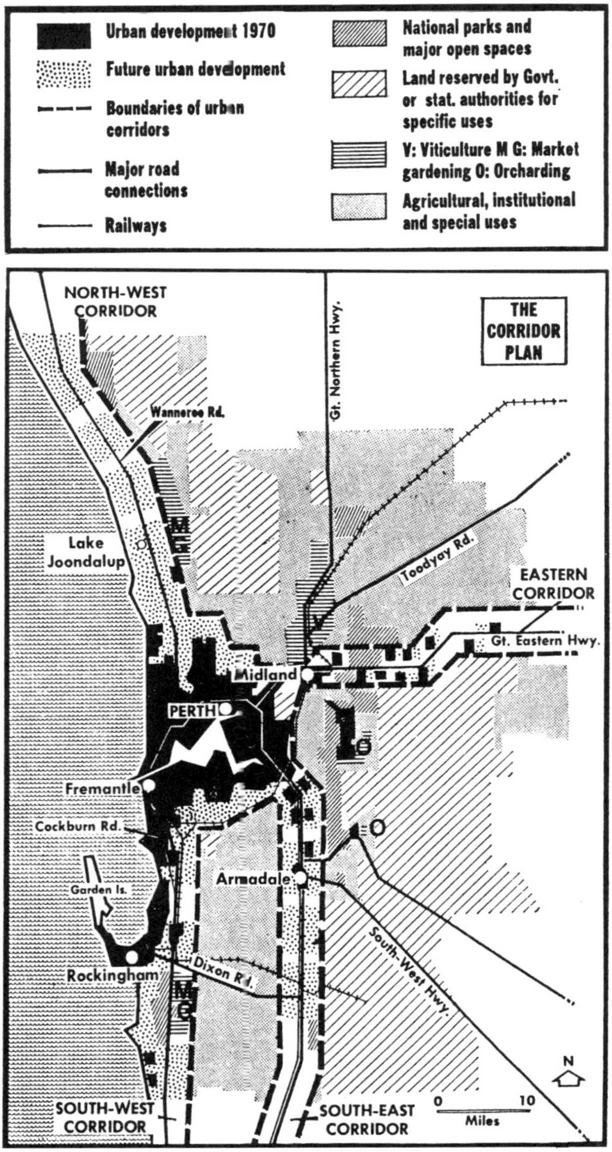

Figure 7.4 Perth's corridor plan (1972)

Source: First published November 1970. *Australian Planning Institute Journal (APIJ)*, July 1972. Courtesy *Australian Planner*.

campaigned on behalf of rural landholders, was noncommittal about adhering to land release programs in designated corridors. The logic of the minister's position came from a non-planning study he had commissioned, the findings of which the MRPA refuted in very clear terms in its *Report on the Corridor Plan for Perth* in July 1972.[43] The MRPA won this fight, but not before political lobbying had secured urban zoning for certain syndicates holding land outside any planned corridor. Subsequent land development and roads planning followed the designated corridors, with existing centres expanding to regional scale at Rockingham, Armidale and Midland. For the most popular but virtually rural corridor, near Perth's northern beaches, planning for the new Joondalup regional centre began in 1976.

The fastest growing sectors of Australia's cities would attract Commonwealth funding from late in 1972 to investigate metropolitan 'growth centres' designed to take up growth pressures and improve quality of life in the cities. They included the south-west and northern corridors of Sydney, the south-west sector of Melbourne and the northern corridor of Perth.[44] States with appropriate organisations used this unprecedented federal bounty to push forward their plans for the development of new communities. Sydney's metropolitan planners would later move out of their city offices to coordinate developments in the growth corridors, gaining an altogether new perspective on their role.[45] Public control over lands needed for commercial and community purposes was the key to attracting to these new centres many of the facilities of a city. Development corporations were established to take charge of Sydney's south-west corridor and Perth's regional centre at Joondalup. The Noarlunga district centre, one of those identified in the 1962 plan for Adelaide, developed on public land to become the primary centre for a large and growing population in the southern part of metropolitan Adelaide.

Conclusion

By the end of the 1960s, metropolitan planning, previously limited to visions of the future and blueprints for the control of land use by local councils, was starting to acquire an *operational* role, producing and managing strategic frames of reference for metropolitan development and protection of the environment. This placed a *developmental* perspective on metropolitan planning and on the players that shape urban change: the planners through their metropolitan strategies; the residents who decide where to live; the employers who decide where to locate; the developers who decide where and when to initiate new urban projects for sale; and the transport and utility service agencies who modify land use potential by creating areas of raised or lowered accessibility.[46]

Under the pressures of growth, urban corridors helped to give these players more room to move and strategic plans helped to integrate their moves. More confident planning and programming of a larger scale of development in defined areas provided a better product for the residents of new suburbs without an undue increase in cost. Urban improvement programs in the mid-1970s shifted attention to the older and poorer suburbs to redress their physical, social and environmental deficiencies. Governments were learning to be coordinators of public investment in urban services and to facilitate private sector investment in houses, shops and factories.[47]

The multi-centred corridor city posed a threat to concentrations of power in the historic city centres, and the corridor city's extended urban perimeter required firm control to resist the tradition of converting peripheral land to urban purposes. The 1960s experience showed that planning agencies with organisational links to state and local government were better placed to meet these challenges and develop new communities. Governments possessing the necessary organisation made extensive commitments within defined metropolitan growth corridors. A growing political spotlight on problems in the cities through the late 1960s drew metropolitan planning towards more overt roles of social reform. After talking to many planners in the late 1960s, historian Hugh Stretton in *Ideas for Australian Cities* saw in 'the long thin corridor city' the means of redressing many of the inequities of life in large cities that result from the quiet transfer of resources from the poor to the well-off.[48]

Urban programs would proliferate in the 1970s in the highly charged political atmosphere of states reacting to federal interventions to improve life in the cities, as considered in Chapter 8. State machinery and priorities for resource allocation for urban purposes would gradually be reorganised, much of it being devoted to community development in nominated growth corridors. Though subsequent achievements on the ground have been patchy, the corridor concept fashioned in the 1960s remains a feature of metropolitan planning in Australia.

8 Administrative coordination, urban management and strategic planning in the 1970s

Margo Huxley

The 1970s were a decade of marked change in economic, political and social conditions from the previous twenty years of post-war growth. In the first half of the decade, the quadrupling of oil prices by the Organisation of Petroleum Exporting Countries (OPEC) in 1973, land price rises and central business district (CBD) building booms in some cities, increases in unemployment, and increases in cheap imported goods, as a result of lowering of the once-hallowed tariff protection, heralded the end of the long boom. The rise and fall of the Federal Labor Government, with its interest in spatial policy and urban affairs, was followed in the second half of the decade by the Liberals' 'new federalism' in which realisation of changed economic fortunes became articulated in federal and state politics and policies. The (largely unrealised) resources boom became the mainstay of economic policy towards the end of the decade, contributing to the growth of cities such as Perth, and prompting activism from green and Aboriginal groups as well as criticism of the neglect of urban problems.[1]

Demographic change became evident in slowing rates of immigration from Europe and in the continued reduction of household size. At the same time, gentrification—having become evident in the late 1960s in Sydney and Melbourne in particular—continued to change the face of the inner city suburbs, while suburbanisation proceeded apace despite increasing house prices. Shortfalls in urban infrastructure provision became more manifest in this period as rising expectations and environmental awareness underpinned demands (by state and market) for serviced land, and planned and sequenced subdivisions.

Over the decade, environmental issues became more salient in both urban and non-urban milieux. In the early 1970s, Sydney's 'green bans' were mounted by building workers at the height of a central city building boom while, in Brisbane and Melbourne, gentrifying inner suburbs were defended from freeway construction. In Melbourne, the middle classes also led the fight against the demolition of cheap inner suburban housing and the construction of high-rise public housing.[2] The efficacy of direct action was demonstrated in the success of the Vietnam moratorium marches, action which also signalled a growing critique of technical dominance in public policy-making. In all these movements, women played increasingly prominent roles, while studies of everyday suburban life began to reveal the double burden of women's roles of household management and paid work.[3]

In such an environment, urban policy and metropolitan planning began to look beyond debates about urban form to locate the 'solutions' to urban problems in the better management of urban systems and, in particular, in the more efficient coordination of government departments and semi-government agencies. This chapter will therefore concentrate on examining the changes to the organisational structures for planning in three urban centres—Sydney, Melbourne and Adelaide—to show how the problem of inter-agency coordination was a dominant concern of the period. But first, no examination of urban planning in Australia in the 1970s can begin without some account of the brief, but extraordinary, period of the Whitlam Government and the influence of the Department of Urban and Regional Development (DURD).

Federal initiatives

It is one of the ironies of history that, just as the post-war long boom came to an end with the OPEC oil shocks, manufacturing downturn, the spread of multinational global investment strategies and the onset of recession, the Whitlam Labor Government was elected in 1972 on a platform directed at redistributing the benefits of economic growth, and dealing with the environmental and social costs and disadvantages of this growth, especially as they were manifested in urban areas.

For the first time in Australian political history, a Federal Government produced explicit urban policies. As early as the mid-1960s, while in Opposition, Whitlam had indicated that issues of locational advantage and disadvantage should be addressed by a social democratic government as part of the social wage. Once in office, the new Labor Government set up DURD under minister Tom Uren and instituted initiatives that played a crucial part in the development of cities and in changing the face of planning during this period. DURD was radical in its approaches; it went beyond the confines of the planning profession in employing and seeking advice from non-planners. Similarly, the Area Improvement Plans (AIPs) and other schemes aimed at by-passing the states (especially the non-Labor ones), gave a new sense of empowerment to local government in undertaking social and community planning initiatives, as well as enabling them to make physical improvements to their areas.

There are numerous accounts of the influence of DURD on urban and regional planning in Australia and of the demise of such initiatives after 1975 with the dismissal of the Whitlam Government, but a brief summary of the most salient reforms will suffice here.[4] In brief, DURD initiatives included the following types of programs: regionalisation of policy delivery; introduction of AIPs; provision of additional funding to reduce the backlog of sewage works, especially in fringe urban areas; new cities and decentralisation initiatives; setting up Land Commissions for the purposes of land banking to stabilise suburban land prices; and coordinating Commonwealth activities in relation to urban policies.

The main result of the many reports on regionalisation in order to increase locational equity was the setting up of Regional Organisations of Councils (ROCs) to make bids for Commonwealth funding and carry out joint planning exercises. In recognition of the unequal distribution of resources in metropolitan areas, ROCs in the western areas of Sydney and Melbourne worked with DURD to administer AIP grants to carry out capital works ranging from sports fields to drainage, and similar programs were instituted in other regions throughout Labor's term. As part of the rectification of locational disadvantage, especially in newly developing urban areas, grants were made to the states to overcome the backlog in providing sewerage systems for the outer suburbs that had emerged in the rapid expansions of the previous decades. DURD funded three urban rehabilitation projects at Glebe and Woolloomooloo in Sydney, and Emerald Hill in Melbourne. These projects, while unable to stem the adverse effects of gentrification, at least had the merit of recognising the issue of conservation, middle class property interests and the rights of low-income residents to live in areas appropriate to their needs. Nowhere was the time-lag of policy more evident than in the Cities Commission's proposals for a new cities program to take the pressure of population growth from the major metropolises and decentralise to regional centres. Of these proposals, only Albury/Wodonga and Macarthur survived, with Macarthur becoming part of an urban 'corridor' for Sydney's expansion, rather than a decentralised new city. In this role, DURD also pursued a policy of locating Commonwealth offices in the states outside the capital city CBDs to further the aims of decentralisation and improving job accessibility. The Land Commissions also focused on population pressures and land availability: their land banking purposes were seen as important in overcoming the inequities of land prices caused at times of high growth and rampant land speculation. South Australia, and later Tasmania and Western Australia, established commissions, but Victoria and New South Wales, with Liberal–Country Party governments, formed advisory Land Councils.

In the implementation of these programs, the issue of the coordination of the multiple Commonwealth departments and agencies involved in urban policy became a matter of some debate. DURD laid claim to the role of monitoring all federal activity with urban implications (which could include almost anything and everything). Coordination was probably one of the most controversial and problematic aspects of DURD's existence, and incurred the wrath of Treasury when DURD attempted to become directive about budgetary allocations.

The Whitlam Government also attempted to influence urban processes through its grants to local government by increasing grants to the state housing authorities and introducing progressive tax rebates on mortgage interest payments. The most ambitious of these initiatives, under the auspices of the Social Welfare Commission, was to set up Regional Councils for Social Development answerable directly to the Commonwealth and by-passing the other two tiers of government. This challenge to traditional ways of governance in the federal system illustrates how the Labor programs produced unresolvable tensions and conflicts between the Commonwealth and the states, and the states and local government, as well as impinging on business interests, the operations of land development industries and the profits from land speculation.

By the time the Fraser Liberal–Country Party coalition came to power after the infamous dismissal of the Whitlam Government in 1975, the recession was well and truly evident so that, for economic and ideological reasons, most of Labor's programs were dismantled. Fraser redefined 'new federalism' in terms that reaffirmed the independence of the states from Commonwealth 'interference' by reducing the policy imperatives of special and tied grants, introducing tax sharing with the states, and signalling the end of federal involvement in urban and regional issues with the disbanding of DURD and the Social Welfare Commission.[5] For the first few years, some of the already-committed funds continued to flow to the cities but, by the end of the decade, spatial and urban policy at the federal level was a memory that was only revived in much muted form at the end of the 1980s (Chapter 9).

Throughout these dramatic events at the federal level, state-based planning continued to grapple with the problems thrown up by the belated recognition of the effects of untrammelled growth in the 1960s. As the decade wore on, the effects of economic downturn rendered the previous trend plans increasingly inappropriate. The implementation of metropolitan strategies began to focus on questions of the organisation of the agencies of planning, and the coordination of government and semi-government bodies having major influences on urban development.

Metropolitan issues

Four major urban issues became apparent to metropolitan planners from 1974 onwards: economic downturn and changes in industrial and employment structure; slowed population growth and decreasing household size; environmental issues; and questions of participation in decision-making about local and regional development. These issues intertwined in the politics of the period.

The changing nature of the workforce resulting from economic restructuring at the end of the long boom had implications for urban areas. The dramatic losses of manufacturing jobs over the decade were particularly evident in Sydney (an 18 per cent loss); Hobart (a 23 per cent loss); Adelaide (a 14 per cent loss); and Newcastle (an 11.5 per cent loss). In contrast, employment in communications, and finance and business grew in all capital cities, indicating a sea change in the nature of urban processes and the increasing importance of quaternary sector functions which favour central city development, employment and property markets. The other area of marked increase in employment was in community service, reflecting both the rising expectations of voters in relation to the provision of government services, and the growing need for such services in the face of rapid economic and social change.[6]

The 1970s saw the end of the 'full employment' that had sustained the suburban expansion and home ownership of the preceding two decades. In 1973, there was an official unemployment rate of 1.8 per cent which climbed to nearly 10 per cent by 1983. During this decade, also, male unemployment began to exceed the rates of female unemployment, as part-time employment, which increasingly involved women, grew at nearly twice the rate of full-time employment.[7]

Accompanying these shifts in the nature of work were a decline in population growth rates of the major cities, short-lived increases in places such as Perth, where mining and resources-related growth was significant, and the beginnings of tourist urbanisation on Queensland's Gold Coast.[8] Even Canberra's government-created post-war growth rates began to slow, despite Labor's expansion of government services, and these rates dropped dramatically with the cutbacks under Fraser in the second half of the decade.

The slowing growth of the major cities (Table 8.1) was related to reductions in rates of natural increase and internal national migration

Table 8.1 Population growth rates of major Australian cities, 1961–81 (%)

	1961–66	*1966–71*	*1971–76*	*1976–81*
Sydney	2.3	2.2	0.3	0.8
Melbourne	2.0	2.6	0.7	0.8
Brisbane	2.9	2.7	1.8	1.1
Adelaide	4.3	2.1	1.2	0.6
Perth	3.5	5.1	2.8	2.0
Hobart	0.6	1.6	0.3	-0.5
Canberra	10.4	8.8	7.6	2.3
Newcastle	2.3	1.4	0.1	0.6
Wollongong	4.2	2.8	1.2	0.8
Geelong	2.8	1.8	1.2	0.5
Gold Coast	n.a.	6.9	9.4	7.9

Source: C. Maher, 'Australian urban character: Pattern and process', in *Urban Planning in Australia: Critical Readings*, eds. J.B. McLoughlin and M. Huxley, Longman Cheshire, Melbourne, 1986.

patterns of exodus from the main centres to places such as Queensland and Western Australia. In fact, as Maher says, without continuing (but slowing) immigration from overseas, 'both Sydney and Melbourne would have suffered population declines'.[9]

Growing concerns about the environmental effects of urban growth were being expressed in government policies and local actions. The corridor plans that had been put in place in most major metropolitan areas by the early 1970s (Chapter 7) were responses to the problems of urban sprawl and unrestrained urban growth, and an attempt to avoid the land price increases attendant upon 'green belt' restrictions on suburban development. Throughout the 1970s, there was continuing concern about the possible long-term effects of oil supply depletion. Policy suggestions to reduce dependence on fossil fuels meshed with calls from environmental and urban development groups alike to reduce air pollution and to create environmentally and economically 'fail-safe' cities.[10]

In turn, the concept of 'urban consolidation'—increasing residential densities in existing urban areas and creating transport-related activity nodes—coincided with the identification of the problem of the 'doughnut city' effect from the loss of inner area population. Policies for increasing inner area densities and revitalising the business and cultural heart of cities became central to political fights over the management and future role of metropolitan CBDs. These fights were also sparked off by the increasingly speculative nature of property development, both in the CBDs and in the land rackets of fringe and ex-urban land development.[11]

The areas around the city centres were now in the full throes of gentrification. The 'green bans' in Sydney in the early 1970s were evidence of the fight to protect traditionally working class areas from the encroachment of 'renewal' (speculative residential redevelopment). Similar struggles took place in inner Melbourne against freeway expansions and public housing schemes, led by the new professional residents and students.[12] By the mid-1970s, the characterisation of the inner areas as slums to be razed and redeveloped, which had dominated urban and housing debates since the turn of the century, had to be finally abandoned, although the public housing authorities returned to earlier strategies of rehousing low-income households and welfare recipients in poorly serviced greenfield estates.

The issue of freeway construction also loomed large in the early part of the decade, with the road authorities' trend planning indicating continued population growth, urban expansion, increased car usage and declining public transport patronage. While Adelaide progressively abandoned its contested 1968 *Metropolitan Adelaide Transport Study Plan* during the Dunstan decade, the transport agencies in Perth, Melbourne, Sydney and Brisbane continued to construct freeways well into the 1970s, until fiscal considerations and tightening federal and state budgets coincided with public opinion and environmental evidence in bringing the freeways to a (temporary) halt.[13]

The gentrification of inner areas, the growing awareness of environmental and gender issues in urban development, and the failure of housing, freeway and utility agencies to produce more equitable urban environments were all influential in bringing the issue of public participation in planning into prominence. DURD's area assistance programs, influenced by the ideas of the Skeffington report on public participation in Britain, had promoted the idea of participation. The desire for participation in planning decisions grew amongst residents of the suburban areas that had voted Labor in, but who were becoming increasingly disenfranchised with pro-growth policies. In the inner areas, too, there was active resistance to large-scale redevelopment, whether publicly-funded freeways and high-rise public housing or private speculative investment. However, not all commentators were convinced of the efficacy of participatory exercises in bringing about grass-roots democracy.[14] Such were the circumstances under which metropolitan planning in the 1970s was debated and carried out.

The metropolitan plans

Although the corridor plans in place by the early 1970s were the offspring of the previous growth period, it was possible to adapt them to more straitened circumstances. Debates about urban form, such as the physical and economic centrality of the CBD, or the relationship between strategic identification of preferred development location and the provision of infrastructure according to agency plans, could be carried on without much change to the strategic plans as formally adopted (or, in the case of the *Sydney Region Outline Plan*, not formally adopted).[15]

The issue of fringe development, however, was still of concern. In different ways in different capitals, developer levies were introduced, preferred development areas were designated, and methods of increasing the population in established areas were debated as funds dried up and infrastructure needs became more urgent. Increasingly, towards the end of the period, urban consolidation became de facto policy. This was seen to be especially necessary in the inner suburbs, where population loss was greatest and infrastructure was presumed to be under-utilised. The urban consolidation debate has proved to be as long-lasting and influential as the suburban solution to the slums had been in the first half of the century (Chapter 3), but less practically effective.

Out of these circumstances grew the re-examination of institutional mechanisms for carrying out strategic planning, the timing of infrastructure provision and the coordination of the various agencies involved in urban development. In part, this emphasis derived from the realisation that, with the demise of DURD, the implementation of plans would always be constrained by the nature of the private land market and the power of property ownership—both the monopolising power of large development corporations and the dispersed power of home ownership. But the experience of DURD also showed the importance of the semi-autonomous agencies in the development process. Systems thinking and agency coordination, in fact, were direct legacies of DURD, as former federal public servants took jobs in the state administrations.

Here they found powerful roads, housing, hydraulic and energy instrumentalities, some with histories going back to the time of colonial administration, accustomed to independent operation and guaranteed budgetary allocations and revenues, and operating at a very long arm's length from government policy. Increasing conflicts over the separate agencies' servicing plans for urban development in the 1960s came to a head in the new fiscal environment. Almost every state embarked on major attempts at institutional and administrative reorganisation of its planning and urban infrastructure agencies. But, as the next section shows, it proved to be no easier to control the independent authorities than to reorient the private market.

Managing the machinery of government

While the 'Mark Two' plans emphasised strategic principles and objectives, and were represented in broad-brush diagrammatic form, the legal mechanism underpinning them was still the statutory regulation of land use, mainly in the form of zoning. Planning departments were now being called on to use the plans as frameworks for urban management, but did not have the legal, budgetary or political powers to bring the agencies to be coordinated into line with the plans.

The planning agencies had to deal with the fact that:

> the reason for the continuation of many of the bodies involved in the management of [urban areas] as independent authorities ... was that their activities were seen largely as being technical ones—building roads, putting in water supplies, running trains on time—which political 'interference' would only hamper. They were ... provided with additional powers which gave them enormous influence and ... led ... to demands that they be co-ordinated and controlled.[16]

Additionally, instrumentalities run by engineers and technical experts had little interest in the social, environmental or equity effects of their activities, and this was true even of bodies such as the state housing commissions (with the honourable exception of the South Australian Housing Trust (SAHT), but even it was unable to deal with the effects of structural economic change).[17]

Wilenski identifies three interrelated administrative problems that the turn to coordination hoped to solve:

> One has been to devise policy machinery to undertake the analysis of the issues so that decision-makers are aware of the choices involved ... The second ... has been to develop information and budgeting systems so that policy choices could be translated into priorities in resource allocation ... The third has been to co-ordinate the implementation and timing of these plans on the ground.[18]

There was considerable debate in later years about the difference between strategic planning, urban management and program coordination, often couched in terms of the difference between 'rational comprehensive' and 'incrementalist' forms of planning.[19] Rather than being conducted in these somewhat abstract terms, it would seem from the examples examined in the following discussion that the real battle, from DURD onwards, was about the claims of planning agencies to coordinate all other urban-related government organisations, including local government.

For the planners' plans to be implemented, infrastructure, roads, schools and other social facilities had to be provided where and when the plan indicated. This was not a matter of the relevant bodies engaging in 'partisan mutual adjustment'[20] to modify their policies incrementally, or to negotiate on an equal footing to achieve agreed outcomes, but of them, or the relevant ministers, accepting the primacy of the planners' plans over their own. This incursion into the agencies' traditional power bases was strongly resisted. As Holmes points out, 'co-ordination is not a policy-neutral activity, but one which requires the co-ordinated to change their policies so as to conform to the policy of the co-ordinator. As such, it inevitably generates conflict.'[21]

Much of the story of metropolitan planning in the 1970s is the story of such conflicts, and the efforts at coordination in Sydney, Melbourne and Adelaide can be taken as examples. To introduce the following city vignettes, some of the antecedent developments of the 1960s detailed in Chapter 7 are briefly recounted.

Sydney

In Sydney, organisational solutions to the implementation of plans were presaged by the demise of the Cumberland County Council and its replacement with the State Planning Authority (SPA) in 1963.[22] The SPA had representation from the Department of Main Roads, the Department of Transport, and the Metropolitan Water and Sewerage and Drainage Board, reducing the number of local government representatives and changing the nature of the deliberations from a form of democratic decision-making to one of technical coordination. But the SPA could do very little more than act as an information-clearing forum and had no powers to direct the independent authorities' planning processes.

The *Sydney Region Outline Plan* was produced in 1968 with the express intention of guiding private sector investment and coordinating the public provision of urban services, but 'there was no machinery provided through the Plan for altering traditional mechanisms for resource allocation'.[23] In particular, the plan expressed the freeway-building intentions of the Department of Main Roads, but was able to do little to modify those intentions in the direction of more equitable and environmentally sound urban outcomes.

However, in its time, the SPA did attempt a number of more interventionist initiatives. In 1970, an attempt was made to introduce a 'betterment tax' to deal with the problems of financing new urban development. This initiative ran into inevitable political difficulties and was abandoned in 1973 (along with the SPA). In the 1960s and early 1970s, the Authority also purchased land in the south and west of Sydney which contributed to keeping land costs down for the provision of a town centre, open space and educational institutions at Campbelltown. In 1976, the Federal Government's Land Commission funding augmented the New South Wales commitment to controlling speculation in fringe land development.

The failure of the SPA to provide coordination and complaints that it was too dominated by government representatives led to its replacement in 1973 by the five-member Planning and Environment Commission (PEC), which acted as an advisory and consultative forum for statutory agencies rather than as a coordinating body. A Ministry for Planning and Environment was set up with responsibility for environmental planning and pollution control and this continued after the election of a Labor State Government in 1976 and the passage of the *Environmental Planning and Assessment Act* in 1979. However, neither the Ministry nor the legislation was able to bring about the sought-after control of the independent authorities, and the staging and timing of infrastructure provision remained a continuing problem.

Sydney's experience with attempts to coordinate urban infrastructure and manage urban development processes was matched in various forms in the other capital cities. So too, it can be noted, was the increase in importance of environmental issues, with almost every state either adding the name 'Environment' to existing departments or creating entirely new ministries.

Melbourne

In Melbourne, the Melbourne and Metropolitan Board of Works (MMBW)—the only planning authority in Australia with infrastructure responsibilities—produced its 'Mark Two' corridors and wedges plan for the metropolitan area in 1971. The government's advisory body, the Town and Country Planning Board, favoured a linear city expanding to the east—an option strongly advocated by activists of the Town and Country Planning Association and the Communist Party, including Ruth and Maurie Crow—while the MMBW, the official planning and hydraulic infrastructure agency, favoured the multiplicity of 'corridors and wedges' formalised in the 1971 Framework Plan. It took until 1974, after consideration of the many objections to the idea of corridors and wedges, for the policy to be confirmed in the *Outline Strategy Plan* (Figure 8.1).[24]

The new Liberal premier of Victoria, Rupert Hamer, began his term in office in 1972 with a reform agenda that included radical restructuring of the machinery of administration and a style of government attuned to environmental issues and urban middle class demands for conservation

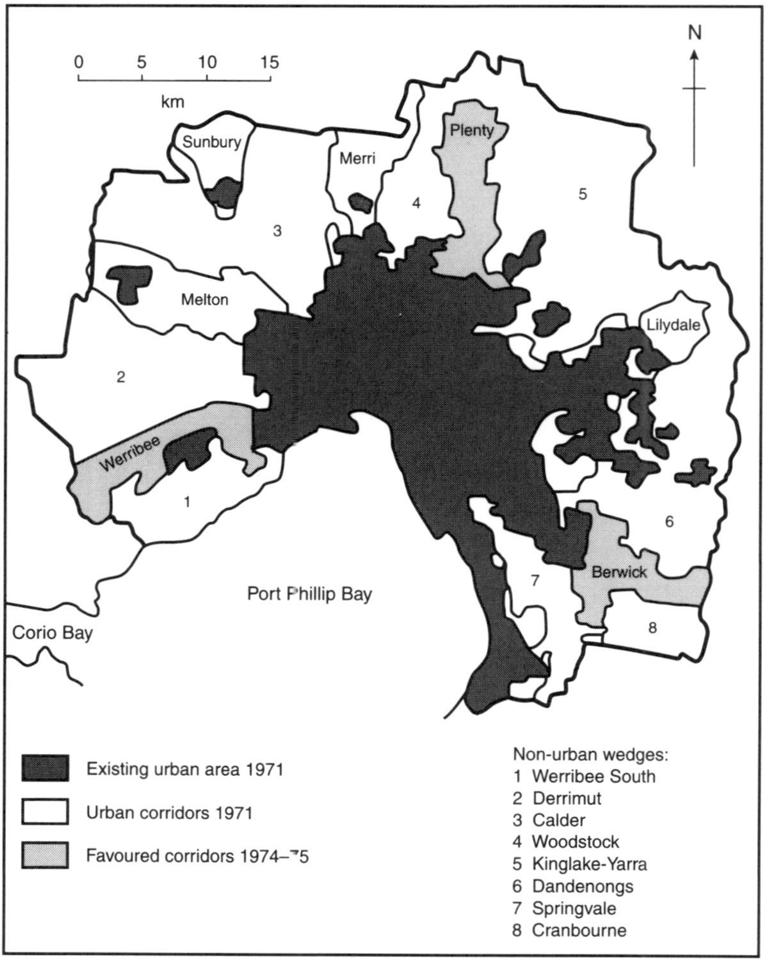

Figure 8.1 The 1971 Board of Works plan for Melbourne indicating preferred development corridors (adopted 1974)

Source: B. Logan, 'The shape of Melbourne: A political geography of Melbourne's planning in the 1970s and 1980s', in *Urban Planning in Australia: Critical Readings*, eds J.B. McLoughlin and M. Huxley, Longman Cheshire, Melbourne, 1986.

and participation. Hamer set up a Ministry of Planning which was to coordinate the activities of the MMBW, the Town and Country Planning Board (already an advisory body), and the State Planning Council (SPC), the technical coordinating body for public authorities, set up in 1968. Figure 8.2 illustrates, in a somewhat idealised form, the relationships between the bodies involved in land use planning in Victoria throughout the 1970s. Such a structure was not atypical of the attempts being made in other states to coordinate the planning process.

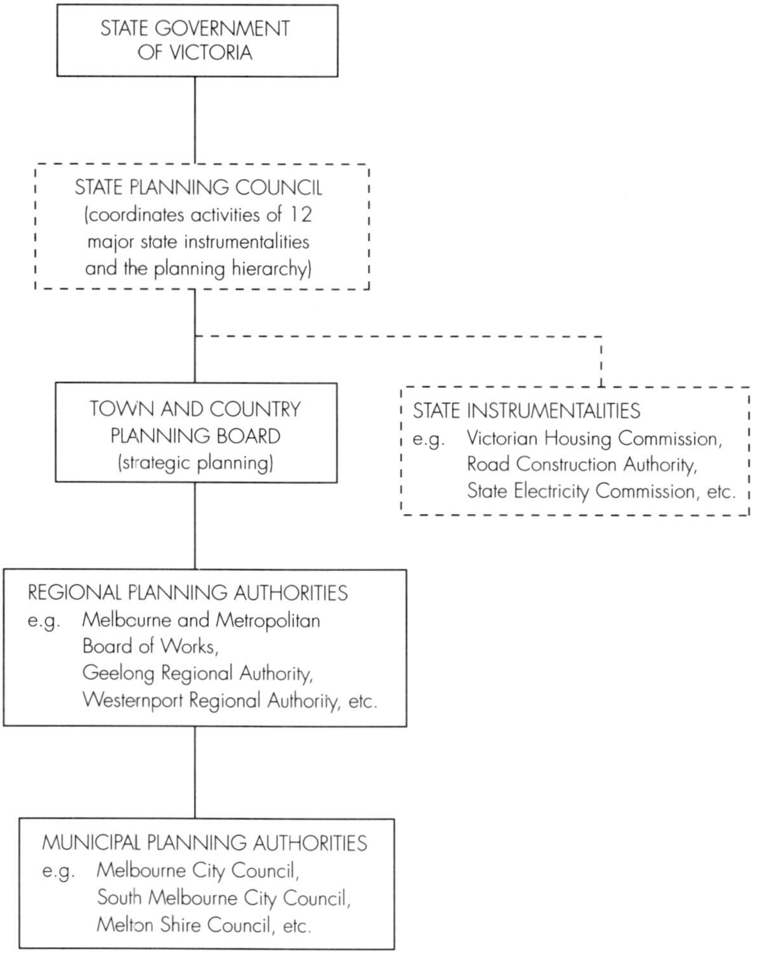

Figure 8.2 The Victorian planning hierarchy, 1968–79

Source: B. Logan, 'The shape of Melbourne: A political geography of Melbourne's planning in the 1970s and 1980s', in *Urban Planning in Australia: Critical Readings*, eds J.B. McLoughlin and M. Huxley, Longman Cheshire, Melbourne, 1986.

Like the State Planning Authority in New South Wales, the SPC was an arena for bureaucratic politics which proved extremely difficult to align with broader planning objectives. In contrast to New South Wales, which reduced the size of the coordinating body when it set up the Planning and Environment Commission, the Victorian solution was to create the State Co-ordination Council (SCC) in 1975, the membership of which included all the SPC members, departmental heads and heads of the new super-ministries. In the end, it too operated mainly as a forum for information exchange with little commitment to an overall coordinated planning approach by its members.

The new Ministry for Planning was to bring together the disparate agendas of the competing service authorities to conform with the strategy plan, but, equally importantly, under the direct control of the minister. But the Ministry was not equipped with the powers to enable it to control either the instrumentalities or the SPC/SCC, and the goal of coordination did not survive the politics of Cabinet. Needless to say, 'agency conflict was the almost inevitable consequence of the structures of government [Hamer] devised'.[25]

The difficulties faced by the Hamer Government's attempts to control and coordinate its statutory authorities is best illustrated by the case of the Mt Ridley land scandals in 1978. The Housing Commission of Victoria (HCV) was caught up in a series of irregular property transactions, in which large tracts of greenfields, non-urban land were purchased by private consortia and on-sold to the HCV at greatly increased prices. Although an inquiry found there was no corruption or direct ministerial or high-level bureaucratic culpability, the minister was forced to resign, signalling a failure of ministerial control over the statutory housing authority.[26] What the land scandals also demonstrated was the impossibility of strategic plans or even administrative coordinating structures to bring about the implementation of metropolitan planning objectives without far wider powers and resources. But this enters the realms of 'socialist intervention', the accusation levelled at Mr Hamer by the Liberal–Country coalition's 'old guard'.

The 1970s were indeed interesting times and much of the commentary on the period revolves around central questions thrown up by the DURD experiment, which continued to influence urban policy debates for the rest of the decade. What is the ability of urban planning to bring about its desired ends in market economies and property-owning democracies? Can there be a socialist city in a capitalist society? To what extent is it feasible for metropolitan planning objectives to depend on the free operation of the land market?[27] These questions were postponed by the increasing emphasis on management and coordination, in the hope that getting the structures right and making small-scale changes might provide alternative answers, but they remain fundamental conundrums for urban planning.

Adelaide

Planning for Adelaide, too, underwent administrative changes in the 1970s as the inadequacies of service provision became manifest and the old technocratic certainties about the political neutrality of spatial trend planning and public works provisions increasingly came under critical scrutiny. Don Dunstan's Labor Government was committed to the same goals of equity in the urban environment as the Whitlam Federal Government and was able to take immediate advantage of the programs and funds offered under the various federal initiatives.[28]

The 1962 *Metropolitan Development Plan*—Adelaide's corridor plan—was adopted with the passage of the *Planning and Development Act 1967* which also established the State Planning Authority. The plan remained the official framework for urban planning throughout most of the 1970s, because the original plan had been extremely long-sighted in the allocation of land for urban development. It was less so in providing the funding and mechanisms for servicing that land.

Dunstan thus began a series of administrative reforms that set up a number of new bodies to undertake his ambitious urban programs. These included the Land Commission and the Monarto Development Commission. In 1975, a senior ministry was created with responsibility for the South Australian Housing Trust and the State Planning Authority and the minister appointed ex-Whitlam staffer John Mant as his policy adviser. Like the Hamer reforms in Victoria, the changes instituted by the Dunstan Government aimed to bring urban policy and, in particular, the activities of the service authorities, under direct Cabinet control. In 1976, the Urban Development Co-ordinating Committee was set up to provide advice to the government and to coordinate activities relating to urban development. In the same year, an entirely new Department of Housing and Urban Affairs was created (renamed Housing, Urban and Regional Affairs (HURA) in 1978) under the directorship of Mant, and incorporating the former State Planning Authority.

The new Department's aims were to provide advice to Cabinet, to coordinate infrastructure provision, and to promote equitable and efficient urban and regional development. Comprehensive, end-state or 'blueprint' planning was to be replaced by a 'systems approach' involving monitoring, forecasting, management and provision of information for decision-making by politicians. These systems did in fact furnish important land monitoring and population forecasting capabilities for the budgeting and coordination of urban infrastructure. However, the Metropolitan Staging Study and the 'sector management' system both impinged on traditional statutory planning procedures and on other authorities' and departments' domains and management styles. There was resistance to HURA's monitoring and coordinating role, just as there had been to DURD and similar attempts at metropolitan strategy implementation. The South Australian experiment came to an end with the election of a Liberal Government in 1979, but the staging and management systems survived in concept at least and became the basis for similar metropolitan development programs in other major cities in the 1980s.[29]

Local–central coordination

Local government, and particularly central city local government, is part of the processes of urban management and, like the major statutory authorities, lack of cooperation or compliance is problematic for the implementation of the planners' strategic plans. Even though local government in Australia is not as powerful or independent as local government in the United Kingdom or the United States, for example, state and federal spatial and land use policies, programs and regulations involve the resources and cooperation of local government if they are to succeed, a fact that DURD and the Whitlam Government understood well.

The most politically prominent and powerful of the local tier of government has always been the central city councils. The struggle for control of the planning and land use regulation of the capital cities' CBDs is a recurring theme in Australian urban history. In all states except Queensland (Brisbane has the only quasi-metropolitan capital city council in Australia), central city councils have vied with their respective state governments for power over the symbolic and economic heart of the state. The sacking of the Sydney City Council in 1967 was over just such issues. The details of the power struggles between central city councils and state governments and the various plans for revitalising central areas cannot be entered into here, but it needs to be noted that with deepening recession and increasing competition between the states for international investment funds during the 1970s, the role of the CBDs became even more crucial. The example of the sacking of the Melbourne City Council in December 1980 over the stalemate between the Council's 1974 strategy plan, the MMBW's metropolitan plan, CBD business interests and local residents provides a poignant coda to the decade.[30]

In summary, it can be seen that attempts at inter-agency coordination in order to implement urban policy and strategic plans were fraught with conflict, since such attempts inevitably disturbed traditional power distributions within the machinery of government. Similar points about the difficulties of implementing strategic planning are made by Yiftachel and Kenworthy in relation to Perth's 1970 corridor plan.[31] They note the lack of coordination between the infrastructure agencies and the requirements of the strategy plan; the lack of political will to tackle the urban services agencies (although the case of Victoria indicates that political will is not necessarily enough); the declining commitment to equitable outcomes; and the persistence of state–local conflicts of interests.

Conclusion

The 1970s were a period of great change, when previous assumptions about the automatic continuance of post-war affluence, the disappearance of poverty and inequality, and the efficacy of technical solutions to social and environmental problems were called into question. Planning turned away from 'moon-shot' single-outcome master planning and began to grapple with the ongoing processes of urban management under changed economic and social conditions.

The Whitlam era and the DURD experiment dominated the first part of the period and influenced almost every aspect of urban policy and planning for many years thereafter. The influence was particularly strong in pointing to the interconnectedness of all government policies with spatial outcomes and the need for policy that takes into account equity as well as efficiency aspects of urban processes.

However, in most states, the strategic plans in place by the beginning of the decade still relied on statutory regulatory mechanisms such as zoning, detached from the broad-brush policy and process initiatives of the new administrative structures. In order to implement plans, most state planning bodies and the respective politicians concentrated on reforming the byzantine machinery of government that had grown up over the previous hundred years. The reforms also attempted to grapple with the perennial problem of central–local responsibilities and jurisdictions at a time when local residents were increasingly sensitised to issues of public participation and local democracy. The growing significance of central city development meant that conflicts over state–local policies were particularly strategically important. However, the political and entrenched bureaucratic power surrounding the attempts to introduce structures for urban management and implement strategic planning was more resistant to change (however technically rational or collectively desirable) than the planners and reforming politicians had imagined.

In general, then, there were some notable improvements in terms of environmental awareness, responsiveness to issues of equity and participation, and attempts to deal with the problems of fringe land development. But, in the end, one of the lessons of the 1970s is that 'the technique of strategic planning, while an undoubted advance [on statutory zoning-based approaches], was inadequate in itself as a device to co-ordinate public investment',[32] let alone as a device to produce equitable urban outcomes.

The period brought into sharp relief the fundamental dilemmas of environmental land use planning in capitalist societies: the tensions between state intervention in the name of collective goals and the operations of market economies based on private property rights; the tensions between centralised control, again in the name of collective goals, and responsiveness to democratic demands for local autonomy; and the irreducible power-plays involved in changing organisational structures in order to implement policies.[33] These tensions inevitably continue to underpin attempts at metropolitan planning in any liberal democracy.

9 The revival of metropolitan planning

Michael Lennon

In the early 1980s, metropolitan planning in Australia was in the doldrums. Most cities still had plans dating from some years earlier which indicated preferred patterns of spatial development and assumed a continuation of car-based suburbanisation. Most plans were closely linked to statutory schemes governing the development of land, with density and subdivision controls as important means of implementation. Metropolitan plans were typically land use zoning plans writ large—'blueprint' or 'trend' plans. The dominant style of planning was that of 'urban management', characterised by incremental growth, 'realistic' objectives and 'by the idea that planners should cease to get in the way of adjustment and "profitability"'.[1] Protectionist manufacturing policies and immigration programs were more influential in shaping the cities than these plans.

By the beginning of the 1990s, the agenda had shifted considerably. Support had grown for long-term, visionary strategic planning which included more concern for environmental protection. The Brundtland report of 1987 was influential in Australia, as elsewhere, in placing issues of environmental sustainability firmly on the policy agenda. The late 1980s and early 1990s also saw a re-engagement with the cities on the part of the Federal Government.

This chapter traces the revival of metropolitan planning in the late 1980s and early 1990s and describes the principal features of federal urban policy under the Hawke and Keating Labor governments. It outlines the significant metropolitan planning exercises of the period and describes the South Australian Planning Review of 1990–92 in some detail as an archetypal example of the new strategic planning with its concern for integrated environmental, social and economic planning. It also places these developments in the broader context of changing patterns of growth across Australia and the rise of economic liberalism with the potential to undermine the aspirations of metropolitan planners.

Urban policy and national affairs

Chapter 8 has shown how the Whitlam Government placed urban policy on the Commonwealth's agenda for a short period and was significant in elevating urban planning to the level of a national priority. However, most of the urban reforms proposed under Whitlam through the Department of Urban and Regional Development (DURD) led to only modest achievements, because, by their nature, programs to bring about major changes in urban areas could only be expected to produce results in the longer term.[2] Moreover, inter-government relations were seriously strained by the DURD experience and the hostility of the states to federal intervention in what they perceived as their affairs created a legacy of enduring suspicion and mistrust.

At the local government level, DURD had made untied funds available from national coffers for the first time. This, too, was resisted by state and local governments as unwarranted federal interference (although all took the money). But in the broad sweep of federal–state–local affairs, there was great significance in the adoption of the principle that the Commonwealth had a responsibility to try to redress the inequalities between places. More generally, the Whitlam period also created an awakening of consciousness about urban issues which was to survive into the 1980s, not least through the numbers of ex-DURD officers who found employment with state governments.

The seven years of Malcolm Fraser's prime ministership after 1975 were concerned with the reining in of public expenditure. DURD was (often rightly) seen as an example of ill-disciplined fiscal excess. Whitlam had sought to realign federal–state responsibilities, but the absence of any reference to cities or regions in the Australian Constitution provided the opportunity for the Fraser Government to assert that there was no role or duty for the Federal Government in such matters.

Given DURD's uneven legacy, it was perhaps not surprising that the Hawke Labor Government, when it was elected in 1983, was unwilling to contemplate a return to strongly interventionist urban policies. Hawke's priorities were, rather, on macro-economic issues—dealing with a currency crisis, unemployment and the need to restructure key industries. There was no explicit urban program in Hawke's election manifesto. However, towards the end of the decade, continuing concerns about rising housing costs and house prices, especially in Sydney, led to measures to improve land supply in the major cities, to simplify planning procedures, and to encourage smaller blocks and denser development in pursuit of 'more affordable' housing.

Brian Howe, minister for social security in the Hawke Government, became a strong supporter of urban consolidation, influenced to a considerable degree by concerns about the social consequences of so-called urban sprawl, the gendered nature of cities and the apparent concentration of deprivation in poorly served outer suburban areas. Howe became an increasingly influential voice arguing for the extension of the Hawke Government's social justice agenda to cities, and for the adoption of a broad approach in which policies to check the outward growth of cities and reduce the costs of new urban development could be better integrated with policies intended to address emerging environmental and transport concerns.

The Better Cities Program, launched in 1991, was to mark the high point of these ambitions. Its focus was on demonstration projects which 'based on fully integrated area strategies, will provide examples for government planners in other areas, and for private investors who will be exposed to new ideas in housing and commercial investment'.[3] These projects, shared around the states, included infrastructure works preparatory to the upgrading of old public housing areas, new public transport investments (heavy and light rail systems, in particular), medium-density housing developments, and a range of other schemes consistent with the overall notion of urban consolidation and the presumed environmental benefits of more compact cities:

> Our housing densities are only one-half to two-thirds of that [*sic*] required to enable efficient public transport systems to operate ... Our reliance on the private motor vehicle, particularly for transport to work, has produced major problems for our cities. These problems include increasing air pollution, congested roads and the ever-growing need to build more freeways. Increased housing densities and improvements to public transport will enable many people to reduce their dependency on the car.[4]

Many criticised the assumptions and limited scope of the Better Cities Program.[5] It was seen, variously, as an instrument of 'crisis management' in response to the economic problems of areas of the major cities,[6] and as part of the outcome of a political deal to provide the Labor Left with the deputy prime ministership in return for Caucus votes in a leadership ballot. Others argued, however, that it was remarkable that its proponents were able to accomplish even this much in the face of a prevailing tide in Canberra in favour of economic rationalism and of limiting government intervention.[7]

The Better Cities Program formed part of a much broader and often confusing array of Federal Government initiatives related to the cities after 1990. In the early 1990s, over 100 Federal Government reports were produced of direct relevance to urban and regional policy. These included studies on locational disadvantage and ecologically sustainable development (ESD), plus reports by the National Housing Strategy and the Industry Commission. From a review of these studies, however, Alexander concluded that, 'given the power of the economic hegemony, questions of equity, social justice, locational disadvantage and even ESD inevitably become lower priorities [and] the proliferation of reports and programs seems to have changed very little on the ground'.[8]

The Better Cities Program also provided funding in the early 1990s to support the 'Multi-Function Polis' (MFP). No account of federal urban initiatives in this period would be complete without some mention of this remarkable project. The MFP began life in early 1987 as a proposal emanating from the Japanese Ministry for International Trade and Industry. It envisaged a utopian combination of physical, economic, and technological innovation. It was to be a settlement of 50 000–100 000 people somewhere in Australia which would represent a new form of city development looking forward to the twenty-first century. It would provide a base for new industries and activities thought likely to be characteristic of the next millennium—information-based and environmental industries, in particular. John Button, Hawke's industry minister, was the driving force behind a joint study with the Japanese Government which had broad aims including technological transfer and the building of new economic relationships in the Asia–Pacific region. The right to host the physical development was decided through a bidding process, won first by the Queensland Government and then, by default, by South Australia. The MFP saga is recounted in more detail elsewhere.[9] Suffice to say that more than $100 million was spent on a project devised in the late 1980s in an atmosphere of euphoria about new global relationships and the benefits of foreign investment. It was cancelled ten years later as a poorly managed public liability and as a monument to the lack of any continuing or consistent policy for Australia's national spatial development.

The broader policy environment

Of all Commonwealth programs relating to urban development, the Commonwealth–State Housing Agreement (CSHA) continued to represent the biggest single outlay of public funds. A major review of the Agreement was undertaken leading to its re-negotiation in 1989 for a further ten-year period. While expressing continuing support for public housing, this review argued for a change in the performance and financing of state public housing authorities and effectively ended the growth of public housing stock which had occurred over the previous 30 years.

A point which has frequently been made is that, for all the expenditure on the various urban programs, including Better Cities, the level of funds transferred to the states under the Hawke and Keating governments actually declined by a factor many times greater than the new funds which came to support demonstration projects. In South Australia, for example, a reduction in CSHA funds of more than $200 million was compensated by Better Cities funds of slightly more than $40 million.

However, the Commonwealth Government's impact on the cities went far beyond its urban programs. Other federal policies of the Hawke and Keating administrations were also to have profound effects on Australian cities. Shifts in federal immigration policies had significant impacts on the attempts by state governments to manage their infrastructure programs and to anticipate housing demand, particularly in Sydney.[10] Immigration surged between 1979 and 1982, and again from 1987 to 1991. The deregulation of the finance and banking sectors, the easing of restrictions on foreign investment in Australian property, tariff reduction and the restructuring of industry all had significant urban impacts.

The increasingly deregulated financial environment and the introduction of micro-economic reforms at all levels saw state governments become adventurous in their attempts to build the economic base of their cities and regions. Faced with industry restructuring, deregulation and the entry of foreign banks, a dangerous spirit of enterprise became evident, particularly in Victoria, Western Australia and South Australia, where state governments became increasingly entrepreneurial in creating new financial institutions and in their attempts to attract footloose capital.[11] Major areas of several cities—Darling Harbour in Sydney, the 'Expo' site on the South Bank of the Brisbane River, the 'Melbourne Central' (later Daimaru) project and the Adelaide Station redevelopment—were redeveloped in the 1980s through a blend of foreign investment and 'fast-track' government approval processes, sometimes with state governments underwriting the risks of speculative ventures.

Metropolitan plans

The shifts which were occurring as a consequence of the deregulation and globalisation of the Australian economy had an impact on the style of metropolitan planning as the 1980s progressed. Old-style, static regulatory plans became inadequate. New ways of engaging the various groups involved in the development debate needed to be found. The 1980s saw a major speculative construction boom in commercial property, which placed pressure on planning authorities for quick approvals and which mobilised community action when heritage values were threatened. There was also a resurgence of environmental activism towards the end of the 1980s which saw governments searching for new ways of planning, new ways of engaging disparate interests and new ways of creating a sense of the future in an increasingly uncertain world.

Table 9.1 indicates the pattern of population growth across major urban centres in the second half of the 1980s. It highlights the significant percentage increases in the populations of South-East Queensland and Perth, in particular. It was not until the 1990s that strategic planning arrangements for South-East Queensland were established, but Perth's corridor plan was reviewed in the 1980s.

The leading idea with regard to metropolitan form in the 1980s was urban consolidation, driven to a substantial extent by the desire of state governments, subject increasingly to tight monetary controls, to reduce their expenditure on infrastructure. In Sydney, as early as 1981, concern was also being expressed at the rate at which housing costs were rising and a debate about the advantages or disadvantages of urban consolidation focused on the implications on housing costs of attempting to increase housing densities.[12] Consolidation was an issue addressed in the *Sydney Region Outline Plan Review* in 1980 and was to be central to most subsequent plans in the 1980s.

Sydney

Sydney's major metropolitan plan of the 1980s, *Sydney into Its Third Century*, was not released until 1988, by which time the Australian economy was in an expansionary phase, with stronger business confidence and investment. It anticipated reduced, although still substantial, growth of one million people in metropolitan Sydney's population to 4.5 million over the years 1986 to 2011. The 1988 strategy was primarily about identifying land for new housing and included a detailed comparison of the advantages and disadvantages of pursuing a 'concentrated' or 'dispersed' urban form to accommodate Sydney's predicted growth. It came down in favour of the 'concentrated' approach because of concerns about the mounting costs of continued fringe expansion, emerging physical constraints to the supply of new urban land, and the under-utilisation of infrastructure in the city's established areas due to population decline. In the context of continuing suburbanisation of employment and retailing, *Sydney into Its Third Century* also sought to achieve a clearer pattern of regional employment and service centres. A brief review in 1989 endorsed the 1988 strategy while bringing forward the likely attainment date of the 4.5 million population to 2006 rather than 2011 as a result of increased overseas immigration in the late 1980s.[13]

Table 9.1 Population change in major urban areas, 1986–91

Urban centre	*1991 population by statistical divisions/ districts (millions)*	*Population change 1986–91 (%)*
Sydney	3.54	5.2
Melbourne	3.02	5.4
Brisbane	1.33	13.4
Perth	1.14	15.0
Adelaide	1.02	4.7
Hobart	0.18	3.9
Canberra	0.30	12.1
Gold Coast	0.29	29.2
Sunshine Coast	0.13	40.0

Source: Adapted from P. Mullins, 'Decline of the old, rise of the new: Late twentieth century Australian urbanisation', in *A Sociology of Australian Society*, eds J.M. Najman and J.S. Western, Macmillan, Melbourne, 1993.

Perth

The 1973 corridor plan for Perth had been prepared at a time when the city's population was 700 000. By 1986, Perth's population had reached one million and a review of the corridor concept was initiated under Max Neutze of the Australian National University. The review was completed in 1987 and its recommendations eventually provided the basis for a metropolitan plan published in 1990 as *Metroplan*.[14] Corridors were retained and broadened in some cases, with a new, fifth north-eastern corridor added along the Swan River Valley (Figure 9.1). Transport spines remained important but public transport access to these spines emerged as a significant policy shift.[15] More housing choice and consolidation were new elements, with 80 000 of a predicted 400 000 required new dwellings to be built within established areas. In some respects, this was an ambivalent plan, simultaneously advocating both decentralisation and the strengthening of central Perth, suburbanisation and consolidation, public transport and continuing road construction, and so on. Ray Bunker commented:

> Metroplan is full of interesting ideas and well-argued contentions, but is short on choices, priorities and decisions like so many contemporary metropolitan plans. It is widely viewed in Perth as a weak compromise between persistent economic pressures from above, demanding optimal conditions for investment, and growing community pressure from below, resisting development, particularly round established residential areas.[16]

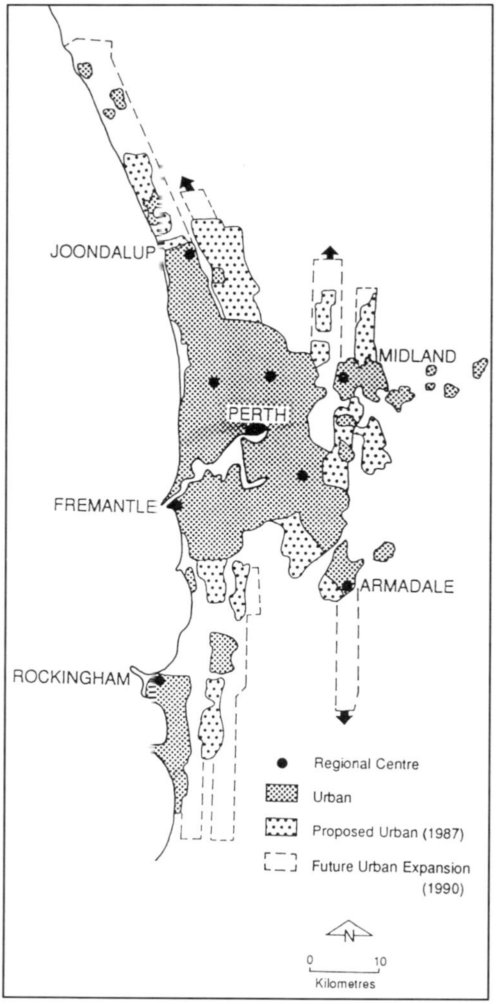

Figure 9.1 Preferred strategy for Perth of the Corridor Plan Review Group (1987) and *Metroplan* (1990)

Source: D. Hedgcock, 'Planning the outward growth of Australian capital cities: Perth', *Urban Policy and Research*, vol. 12, no. 2, June 1994, p. 127.

Canberra

In the early 1980s, the National Capital Development Commission (NCDC) initiated a review of Canberra's planning in response to a number of factors. Population growth was slowing, but as the average size of households declined more steeply than expected, the population capacities of Canberra's towns turned out to be lower than originally planned. More married women were working and the workforce was also now expected to rely principally on government and tertiary sector jobs, without the growth in industrial employment that had been anticipated earlier. The review eventually led to the publication by the NCDC of the *Metropolitan Canberra Policy Plan* in 1984. This envisaged Canberra's population growing at a rate of about 2.5 per cent per annum and reaching about 380 000 by the beginning of the twenty-first century. To accommodate this growth, the completion of Tuggeranong and the development of a major new settlement at Gungahlin were proposed. Other principles of the 'Y Plan' (Chapter 7) were retained, but restrictions were placed on the amount of government and other employment to be located in the central Civic precinct, because of the desirability of providing more jobs in the new town centres on the assumption that this would allow people to work closer to their homes.

The Parliamentary Joint Committee on the Australian Capital Territory (ACT) conducted a further review in 1987. This Committee's report, published under the title of *Metropolitan Canberra*, endorsed the planned metropolitan structure of Canberra but 'strongly urged that the benefits of urban consolidation in the established areas of the city should be fully exploited as an alternative to continued, rapid peripheral expansion'.[17]

In 1989, the ACT was made self-governing and the NCDC was abolished. Arrangements for shared planning responsibility between the Commonwealth and territory governments were set out in the *ACT (Planning and Land Management) Act 1988*. A National Capital Planning Authority was given responsibility by the Commonwealth Government for the preparation of a National Capital Plan dealing with those parts of Canberra which were of national significance, with the ACT Government dealing with local and day-to-day planning matters elsewhere.[18]

Melbourne

Urban consolidation was a central policy concern of Melbourne's major metropolitan plan of the 1980s, *Shaping Melbourne's Future*, prepared in 1986–87. Consolidation was to be fostered by assisting the development industry in site assembly and by facilitating the planning process for medium-density developments. Surplus government land was identified for infill housing and a public awareness campaign was proposed to explain the benefits of smaller lots. Other themes were: managing development within urban growth corridors, a balanced pattern of activity centres, new job opportunities in areas of declining employment in the north and west, and a wider range of housing choices. The key spatial concern was that the eastern municipalities were running short of residential land and there was thus a desire to increase the amount of development to be accommodated elsewhere. The Plenty Valley was identified as a likely area for new residential development, and a western growth area extending through Werribee was also defined as a complement to the south-eastern corridor (Figure 9.2). Another important objective was the strengthening of central Melbourne's role as the major focus for metropolitan activity at the apex of a hierarchy of activity centres, although government offices were to be decentralised to major suburban centres, especially the outer 'strategic' centres. Measures were proposed to encourage higher rates of employment in the northern and western suburbs and in employment areas along the outer north-western ring roads.

Shaping Melbourne's Future was a coherent statement of a possible pattern of physical development, but implementation was always going to be difficult because of continuing problems of power and coordination:

> With no single body empowered to coordinate metropolitan issues across all State Government departments and municipal jurisdictions, Melbourne probably has the most fragmented metropolitan area among all world cities. This undoubtedly made the implementation of Shaping Melbourne's Future much harder than it might have been.[19]

Brian McLoughlin published a substantial review and critique of post-war metropolitan planning in Melbourne in 1992, ironically titled *Shaping Melbourne's Future?*[20] McLoughlin emphasised the power of private interests and of public agencies such as the Melbourne and Metropolitan Board of Works, the Urban Land Authority and road construction agencies rather than the state government's strategic planners in influencing Melbourne's form and structure. He argued that Melbourne's planners had been least effective in controlling central city development and imposing order on fringe growth, and that planning had been most effective in protecting and enhancing suburban environments. McLoughlin's work suggested a number of necessary conditions for more effective planning:

> [The] development of policies in each and every field ... housing, transport, recreation, heritage, land-use planning and so on ... must ... be explicitly conscious of all others. This is a tall order ... However what we can easily do is to specify a set of types of policy vehicle which are identified as 'strategic' and so require that each of these be prepared as a result of consultation with all the others. In this way we might ensure the elimination of gross inconsistencies and the building up of a better integrated combination of community and government views. Clearly the place where the buck stops is in the [State] Cabinet who must approve all strategic policies before they become operational.[21]

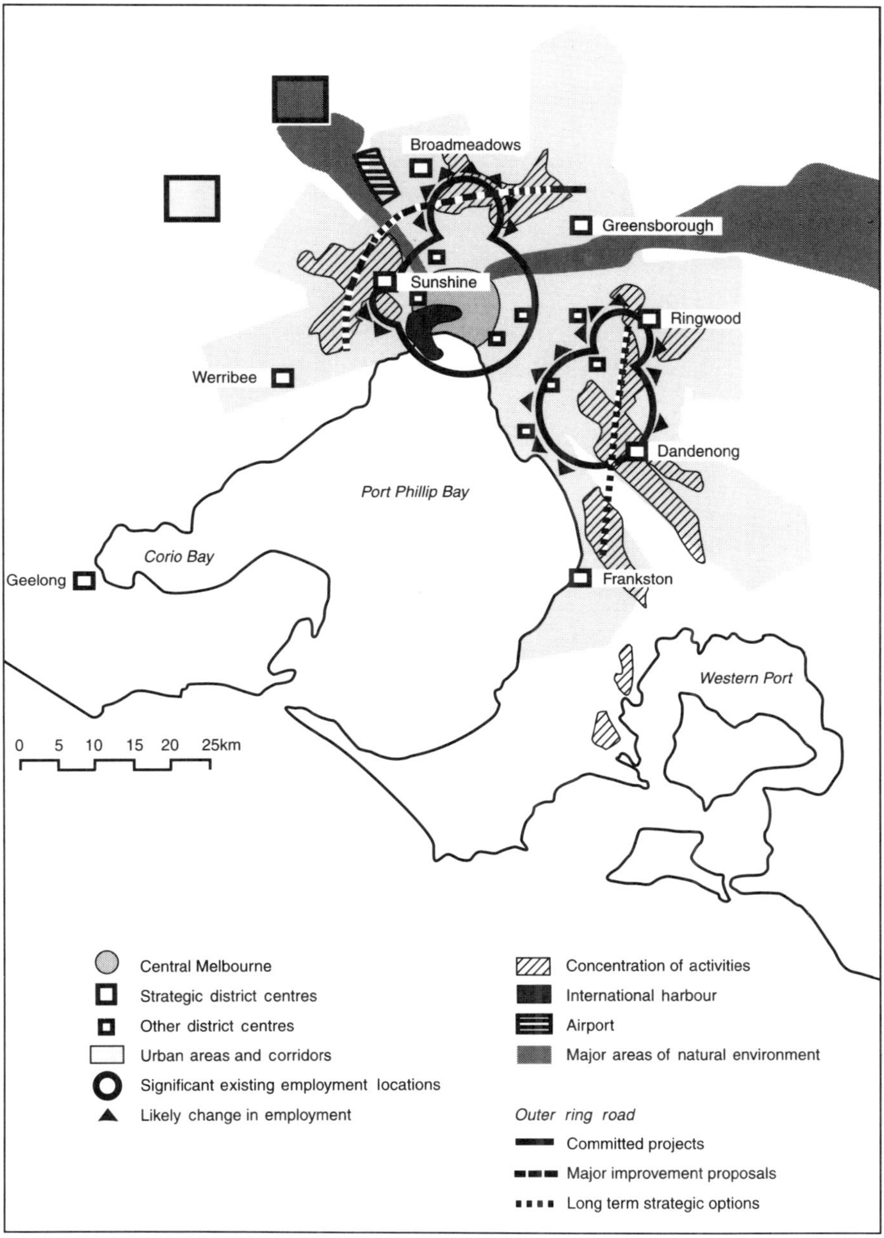

Figure 9.2 Pattern of future metropolitan development for Melbourne (1987)

Source: Shaping Melbourne's Future, Victorian Ministry for Planning and Environment (MPE), Melbourne, 1987. (This figure reproduced from K. Seibert and V. Sposito, 'Strategic planning for metropolitan Melbourne', unpublished conference paper prepared for Metropolis '93, Conference of the World Association of Metropolises, Montreal, Canada, 1993.)

Adelaide

A new growth strategy for metropolitan Adelaide was released in September 1987, once again with a heavy emphasis on urban consolidation, but also identifying substantial areas for further fringe growth. This strategy favoured urban consolidation because of its presumed potential to reduce infrastructure costs and the state government's public transport deficit. It also leaned heavily on consultant reports which strongly recommended against sending low-income households to new suburbs at a distance from the city centre,[22] although there were strong voices raised to criticise urban consolidation in turn as regressive.[23] To many it appeared to be the latest example of planning to provide land for housing on the basis of trend projections, with 'no evidence to suggest that any serious attempt has been made by the Government to integrate state development with metropolitan planning'.[24] But the mood of the times was beginning to swing in favour of a more ambitious approach to metropolitan planning which attempted, once again, to address the coordination problems seen in Melbourne and the lack of a long-term context for land release programs such as Adelaide's. Neutze expressed this mood in a paper delivered to a 1988 seminar on metropolitan planning:

> The criticisms that were levelled at the performance of urban planning have been used as a justification for retreating from some of its more ambitious attempts to determine urban futures. Some recent writings on the topic imply that a retreat from 'blueprint' planning would bring unambiguous gains. It is the contention of this paper that the gains in flexibility which come with the kind of urban management which is less oriented to a long-term vision of the future will necessarily be accompanied by losses in efficiency through less effective coordination between different investment decisions, and an inability to consider large scale alternatives in patterns of development.[25]

Brisbane

Robert Stimson, the director of the Brisbane Plan Project, carried out for Brisbane City Council between April 1990 and September 1991, observed that planning had 'rarely succeeded' because of

> a lack of political will to implement plans; methodological deficiencies in the way plans were devised; and a failure both to recognise the rapidly changing nature of economic, environmental, demographic, social and technological forces at the global, national and regional ends and to understand how these processes are restructuring and re-shaping the way cities and their regions function and evolve.[26]

The Brisbane plan had broad aspirations to be strategic, integrated and holistic, and to span the full range of government activity. It was also underpinned by ambitious notions of community consultation and began to use the language of pluralism, acknowledging both the limitations of earlier plans which rested on a unitary idea of the public interest and reflecting the growing significance of gender, multiculturalism and diversity generally in public policy debates. Its rosy vision for Brisbane's future is set out in Figure 9.3. The Brisbane plan fell foul of political changes in the City Council in 1990 and was eventually published in 1991 simply as a discussion document under the title, *Brisbane—Magnet City*.[27] However, it represented one of the first attempts at a new style of metropolitan plan which emerged full-grown the following year in the work of the South Australian Planning Review.

The South Australian Planning Review

The South Australian Planning Review was carried out between 1990 and 1992. Its major products were a metropolitan planning strategy and a new Development Act. Its draft metropolitan strategy, *2020 Vision: A Planning Strategy for Metropolitan Adelaide*, drew upon extensive public consultation to distill and express a set of broad values and choices, followed by strategies about 'living', economic activity, the use and conservation of natural resources, access, heritage, and urban design. The metropolitan strategy proposed measures to slow Adelaide's outward growth and to shift the balance of future urban development to the northern suburbs, away from the vulnerable vineyards to the south (Figure 9.4). It sought to promote a more diverse housing stock and to redevelop old public housing areas with a mix of public and private dwellings. It argued for the promotion of a multi-centred city, with regional centres taking a greater share of employment and public services, and developing as 'real town centres' for their surrounding suburbs. And it espoused a series of travel demand management strategies intended to make better use of the existing road network, while firmly ruling out any future expressway development.

The Planning Review also made some explicit statements about what it regarded as an appropriate style of planning. It proposed a new planning system, key elements of which were a long-term perspective, a strategic focus, and a new set of arrangements within government to ensure that the actions and budgets of individual government agencies were coordinated to support the agreed purposes of metropolitan development—a 'whole of government' approach. The responsibility for maintaining the strategy was to lie with an agency close to the centre of government—the Premier's

Do you want a City like this? . . .

A system of largely self-contained cities make up the megalopolis with a regional population that is over 3 million and growing.

Agricultural lands, natural parks, wide open spaces and waterways separate the urban areas. But getting from one to another is easy and quick on the rapid transit rail or by the attractively landscaped freeway.

Leaving for work after a leisurely breakfast, an office worker with a computer company walks for 10 minutes to the rail station from the family's townhouse, set in a landscaped area with pool and tennis court shared with 19 other families who collectively come from four states of the nation and half a dozen overseas countries.

Arriving downtown after 20 minutes and with the morning paper read, the worker reaches the office by a short ride on the city light rail to the high tech office block by the River.

After work the family members reunite to enjoy a meal in an outdoor café and to discuss which of a large number of cultural, recreational, artistic and sporting events they will go to at the weekend.

Each of the cities that make up the region have excellent health, education, recreation and sporting facilities which are easily accessed by the mini-bus or family car. A trip to the beach is either by the freeway or the fast train, with a fun ride by light rail to the sparkling surf.

On leaving school, the kids have the choice of many universities and TAFE colleges, and a diverse range of high tech industries and service sector jobs means their future looks promising. Investment is pouring into the region and its industries, tourism and offices.

Men and women alike have modern and attractive working environments in major employment nodes, from the CBD to the Regional Business Districts and the Office/Industrial parks in the region's new towns.

The booming International Airport brings tourist and business travellers from all over the Pacific Rim and the nation. Downtown, they can stroll through the pedestrian malls, gardens and along the River. They might marvel at the architectural diversity of urban villages vibrant with activity day and night. These are reached after a five to ten minute ride on the underground or light rail. Or they might take a tour to one of the many national parks, theme parks or integrated resorts in the region.

Life in the 'sun belt' metropolis is great. Services are good. Housing is affordable. There is a good sense of community and the quality of the built and natural environment is unsurpassed elsewhere in the country. Civic pride is high in the livable city.

Figure 9.3 A Vision of Brisbane's Future (1991)

Source: R.J. Stimson, *Brisbane—Magnet City: A Report on Strategies for the Development, Growth and Management of Brisbane City into the 21st Century*, Brisbane City Council, Brisbane, September 1991.

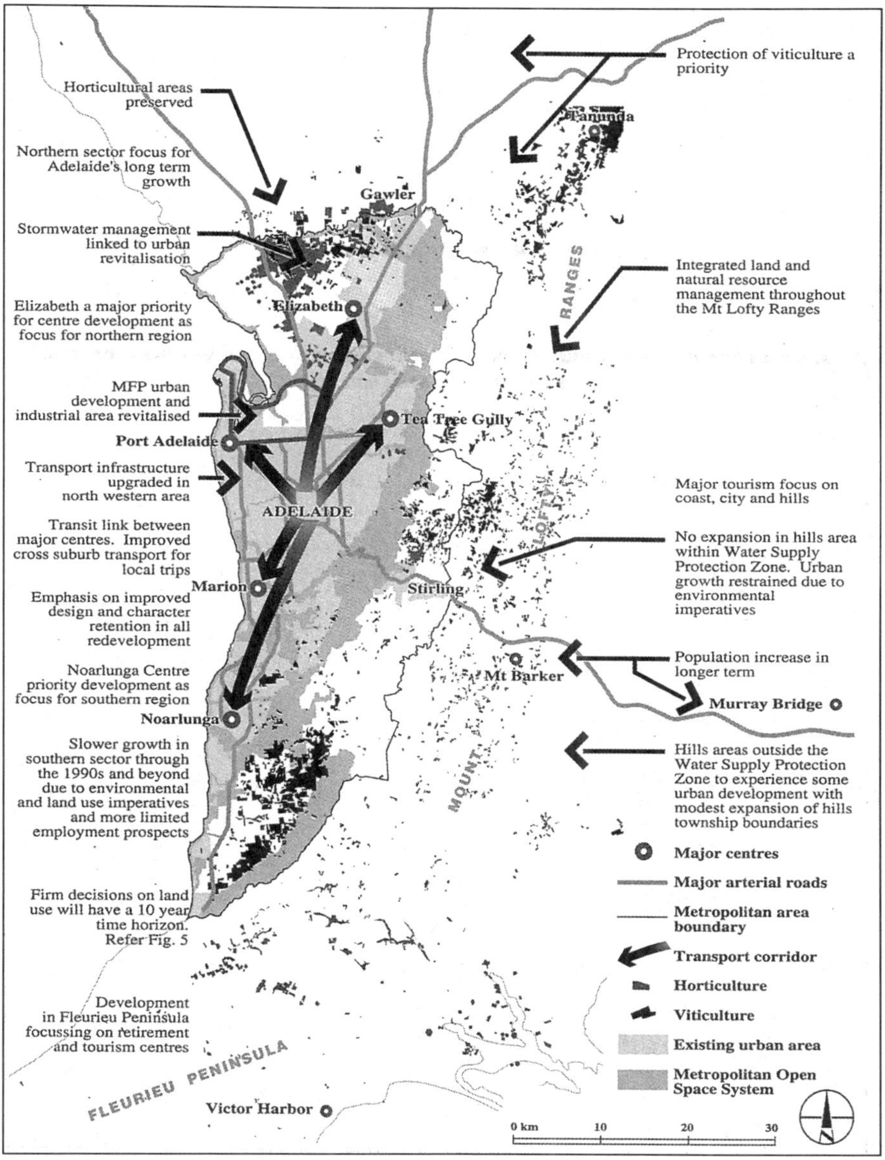

Figure 9.4 'Visions of Adelaide' (1992)

Source: South Australian Planning Review, *2020 Vision: A Planning Strategy for Metropolitan Adelaide*, SA Department of Premier and Cabinet, Adelaide, 1992.

Department—and this responsibility was to include continuing and extending the arrangements for public involvement developed during the Review.

One of the major purposes of the legislative changes which were proposed by the Planning Review was the creation of a framework in which the many approvals needed for private development of land could be simplified. Significant changes were also proposed to the way in which disputes over planning matters were to be resolved. The Planning Review also addressed the need to resolve some of the role ambiguities of state government departments charged with both promoting and regulating development. The Planning Review encouraged reorganisation to bring together most of the government's urban development functions and agencies, such as the South Australian Housing Trust and the Urban Land Trust, into a single portfolio.

The government's own locational decisions were also seen as important. The state in its various forms was an important employer in South Australia. Proposals in the strategy to increase the amount of employment in sub-regional centres were dependent to a significant extent on the cooperation of government agencies. Incremental locational decisions were intended to be taken within a long-term strategic framework and to lead, eventually, to the achievement of a polycentric city.

The Planning Review's report supported the continuation of the public–private joint venture approach to urban development which, especially since the 1980s, had provided the basis for most large new residential developments on fringe land acquired and assembled by the Urban Land Trust or on surplus government land within the metropolitan area. The future application of such an approach to the redevelopment of old public housing areas was also advocated. The Planning Review favoured a pragmatic approach to the question of how infrastructure should be funded, allowing scope for negotiation at the time of establishing joint ventures. However, it basically aligned itself with arguments in favour of retaining a strong public presence in the funding and provision of urban infrastructure on equity grounds.[28]

The South Australian Planning Review was, in retrospect, a remarkably ambitious attempt to bring together major elements of emerging planning orthodoxy at the beginning of the 1990s. It sought to provide a 'community-shared' vision of the future metropolitan area as a context for short- and medium-term development programming and to provide the long-term development framework which had been argued to be lacking in the 1980s. It sought to place equity considerations back on the metropolitan planning agenda and to resolve tensions between economic investment and environmental planning. Its central notion of strategic planning was meant to symbolise a shift from reactive, short-range thinking, dominated by sectoral issues, to a proactive, long-range and citizen-oriented style of planning, tackling multiple issues and their interrelationships, and seeking to build consensus around community priorities and aspirations. Overall, the Planning Review consciously aligned itself with its interpretation of South Australia's tradition of a strong public sector framework for private sector investment, allied to an inclusive and socially just focus appropriate to the 1990s. In retrospect, this was clearly out of step with the emerging trend towards smaller government and market outcomes.

Economic disaster overtook South Australia as the Planning Review's preliminary conclusions were being drafted. Following the deregulation of the banking system, the State Bank of South Australia had grown dramatically between 1985 and 1990, increasing its total assets by an average annual rate of 43.9 per cent. In the 1990/91 financial year, however, huge losses of the order of $2.2 billion were recorded.[29] Confidence in public sector management fell sharply and the climate became one in which investment attraction became an ever greater priority.

Conclusion

The new metropolitan plans (Table 9.2) which began to appear at the start of the 1990s were characterised by several attributes, notably the desire to integrate social, economic and physical policies; the coordination of land development with transport, water supply, schools, hospitals and other community services; more explicit strategies for developing employment and attracting investment; policies designed to ameliorate the

Table 9.2 Major metropolitan plans of the 1980s and early 1990s

City	*Major plan*
Adelaide	*Long Term Development Strategy for Metropolitan Adelaide*, 1987 *2020 Vision: Draft Planning Strategy for Metropolitan Adelaide*, 1992
Brisbane	*Brisbane—Magnet City*, 1991
Canberra	*Metropolitan Policy Plan*, 1984 *Metropolitan Canberra (Report of the Joint Parliamentary Committee on the Australian Capital Territory)*, 1987 *National Capital Plan*, 1989
Darwin	*Darwin Regional Land Use Structure Plan*, 1990
Melbourne	*Shaping Melbourne's Future*, 1987
Perth	*Planning for the Future of the Perth Metropolitan Region*, 1987 *Metroplan: A Planning Strategy for the Perth Metropolitan Region*, 1990
Sydney	*Sydney into Its Third Century*, 1988

problems of areas of social disadvantage; and a new emphasis on environmental protection and natural resource management.

The new plans emphasised the need for more effective implementation measures and the phrase 'whole of government' began to appear in documents around 1991, signifying the coordination of all relevant government agency programs and implying a close relationship between strategic infrastructure proposals and state government budgetary processes. Metropolitan development programs for matching land release and infrastructure requirements to population and household growth were retained and refined, but now set within the context of integrated plans setting out long-term spatial patterns.

These new plans were impressive to look at. They rested typically on higher levels of research and analysis than their predecessors, with environmental and social scientists working alongside planners and urban designers. And they involved determined efforts to secure community involvement. But with hindsight, it appears that the authors of these plans were too easily convinced by their own rhetoric and ambition. The decade was one in which major projects, often driven by foreign investment, were increasing features of the Australian urban landscape and, in practice, competitive state governments invariably bowed to pressure to facilitate these projects through hurried ministerial approvals, special legislation, the excising of key sites within cities from state-wide planning regimes and the establishment of development corporations.

Even while the plans were in preparation, the main game was elsewhere. Most plans lacked the means to effectively blend economic priorities with land development and service requirements. In the midst of major economic change, state governments found economic policy and programs difficult to express. Targets for employment were based on thin evidence and on limited understanding of the depth of industry restructuring and its impacts. As the effects of economic restructuring and globalisation became manifest, it was clear that communities across the country faced new issues and challenges. The impacts of the information economy and the factors encouraging clustering of new high-technology industries, for example, were poorly understood, but the zoning of additional land was unlikely to be the most important factor in planning for such industries. The planning strategies of the early 1990s also rested on 'community shared visions' which were increasingly at odds with the diverse and fragmented images of community which post-modern views of the city were presenting. Peel has criticised the 'wishy-washy pluralism of "community desires"' which underpinned some of these documents and notes that 'in working-class suburbs like Adelaide's Elizabeth, there is strong evidence that these people do not feel part of a "consensus" on Adelaide's future, even if they have been consulted'.[30]

In the early 1990s, the challenge to the public provision of infrastructure and services was expressed by introducing a 'user pays' approach where appropriate and in exploring new forms of development charges, statutory contributions and joint ventures. Within a very short time, this had evolved into a full-scale retreat from the notion of public ownership and government service provision. In this environment it was hard to see how, and by whom, integrated metropolitan planning strategies were to be implemented.

At the national level, in the ebb and flow of federalism, the Commonwealth was never willing or able to address the primary impacts of its policies on cities and regions. Population policy, the consequences of changes to immigration quotas, the effects of declining public capital and infrastructure provision, and the location of Commonwealth activity were never seriously assessed in terms of their spatial and urban impacts.

In summary, the years around 1990 saw a renewed interest in a form of strategic planning through which state governments and bureaucracies began to embrace the benefits of a systematic approach to coordination, underpinning a long-term and integrated vision of metropolitan development. The aspirations of the proponents of this new style of planning have only been realised to a limited extent, however, in the face of an ideology which is fundamentally antithetical to public sector planning and leadership. The plans had certainly changed. But the rest of the world had changed faster.

10 The late 1990s: competitive versus sustainable cities

Stephen Hamnett

Australia's cities in the late 1990s face some daunting problems. The ageing of the population has significant implications for the housing stock, for notions of access and for the provision of services. Cities are becoming more obviously divided along social, ethnic and generational lines. Economic restructuring has left some communities with long-term problems of unemployment and disadvantage. And there is growing recognition of the urgent need to address poor urban air and water quality, and to give a higher priority to the management of natural resources.

These issues are common, but there are also significant differences in the experiences of cities. In Sydney, for example, the Olympic Games are providing a short-term boost to infrastructure investment, but development pressures in the city centre continue to cause problems of congestion, and concerns about heritage and cultural values. In Adelaide, stagnation is the major challenge. Brisbane is at the heart of Australia's fastest growing metropolitan region. And Canberra is struggling to adjust to a dramatic decline in public investment and employment.

The 1996 census showed that some 15.3 million people, or 86 per cent of Australia's population, now live in urban areas. Queensland accounted for 37 per cent of the national growth between 1991 and 1996. There is evidence of the continuance of the movement, which, over the past two decades, has seen a westward and, especially, a northward drift away from south-eastern Australia. The outer parts of cities and peri-urban areas continue to grow quickly, but some evidence has emerged recently of a slowing of fringe growth and of increases in the proportion of new housing being built in established areas.[1] Some early signs of a revival in inner city populations are appearing, but their significance cannot yet be assessed.

While these trends are occurring, the importance of public planning is being further questioned. Australia is dominated once again by a conservative political agenda as it approaches the end of the first century of Federation. The Federal Government has no explicit interest in urban affairs and public planners now work in a landscape dominated by privatisation, national and state competition policies, the 'contracting-out' of public services and, overall, a diminishing role for government in the regulation of urban form and development. Cities are increasingly portrayed as economic and cultural entities which need to undertake entrepreneurial activities in order to enhance their competitiveness,[2] with the principal role for planning being to support a new round of civic boosterism and deregulatory place marketing.

Twentieth-century urban planning is an activity which sits squarely in the tradition of modernity. Modernity implied that individuals could combine democratically to manage their collective affairs and, through the application of scientific knowledge and reason, increase the sum of human happiness and welfare. Planning was seen as a way of furthering progress by managing public affairs, and occasionally overriding private property rights, so as to avoid the externalities of unfettered economic development. As previous chapters in this book have shown, ideas relating to the specific field of urban planning were formed largely in reaction to the adverse consequences of uncoordinated nineteenth-century urban development and early twentieth-century problems such as traffic congestion, design chaos and poor housing conditions.

But the modernist notion of collective action through government planning is under attack, undermined by 'market triumphalism'—the current political and ideological preference for a smaller role for government.[3] It is also challenged by postmodernist critics who argue that, rather than expressing a recognised and general public interest, planning's collective values and prescriptions 'appear to be partial, to come from fallible experts rather than citizens'.[4] Its institutional forms are criticised as being too technocratic, paternalistic and bureaucratic to accommodate the diversity of contemporary society. From this perspective, the notion of a homogeneous public interest is rejected in favour of an alternative view which recognises 'multiple publics' as the basis for an inclusive democracy.[5] The notion that 'cities can be made better'[6] is replaced by a relativism which provides no basis for intervention in market processes.

This chapter begins by describing the character of recent federal initiatives related to the cities, and then examines metropolitan planning arrangements and plans in the closing years of the century. An important theme is the convergence around Australia on a style of strategic planning which aspires to the integration of economic, social and environmental concerns, the pursuit of more 'compact' cities and the balancing of investment attraction with 'quality of life' issues. This sits uneasily, however, with current government preferences for urban outcomes which are determined by market and individual choices, with the trend towards simplified planning legislation intended to facilitate investment, and, in some places, with the dismantling of the agencies and arrangements which have delivered integrated planning in the past. The chapter ends with some reflections on the future of Australia's cities and their planners, and raises the prospect of a redefined collective interest in planning based on the imperatives of environmental sustainability.

Planning for Australia's cities in the late 1990s

The federal level

The Better Cities Program of the early 1990s marked a significant renewal of interest in the cities on the part of the Federal Labor Government, but under very different circumstances from those of the Whitlam period. In the early 1990s, there was a revival of some earlier ideas about urban and regional reform, but 'the capacity to actually address many of the problems had been dramatically eroded both politically and institutionally'.[7]

What had changed also was that an explicit relationship was now drawn between the costs of urban development and the broader productivity of the economy:

> [G]iven the need to make our economy more competitive in the Asian Region, we need to adopt less expensive forms of urban development which allow more of our national wealth and savings to be spent in supporting new, productive forms of economic activity.[8]

The early Better Cities initiatives have been described in Chapter 9. By 1994, the language of federal policy was clearly evolving, and a dominant idea was that of cities as 'engines of economic growth'. A host of international speakers came to Melbourne at the invitation of the Federal Government in 1994 to speak to this theme at the Organisation for Economic Cooperation and Development/Australian Government conference on 'Cities and the New Global Economy'. Prime Minister Keating set the tone:

> We want cities of both efficiency and beauty. Quality of life is just as much bound up with the development of cities as is economic advancement. Our cities must enable us to respond effectively to developments in the global economy. But they must also offer a quality of life that enhances our work and recreational well-being. They must be great places both to live in and do business in.[9]

The OECD conference saw the launch of the report of the Prime Minister's Urban Design Task Force.[10] Keating's interest in improving the appearance of Australian cities had provided the impetus for this report, but its definition of urban design went well beyond aesthetics, fitting seamlessly within the Better Cities agenda by providing support for the compact city notion and for the 'New Urbanist' formula of traditional grid street layouts, housing densities supportive of public transport and mixed-use forms of development.[11]

Better Cities was reviewed and judged a success in 1994–95, and the 1995–96 federal budget announced a $236 million extension to the program, which came to be known as Better Cities II. Most of the new funding was to go towards planning strategies and to feasibility studies of investments required in selected areas of the nation's major cities—'gateway' zones experiencing rapid growth and urban renewal projects.[12] Strategic planning was required because 'good planning removes policy risks which inhibit private sector investment'.[13] Shortages of funds for capital investment needed to be made up by giving the private sector a bigger role in the provision of infrastructure.[14]

In practice, little came from Better Cities II. In 1996, the Keating Government was replaced by a Liberal–National coalition led by John Howard and the Better Cities program was immediately abolished. On taking office, the Howard Government had no explicit urban policies, apart from an inherited lukewarm commitment to urban design, soon abandoned, and took the traditional conservative view that urban policies are a state concern.[15]

So ended the third brief episode of national government engagement with Australian cities in the twentieth century. The funds provided for Better Cities and associated federal urban policy initiatives in the early 1990s were modest. Orchard has argued, however, that this period was significant in representing a substantial shift in intellectual and policy approaches to Australia's cities 'towards a view which challenged Australian housing preferences and city structure as too expensive and inefficient, not environmentally sustainable and as reproducing social disadvantage'.[16]

Reforms to legislative frameworks for state and local planning

At the state government level, there has been a spate of reforms to planning legislation since 1994, extending the micro-economic reform arguments which, since the mid-1980s, have supported the pursuit of standardised and simplified development assessment frameworks.

Changes to the New South Wales Government's *Environmental Planning and Assessment Act*, which came into effect in July 1998, were explicitly driven by national competition policy.[17] Private certification of building code approvals was introduced, following the lead of a number of other states. In addition, the 1998 changes offered the prospect of allowing private 'certifiers' to make decisions on routine planning matters. There was also provision for an integrated consent process, intended to simplify the task of applying for development approval by providing applicants with a 'one stop shop'—a single application to address planning, building, environmental and other relevant matters. There was an expectation that these reforms would encourage local and state organisations to move towards flexible administrative structures using 'multi-skilled' staff, rather than retaining control systems essentially for 'the purpose of advancing the interests of members of the guild or pressure groups they represent'.[18]

Similar ideas underpinned legislative reforms in other states. The principal purposes of Queensland's *Integrated Planning Act 1998* were to focus on the effects of development and to provide a 'one stop shop . . . to attract job-creating investment'.[19] South Australia's *Development Act*, in effect since January 1994, also included building construction provisions, previously treated in a separate Act. A significant amendment to this Act was made in 1996 with the purpose of protecting certain decisions relating to the assessment of major projects from judicial review. Legislative changes were also under consideration in Western Australia in 1997 with the intention of achieving 'simplification and greater integration of land use decision-making'.[20]

The impacts of micro-economic reform on planning legislation have perhaps been most dramatic in Victoria. When the Kennett Government was elected in 1992, its view of the role of planning was unambiguous:

> Wealth creation is a first priority in Victoria. The statutory planning system should not contain unnecessary deterrents to development or innovation and the decision-making process should give additional weight to protection and promotion of wealth creating activity . . . There are many Victorians to whom real and sustainable employment prospects are of more immediate importance than increased residential amenity.[21]

Local government boundaries and responsibilities have been radically altered in Victoria, and enlarged local councils have been given responsibility for administering a new planning system created under the *Planning and Environment (Planning Schemes) Act 1996*. Key elements of this are a number of statewide 'planning provisions' and a set of 25 standard zones, from which local councils may select but not depart.[22] The Property Council of Victoria, which represents private development interests, has welcomed these provisions as a move away from 'command and control regulatory planning' towards a more performance-based system.[23] Some critics take a different view. Ogilvy suggests that the new arrangements represent 'the withdrawal of the State and local government from any meaningful role in the regulation of land use and development; "prohibited" has become a dirty word in the planning machinery and Central Melbourne is fast becoming a planning free zone; almost everything can be negotiated'.[24]

Metropolitan planning

In the late 1990s most Australian metropolitan areas have strategic plans (Table 10.1). Their aims are those of the late 1980s and early 1990s—all aspire to bring together environmental, social and economic concerns—but there is a stronger emphasis on economic policy, on the purpose of plans to provide a framework for investment and on their means of implementation. Urban containment and consolidation policies are now subsumed in the general pursuit of the compact city, which involves the desire to slow the outward growth of cities and suburbs, create a more diverse housing stock and protect the viability of central cities. Environmental issues, although less politically salient at the federal level than a decade or so ago, express themselves in state and city strategies through increased concerns for air and water quality, while the integration of land use and transport planning is again fashionable.

Most state governments now seek to pursue 'whole of government' approaches, the current shorthand for seeking greater coordination of the planning of services and development as well as the funding of infrastructure. Recent years have also seen the development of a series of separate planning statements for the central areas of some major cities. A significant feature of the late 1990s is the continuing tension between the competitive desire to attract major projects to inner areas and the requirement to comply with plans and processes. Current metropolitan plans for Sydney, Brisbane, Melbourne and Adelaide are discussed in this chapter, with a briefer review of developments in Canberra and Perth.

Sydney

In 1995, the New South Wales Government released *Cities for the 21st Century*, a strategy for the greater Sydney metropolitan region, extending north to Newcastle and south to Wollongong. Based on an earlier discussion paper released in 1993 entitled *Sydney's Future*, this assumed that greater Sydney's population would reach about 5.3 million by the year 2021. A key purpose of this strategy was to slow urban expansion by accommodating the greater part of projected growth within existing

Table 10.1 Major metropolitan plans, 1993–98

City	*Major plans*	*Planning agency*
Adelaide	*Planning Strategy for Metropolitan Adelaide*, 1994	Department of Premier and Cabinet
	Planning Strategy for Metropolitan Adelaide, 1998	Premier of South Australia/ Department of Transport, Urban Planning and the Arts
Brisbane	*Brisbane 2011*, 1996	Brisbane City Council
	SE Queensland Regional Framework for Growth Management, 1998	SE Queensland Regional Co-ordination Committee
Canberra	*Canberra: A Capital Future*, 1996	Chief Minister's Department
Darwin	*Central Darwin Land Use Objectives*, 1996	NT Department of Lands, Planning and Environment
Hobart	*Hobart—Sustainable City*, 1994	Department of Environment and Land Management/Urban Management Programme Group
Melbourne	*Capital City Policy*, 1994	Department of Planning and Development
	Living Suburbs, 1995	Department of Planning and Development
Perth	*State Planning Strategy*, 1996	Western Australian Planning Commission
Sydney	*Sydney's Future*, 1993	Department of Planning
	Cities for the 21st Century, 1995	Department of Planning
	A Framework for Managing Growth, 1997	Department of Urban Affairs and Planning

urban areas through fairly heroic increases in housing densities and through a shift away from single-family housing to 'multi-unit' dwellings. The other priority was to develop a more ecologically sustainable region, particularly by improving air and water quality.

The strategy stressed the importance of reinforcing existing employment concentrations, supporting and improving public transport, and locating housing close to jobs, transport and services. This strategy represented a shift from 'plan-making to urban management'—here understood as coordinated infrastructure planning achieved as part of a 'whole-of-government' approach to metropolitan growth (Figure 10.1). The simultaneous preparation of an 'Integrated Transport Strategy' for the

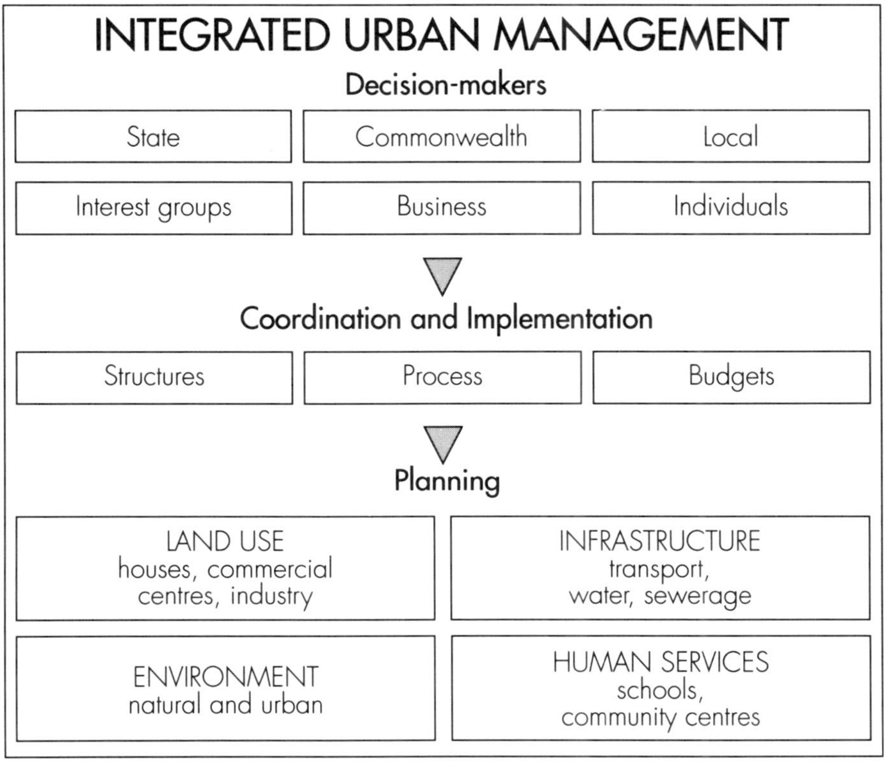

Figure 10.1 Integrated urban management

Source: NSW Department of Planning, *Cities for the 21st Century*, NSW Government, Sydney, 1995.

greater metropolitan region was cited as an important indicator of what this meant. *Cities for the 21st Century* was celebrated within and outside government as involving 'a change in emphasis in the role of the planner away from a directive central role . . . and towards a role which centres on building links across government and facilitating consensus in approach and action'.[25]

Following changes of government at state and commonwealth level, a review of metropolitan strategy for Sydney was published in 1997 under the title, *A Framework for Growth and Change*. The 1997 planning framework reasserted the importance of a strategic plan to guide agencies of state government in setting their infrastructure funding priorities, although the implementation of new road and other infrastructure projects would increasingly become the responsibility of private providers.[26]

Sydney's status as a 'global city' loomed large in contemporary government documents[27] and planning was seen to be important 'in maximising the positive aspects of amenity, environment and image in attracting international investment'. The importance of 'quality of life' issues in securing investors and major events had been underlined earlier by the emphasis placed on principles of ecologically sustainable development in Sydney's successful bid for the Olympic Games for the year 2000 and in the detailed proposals for the major venue for the Games, a 760 hectare site at Homebush Bay, fourteen kilometres west of the central business district (CBD).

A Framework for Managing Growth restated the arguments of the earlier strategy in support of a more compact city. The overall spatial pattern proposed for Sydney's greater metropolitan region has elements of previous urban containment and corridor plans, with the intention being to define four 'distinct, interdependent subregions'—Sydney, Newcastle, Wollongong and the Central Coast—separated by green spaces to prevent the establishment of a continuous conurbation and with urban expansion contained within linear corridors along major transport routes, principally the rail network.[28]

Sydney has experienced a development boom in its central area from the 1970s to the 1990s, linked to the rapid economic growth of the Asia–Pacific region, and reflecting its attractiveness to financial services, tourism and the regional headquarters of international firms. Since 1991, pro-development pressures have been somewhat restrained by the influence of strong amenity and heritage groups at local council level. And, since 1996, central Sydney has had a city plan which is notable for a strong emphasis on urban design as well as providing for substantial expenditure on public space by the City Council, in readiness for the 2000 Olympic Games.[29] As Searle has observed, however, 'such activity has its limits, set by Sydney's possibilities for capturing global investment and by the continuing legal subordination of local government by the state government'.[30]

Brisbane

The issues facing the greater Brisbane metropolitan area in the last years of the century are those of coping with growth. There has been a recent shift in focus to planning for the expanded metropolitan region of South-East Queensland. Queensland has a long tradition of minimalist state involvement in local government planning and this has been reflected in the cooperative nature of relationships underpinning the growth management frameworks developed for South-East Queensland since 1990, when the 'SEQ 2001' project commenced in response to the pressures of high population growth in the region. The early years of the SEQ 2001 project involved substantial Federal Government involvement through the Better Cities Program. The latest in a series of framework plans for South-East Queensland, the *Regional Framework for Growth Management*, was released in 1998. It assumes a population for the region of more than 3 million by 2011, at which time around 2 million will be in the Brisbane metropolitan area. Twenty-nine per cent of Australia's population growth between 1991 and 2011 will occur in South-East Queensland.

The principal concerns of the framework are with accommodating growth while preserving the identity of four distinctive urban areas—Brisbane, the Sunshine Coast, the Gold Coast and Toowoomba—by maintaining rural, open space and water catchment areas between them. A hierarchy of centres have been identified, with the Brisbane CBD as the dominant centre in the region and seven key centres at the next level down providing the focus for employment growth, government services and facilities. The language is familiar—'self-contained' centres to assist in reducing private vehicle demand, with a parallel integrated regional transport policy providing supporting measures intended to increase substantially the proportion of trips made by public transport, cycling and walking. The *Regional Framework* seeks greater choice and diversity in housing, and increased housing densities where appropriate, but notes that 'most new residential suburbs will, however, continue to offer detached homes on single allotments'.[31]

A complementary strategy for the Brisbane City area was released in May 1996, under the title *Brisbane 2011: The Livable City for the Future*,[32] and placed the same high priority on creating an urban environment less dependent on cars. 'Transit-Oriented Development' is to be pursued in new suburbs and also as part of ambitious proposals for the renewal of Brisbane's inner north-eastern suburbs. Agreement on broad strategic directions will need in future to overcome long-standing tensions between the state government and the Brisbane City Council over infrastructure investment priorities.

Melbourne

A new strategy for Melbourne appeared in 1992 under the title *A Place to Live, Urban Development 1992–2031: Shaping Victoria's Future*.[33] This sought to place Melbourne's growth in a broader regional context and, like the contemporary plans for Brisbane and Adelaide described in Chapter 9, concentrated less on alternative patterns of spatial development and more on 'the processes that give rise to urban development'.[34] *A Place to Live* soon became irrelevant, however, as the Kirner Labor Government was replaced by the Liberal-led Government of Jeff Kennett, which came to power committed to a major overhaul of Victoria's planning arrangements.

Since the mid-1990s, Melbourne's metropolitan planning strategies have been separated into two principal documents. Proposals for the central city were set out in 1994 in *Creating Prosperity: Victoria's Capital City Policy*.[35] Melbourne City Council was replaced the previous year by state-appointed commissioners who oversaw a period of intense development along the banks of the Yarra—with the Crown Casino as the centrepiece of both economic and city development strategies—recognising that Melbourne's centre, like other city centres, is likely to become increasingly dependent on tourists and visitors to generate trade.

A complementary policy—*Living Suburbs: A Policy for Metropolitan Melbourne into the 21st Century*—was released in December 1995.[36] It proposed a 'whole-of-government and community approach' to cater for development and 'the lifestyle requirements of suburban neighbourhoods'.[37] The language, thereafter, was principally that of economic development, however, with four of the document's five aims having to do with improving Melbourne's business environment and competitiveness. In its urban form proposals, *Living Suburbs* is conventional, promoting a hierarchically structured city organised around activity centres located at key transport nodes around the suburbs. Transport corridors remain as important structural elements, with a particular emphasis on providing easy access to ports and airports. *Living Suburbs* notes that Melbourne has ample land—twenty years supply—already set aside for urban development in fringe growth areas. However, half of Victoria's households are now made up of only one or two people, and this leads once again to arguments for a greater diversity of housing across the metropolitan area and for an increase in the proportion of medium-density housing. As in most other cities, there has been some increase in the residential population of inner Melbourne recently, leading to state government claims of 'fundamental shifts occurring in Melbourne's economy, culture and socio-demographic profile',[38] although the significance of these shifts is questioned by some observers.[39] *Living Suburbs*, like other contemporary plans, also proposes improvements to energy efficiency and water management through concept plans for 'urban villages', which demonstrate the feasibility of low-energy urban development and water-sensitive design guidelines. Proposals for enhancing Melbourne's parks and streets build on the leadership which Melbourne has shown over the past decade in urban design, both at state and local levels.

The Melbourne City Council was reinstated in 1996 and produced a municipal planning scheme—*CityPlan*—in 1998. *CityPlan* is an extension of the *Creating Prosperity* document and its objectives are expressed in a serious of adjectives relating to the sort of city that the council would like Melbourne to become: 'prosperous', 'innovative', 'culturally vital', 'attractive' and 'sustainable'.[40]

But the driving force in the development of Melbourne's central city continues to be a succession of major waterfront projects, of which the most significant at present is the Docklands redevelopment. Docklands is the responsibility of a separate, specially established authority, and receives only passing mention in Melbourne's municipal strategic statement, despite its significance to the city centre—220 hectares of land and water, and seven kilometres of water frontage adjacent to the CBD. It represents, according to Long, the 'privatisation of the planning process', and

> one of the crucial questions that must be asked when the planning system is so thoroughly subject to private control is how the public interest is to be protected. Of course, for the Government this question may not even arise, given its propensity to conflate private and public good . . . It's an old argument: the public good is best satisfied by individuals seeking to maximise their own interest in market relationships. The only problem is that the history of urban development demonstrates that it's simply not true.[41]

Adelaide

Some saw in the 1992 report of the Planning Review a continuation of South Australia's tradition of conscious purpose and planning—perhaps 'the last gasp of the visionary tradition'.[42] As described in Chapter 9, the Planning Review proposed a new planning system for the state, the major components of which were a metropolitan planning strategy, a new Development Act and proposals for a 'whole of government' approach in which strategic planning had a key role. These proposals anticipated, and probably influenced, those in other states a few years later. But not much of the spirit of these reforms survived into the second half of the 1990s.

In December 1993, the Arnold Labor Government was replaced by the Brown Liberal Government and the *Planning Strategy for Metropolitan Adelaide* was issued early in 1994. The strategy was essentially the document prepared under the previous government but with some hastily inserted new economic objectives. The strategy's key proposals included the development of strong metropolitan centres, managing travel demand, protection of important rural and water catchment areas and the redevelopment of middle ring suburbs. New areas for urban expansion beyond the metropolitan fringe were not identified, given Adelaide's slow growth and the availability of large amounts of vacant land within the metropolitan boundary.

Thereafter, successive Liberal governments showed little interest in their metropolitan strategy, other than as 'a display case for the Government's success in attracting individual businesses to Adelaide'.[43] Infrastructure projects proceeded without regard to longer term strategic purposes—most notoriously, the unnecessary Southern Expressway—and the picture was one of 'a mixture of broad ideology and *ad hoc* projects'.[44] A more thorough review of the metropolitan planning strategy was released in January 1998. Like its predecessors, it begins with a fine statement of the values that should guide urban development and provides a coherent, if largely unchanged, set of policies for guiding Adelaide's future growth. But to many it seems incidental, rather than central, to the processes shaping Adelaide's development.

The picture is not one of unredeemed gloom. New catchment management boards now provide the scope for an integrated approach to water management. After a fairly long gestation period, programs for the regeneration of the Adelaide city centre, resulting from the 'Adelaide 21' project,[45] are progressing. And the state government, which sought to remove the powers of the Adelaide City Council in 1996, now appears to be working harmoniously with a populist lord mayor.

But some of Adelaide's more effective vehicles for managing urban growth have been dismantled. The South Australian Housing Trust is now a small and hard-pressed welfare housing agency, responsible to a minister of social services, with many of its functions 'out-sourced'. The Urban Land Trust, responsible for managing the land bank built up since the 1970s, has been abolished and its functions taken over by a Land Management Corporation which has a clear charter to dispose of public land. Responsibility for managing complex urban projects has been dissipated with the demise of the state's Urban Projects Authority and with the scrapping in 1997 of the utopian and tragi-comic 'Multi-Function Polis'.[46]

Like Victoria, South Australia inherited serious debt burdens from the financial crisis of the early 1990s. Attraction of private capital for investment remains a major priority and it is understandable that governments have been preoccupied with this issue. However, an accumulation of unrelated investment projects as part of a deregulatory 'race to the bottom' will not preserve or enhance the distinctive urban qualities on which Adelaide's future place marketing is likely to depend.

Canberra

Canberra is enduring a difficult transitional period in the late 1990s. The nation's capital, for much of the post-war period, experienced population growth and development driven by public investment and public sector employment. Population growth has now slowed. About 307 000 people live in the Australian Capital Territory (ACT) and this is estimated to increase to somewhere between 325 000–380 000 by 2010. The Commonwealth public service has been cut back hard in the 1990s and the fledgling territory government has to pay for services in the same way as the rest of Australia. Unemployment in the ACT has been higher than the national average recently and there is a growing gap between the cost of maintaining and providing new infrastructure, and administrative revenue. With slowing population growth and an ageing population, assumptions about employment locations, shopping habits, travel demand and housing preferences built into the 'Y Plan' in the 1970s and 1980s are now under review. Households are smaller, more people live on their own and fewer families have children. Central Canberra now has a much smaller population, but more jobs, than originally planned.

Strategic planning in the ACT is undertaken by the Chief Minister's Department which, needless to say, adopts a 'whole of government' approach to the provision and coordination of advice to the territory government. A strategy entitled *Canberra: A Capital Future* was released in December 1996. It expresses a concern that 'Canberra is in danger of being isolated—and being seen to be isolated—as a monument to the bureaucratic state'.[47] In the light of growing competition between cities, Canberra's image is seen as needing to be reshaped. Part of this involves the revitalisation of the central core of Canberra as a destination and as a location for major events. Elsewhere, no further urban land releases are anticipated in the foreseeable future, with demand for urban growth being accommodated within the existing 'urban envelope'—established areas, plus undeveloped parts of Tuggeranong and Gungahlin. Locations near town, district and local centres, and along transport corridors are favoured for new development in established areas, with higher residential densities encouraged close to Civic and the other town centres.

Perth

Perth's principal planning document remains its long-established Metropolitan Region Scheme, but the Western Australian Planning Commission has completed a State Planning Strategy which places Perth's future growth in a broader regional context. Perth itself is to become a 'city of world renown for livability, environmental quality and wealth'.[48] The State Planning Strategy has a planning horizon of 2029, Western Australia's bicentenary year, by which time Perth should reach a population of about 2 million, slowed by deliberate policies to develop a number of smaller towns and communities to the east and south-west of the capital (Figure 10.2).

In other respects the State Planning Strategy echoes plans elsewhere—more priority for freight and high-occupancy vehicles, closer integration of land use planning and transport, mixed development in district and neighbourhood centres, and strategic public transport systems along corridors linking activity centres. New development will be based on 'urban villages'—sustainable compact, identifiable residential areas with clear centres. Heretical and unfashionable views are buried here and there in the strategy, however, most obviously in the suggestion that government agencies should make strategic land acquisitions to facilitate the development of new settlements beyond the current urban fringe of Perth. In discussing rural areas, the strategy also notes that smaller communities are likely to find it difficult to sustain services as considerations such as economies of scale and corporatisation are taken into account and 'this may raise a difficult problem for government and the land use planning system, as the preferred settlement pattern may not be supported by purely economic calculations of efficiency'.[49] Indeed it may not.

Strategic planning and urban reform

Twenty years ago the political scientist Martin Painter observed that 'urban policy is fundamentally too complicated to be successful. Given the inherent limitations of co-ordination and implementation, it makes no sense to engage in futile acts of administrative heroism.'[50] Nevertheless, in the late 1990s, the prevailing planning style is one that aspires to the integration of broad economic, social and environmental objectives (Figure 10.3).

Most metropolitan plans contain ambitious vision statements which seek to bring together economic development with sustainability, and use the language of diversity, community empowerment and choice. These are underpinned by a 'whole of government' approach, referred to in New South Wales, and elsewhere, as 'urban management', but this is not the urban management based on incrementalism and trend-projection of the 1970s and early 1980s.[51] Rather, it implies a broadening of the scope of urban policy, the creation of a strategic framework for metropolitan planning and attention to the budgetary requirements for implementation.

The 1990s are quintessentially the decade of strategic planning. As previous chapters have shown, this is not a new notion, but its ubiquity can scarcely have been matched before. It is also an elusive concept. Its central idea is that of a long-term perspective and it is distinguished from

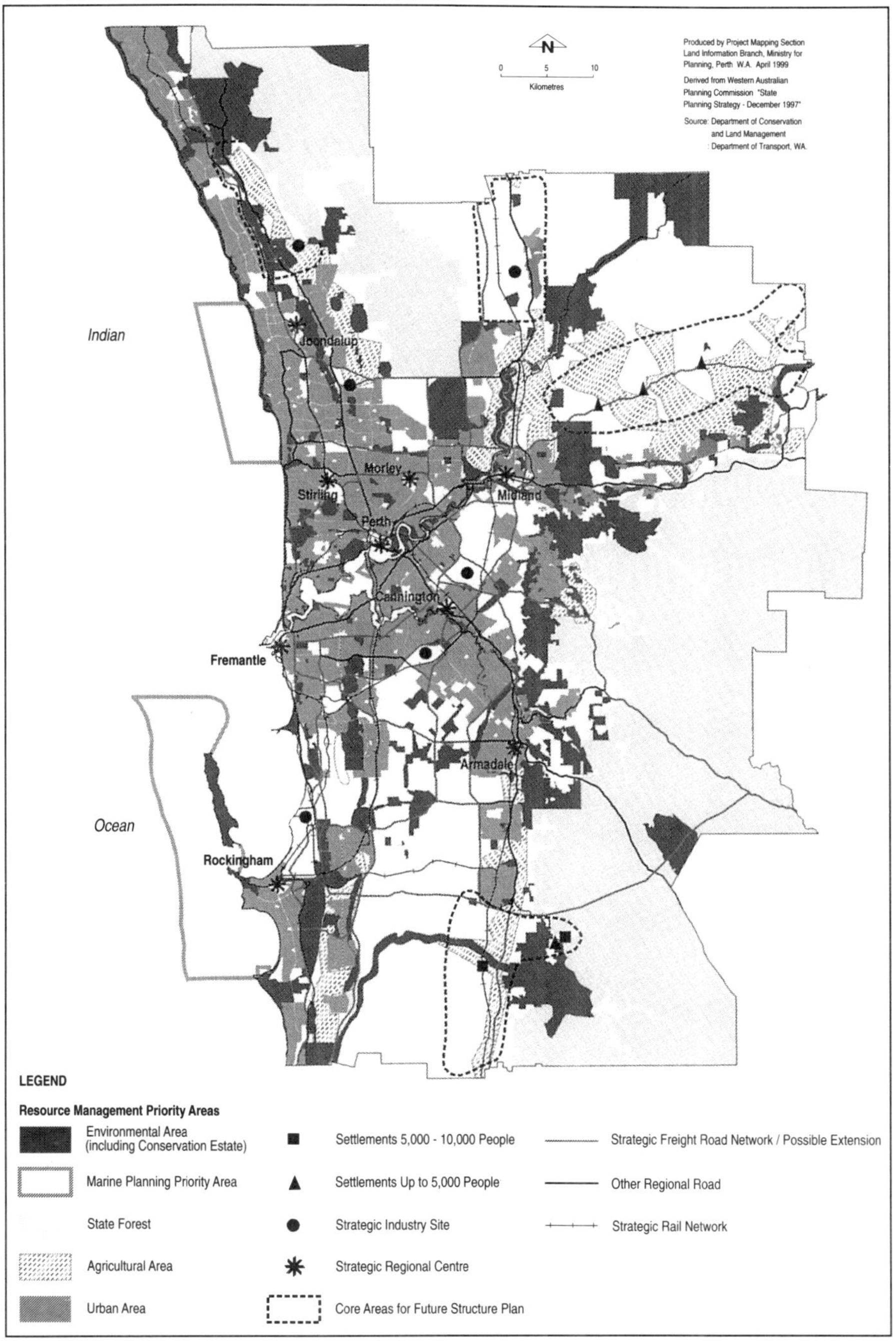

Figure 10.2 Perth region (1997)

Source: Department of Conservation and Land Management, Department of Transport, WA.

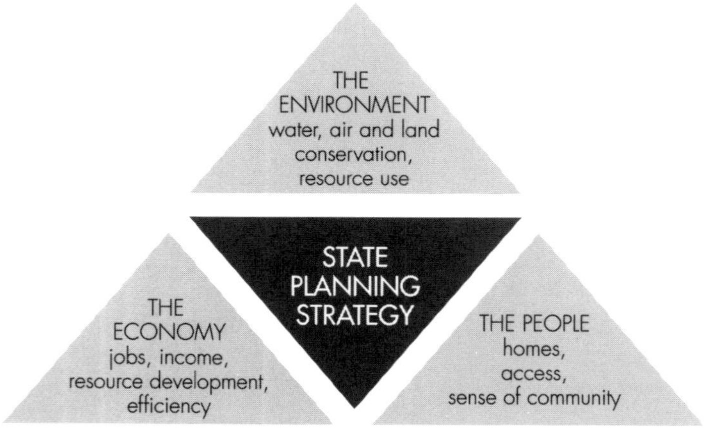

Figure 10.3 Integrated decision-making

Source: Western Australian Planning Commission, *State Planning Strategy*, WAPC, Perth, 1996.

earlier concepts of comprehensive planning by a focus on *key* areas for action and intervention. Some have suggested that the military and business origins of strategic planning make it unsuited to government where the art 'is to pick a path between competing interests and the notion of coördinating clear corporate goals sits uneasily'.[52] Others express the view that strategic planning and long-term vision statements are exercises in 'banalization—"woolly thought" and pseudo-legitimization for a number of measures and projects connected only on paper'.[53]

Meanwhile, governments in practice pursue a deregulatory agenda, the principal purpose of which is to facilitate development. Environmental aims are accorded importance in contemporary metropolitan plans, but many criticise their central tenet—the compact city notion as a response to pressing problems of sustainability—on the grounds both of the impracticality of seeking to change Australia's low-density settlement pattern in the short term and also because of the threat to egalitarian principles which they see in higher density cities. Australians may well 'continue to choose where they want to live',[54] as claimed in the Western Australian State Planning Strategy. But choice is invariably limited in practice by ability to pay and 'commitments to market principles ... so constrain the interventionist scope of public policy that goals like 'increased equity' or 'social justice' are effectively marginalised and maintain a mostly rhetorical presence'.[55] The optimistic and inclusive visions of official metropolitan plans are matched by as many dystopian views of the current and future Australian metropolis. Long, for example, sees Melbourne in these terms:

> So we approach the end of the 20th century, the century in which urban planning has played such a major role, to find that it all amounts to this: the city of spectacle, a shining Oz of footloose global capital, of waterfront showpieces inhabited by the post-industrial bourgeoisie and frequented by credit card consumers, a central city citadel of secure apartments and boutique cafes. Meanwhile, the ranks of the poor swell as the gap between rich and poor widens; homelessness grows and housing poverty in the face of rising rents and house price increases; unemployment, especially among the young, persists at soul-destroying levels and wages for those who have jobs stagnate while unionists are persecuted. Urban planning cannot solve these problems, but once some planners used to think that it could help ameliorate some of the ravages of the free market. Now politicians, planning bureaucrats and their underlings aren't even interested. Planning is about facilitating development, with a bit of urban design thrown in to keep things nice: ethics sacrificed to aesthetics in the global competition between cities.[56]

It might be argued that this is nothing new and that conditions were much worse at the end of the nineteenth century. As we have seen, however, the nineteenth century also produced a blend of 'socialist sentiments, anarchist ideas, notions of bourgeois reformism and social responsibility'[57] which came together in visions, such as the city beautiful and garden city movements. There are fewer influential voices raised on the side of reform today. And as long as we refuse to acknowledge that the urban condition can be ameliorated, or as long we see the public interest as identical with the interests of business, it is hard to see a new reform movement emerging.

Towards the twenty-first century: environmental planning?

In 1919, John Sulman concluded his series of lectures at the University of Sydney, published as *An Introduction to the Study of Town Planning in Australia*, by observing that 'In all walks of life the specialist is coming to the front wherever efficiency is desired, and most of all it is required in the management of municipal affairs'.[58] Sulman's lectures provided detailed prescriptions for the physical planning of town expansions and for the improvement of existing cities and towns.

Thirty years later, in 1949, Australia's first organised program of planning education commenced in Adelaide at the South Australian School of Mines and Industries. Much of its content would have been familiar to Sulman. The Adelaide course was instigated by the newly established Town Planning Institute of South Australia and its purpose was to train professional town planners—'specialists'— along the lines of other relevant professions. Entry was restricted to persons qualified in architecture, engineering or surveying. Subjects covered in the course were 'History of Town Planning', 'Town Planning Practice', 'Town Planning in Relation to Architecture and Amenities', 'Town Planning in Relation to Engineering', 'Town Planning in Relation to Surveying', and 'The Law Relating to Town Planning'.

Half a century further on, in 1999, the Royal Melbourne Institute of Technology is offering a postgraduate course which aspires to cover 'the latest in professional planning and environmental practice'. Among a list of twenty or so subjects included in this program are 'Environmental Policy and Globalization', 'Ecological Economics, Conflict Resolution and Mediation', 'Catchment Management and Planning', 'Working with Communities', 'Mega-Projects: Planning for Change', 'Planning Systems and Public Policy', 'Environmental Management and Impact Assessment Systems' and 'History, Theory and Contemporary Practices of Planning'.[59]

The changing definition of the scope of planning in the twentieth century is illustrated in a shorthand way by comparing these two lists of subjects. The town planning education codified by mid-century was still largely a technical matter, but at the end of the century, its boundaries have expanded enormously. The eclectic curriculum leads some to question whether the planner, in fact, has any sort of technical expertise and to suggest that the continuing existence of professional planners rests primarily on the ability of their professional body to shape the job market or on the alternative notion that planners can play a useful role in managing the land development process and in 'identifying and mediating between different interest groups'.[60]

But what is also clear from the Melbourne program—and from other planning programs around Australia—is the importance which is attached to environmental issues and values in the contemporary planning curriculum and in recent metropolitan plans (Figure 10.4). And it is the case that the growing concern about the environmental sustainability of cities and communities seems to some to lead back in the direction of *more* rather than less interventionist policies, to the reassertion of the idea of a collective interest, and to a society in which people may need to be encouraged to behave in ways which run counter to their short-term preferences and interests. Environmental goods are demonstrably public goods which cannot be secured by private action and 'sustainable development will require . . . an enhanced role for governments to intervene on behalf of the community as a whole to secure environmental protection, when individual action is incapable of achieving it'.[61]

Environmental planning—the planning of more sustainable cities,

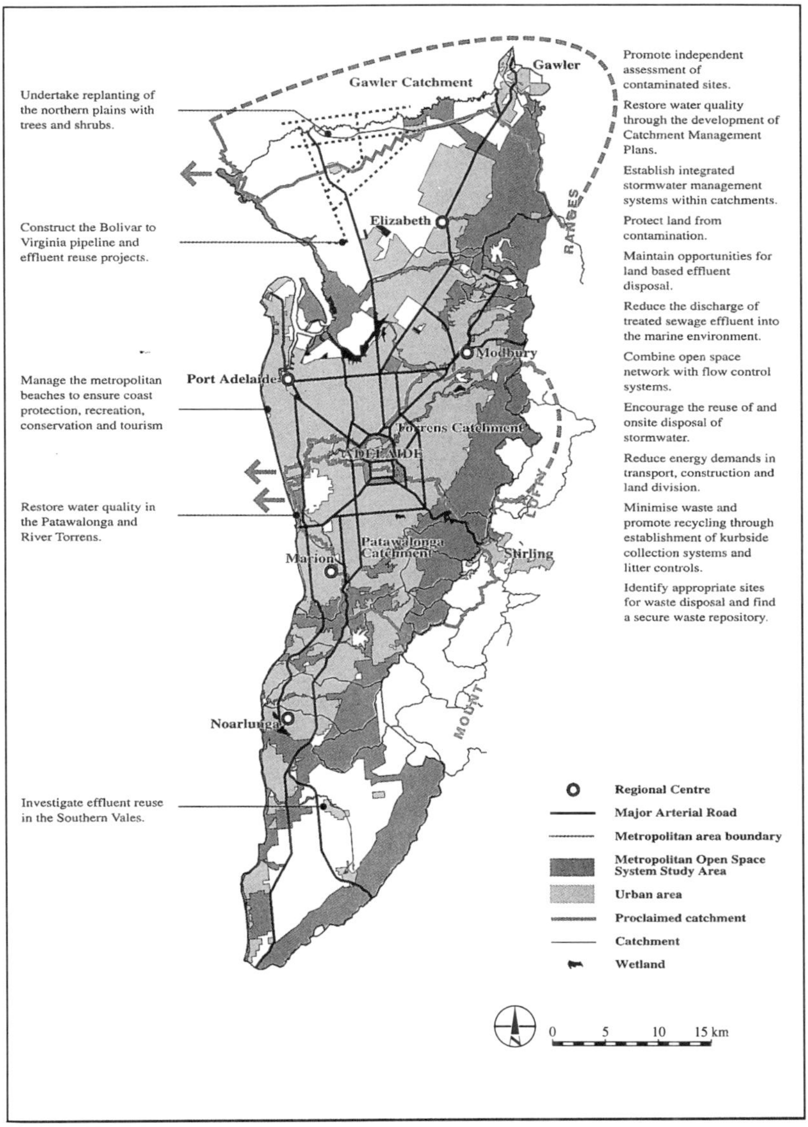

Figure 10.4 Natural resources management strategies for metropolitan Adelaide

Source: Premier of South Australia, *Planning Strategy for Metropolitan Adelaide*, Department of Transport, Urban Planning and the Arts, Adelaide, 1998.

whether compact or not—will require a wide range of skills and expertise which go well beyond those of the traditional land use planner, embracing technical, political, and, above all, ethical concerns.[62] It will pose a serious threat to the twentieth-century notion of planning as an exclusive professional activity. But an environmental planning which is interdisciplinary and which aspires to be genuinely, rather than rhetorically, strategic and integrative offers the opportunity to rekindle a reformist zeal which challenges the values and practices embodied by modern technologies and economic orthodoxies, in much the way that the early twentieth-century pioneers of Australian planning challenged the orthodoxies and problems of their colonial cities.

Notes

Introduction

1 H. Stretton, *Ideas for Australian Cities*, Georgian House, Melbourne, 1970.
2 M. Neutze, *Urban Development in Australia: A Descriptive Analysis*, George Allen & Unwin, Sydney, 1977. A companion volume, *Australian Urban Policy* (George Allen & Unwin, Sydney), was published the following year.
3 Notably J.W. McCarty and C.B. Schedvin, eds, *Urbanisation in Australia: The Nineteenth Century*, Sydney University Press, Sydney, 1974.
4 D.L. Johnson, *Canberra and Walter Burley Griffin: A Bibliography of 1876 to 1976 and a Guide to Published Sources*, Oxford University Press, Melbourne, 1980. The most planning-orientated historical account remains K. Fischer, *Canberra: Myths and Models. Forces at Work in the Formation of the Australian Capital*, Institute of Asian Affairs, Hamburg, 1984.
5 L. Sandercock, *Cities for Sale: Property, Politics and Urban Planning in Australia*, Melbourne University Press, Melbourne, 1975; republished with a new introduction as *Property, Politics and Urban Planning: A History of Australian City Planning 1890–1990*, Transaction, New Brunswick, 1990.
6 A. Hutchings and R. Bunker, eds, *With Conscious Purpose: A History of Town Planning in South Australia*, Wakefield Press, Adelaide, 1986.
7 P. Ashton, *The Accidental City: Planning Sydney since 1788*, Hale & Iremonger, Sydney, 1993.
8 J.B. McLoughlin, *Shaping Melbourne's Future? Town Planning, the State and Civil Society*, Cambridge University Press, Melbourne, 1992.
9 R. Freestone, *Model Communities: The Garden City Movement in Australia*, Thomas Nelson, Melbourne, 1989.
10 T. Stannage, *Lakeside City: The Dreaming of Joondalup*, University of Western Australia Press, Nedlands, 1996.
11 P. Harrison, *Walter Burley Griffin: Landscape Architect*, National Library of Australia, Canberra, 1995.
12 R. Freestone and A. Hutchings, 'Planning history in Australia: The state of the art', *Planning Perspectives*, vol. 8, 1993, pp. 72–91. Planning and urban historians have organised national conferences in 1993, 1995, 1996 and 1998. The fourth conference was held in conjunction with an international

symposium (see note 21). The proceedings of the 1996 Melbourne conference provide a good illustration of the variety and depth of contemporary interest: T. Dingle, ed., *The Australian City—Future/Past: Proceedings of the Third Australian Planning History/Urban History Conference*, Monash University, Melbourne, 1996.

13 Sandercock, *Cities for Sale*, p. 1.

14 P. Fitzgerald, *The Sydney Airport Fiasco: The Politics of an Environmental Nightmare*, Hale & Iremonger, Sydney, 1998.

15 A classic study in the planning history genre is P. Hall, et al., *The Containment of Urban England*, 2 vols, George Allen & Unwin, London, 1973.

16 C. Abbott and S. Adler, 'Historical analysis as a planning tool', *Journal of the American Planning Association*, vol. 55, 1989, p. 473.

17 A. Hutchings, 'Planning history in practice', *Australian Planner*, vol. 35, 1998, pp. 122–6.

18 P. Hall, *Cities of Tomorrow: An Intellectual History of Urban Planning and Design in the Twentieth Century*, rev. edn, Blackwell, Oxford, 1996, p. xiii.

19 A. Sutcliffe, 'Why planning history?', *Built Environment*, vol. 7, no. 2, 1981, p. 65.

20 G. Davison and R. Fincher, 'Urban studies in Australia: A road map and ways ahead', *Urban Policy and Research*, vol. 16, 1998, pp. 183–197.

21 A. Sutcliffe, *The History of Urban and Regional Planning: An Annotated Bibliography*, Mansell, London, 1981. The British-based journal *Planning Perspectives* is the leading journal for studies in 'history, planning and the environment'. The International Planning History Society, formed in Britain as the 'Planning History Group' in the late 1970s, held its 1998 biennial conference in Sydney and over 200 papers were presented. A large number of these are reproduced in R. Freestone, ed., *The Twentieth Century Urban Planning Experience: Proceedings of the Eighth International Planning [History] Society Conference and Fourth Australian Planning/Urban History Conference*, University of New South Wales, Sydney, 1998.

22 M. Scott, *American City Planning since 1890*, University of California Press, Berkeley, 1969.

23 R. Fogelsong, *Planning the American City: The Colonial Era to the 1920s*, Princeton University Press, Princeton, 1986.

24 C. Boyer, *Dreaming the Rational City: The Myth of American City Planning*, MIT Press, Cambridge, 1983.

25 L. Sandercock, ed., *Making the Invisible Visible: A Multicultural Planning History*, University of California Press, Los Angeles, 1997.

26 D. Krueckeberg, ed., *The American Planner: Biographies and Recollections*, 1st edn, Methuen, New York, 1983; and D. Krueckeberg, ed., *Introduction to the Study of Planning History in the United States*, Center for Urban Policy Research, Rutgers University, New Brunswick, NJ, 1983.

27 D. Schaffer, ed., *Two Centuries of American Planning*, Johns Hopkins University Press, Baltimore, 1988.

28 M. Corben Sies and C. Silver, eds, *Planning the Twentieth-Century American*

City, Johns Hopkins University Press, Baltimore, 1995. The editors' introduction, 'The history of planning history' (pp. 1–34), provides a more detailed discussion and interpretation of major American contributions.

29 H. Liggett and D.C. Perry, *Spatial Practices: Critical Explorations in Social/Spatial Theory*, Sage, Thousand Oaks, 1995.

30 S.T. Roweis, 'Urban planning in early and late capitalist societies: Outline of a theoretical perspective', in *Urbanization and Urban Planning in Capitalist Society*, eds M.J. Dear and A.J. Scott, Methuen, London, 1981, pp. 159–77; see also Sutcliffe, 'Why planning history?', pp. 65–6.

31 McLoughlin, *Shaping Melbourne's Future?*, p. 240.

1 Founding cities in nineteenth-century Australia

1 I am grateful to Lester Hiatt for clarifying this interpretation.

2 C. Maher, 'The changing character of Australian urban growth', in *Urban Australia: Planning Issues and Policies*, eds S. Hamnett and R. Bunker, Mansell/Nelson Wadsworth, Melbourne, 1987, p. 10.

3 L. Hartz, *The Founding of New Societies*, Harbinger, Harcourt, Brace & World, New York, 1964, especially Chapter 8 by R.N. Rosecrance on Australia.

4 For detailed case studies of the foundation and early development of Australian capital cities, see P. Statham, ed., *Origins of Australia's Capital Cities*, Cambridge University Press, Cambridge, 1989. For another interpretation see L. Frost, *The New Urban Frontier: Urbanisation and City-Building in Australasia and the American West*, University of New South Wales Press, Sydney, 1991.

5 R. Home, *Of Planting and Planning: The Making of British Colonial Cities*, E & FN Spon, London, 1997, p. 9.

6 Maher, 'The changing character', pp. 10–13.

7 H. Proudfoot, 'Town plans and their impact on the settlement process 1788–1849', PhD thesis, Macquarie University, 1995. The *cardo-decumanus* orientation was based on a principal north axis overlaid with the east–west axis which echoed the daily passage of the sun through the skies.

8 Home, *Of Planting and Planning*, pp. 8–9.

9 Proudfoot, 'Town plans and their impact', Chapter 9.

10 G. Sharp, *A General Plan for Laying Out Towns and Townships*, 2nd edn, n.p., London, 1794.

11 Home, *Of Planting and Planning*, pp. 21–3.

12 L.R. Hiatt, *Arguments about Aborigines*, Cambridge University Press, Cambridge, 1996, Prologue. Information on Granville Sharp was much enhanced by Hiatt's work, augmented by personal correspondence with the author.

13 Proudfoot, 'Town plans and their impact', Chapter 7; also H. Proudfoot, 'Fraternal twins', *Australian Planner*, vol. 35, 1998, pp. 75–80.

14 Copy in Mitchell Library, State Library of New South Wales. Full title is 'Map of the Colony of New South Wales, compiled from actual measurements,

with the chain and circumferenter, and according to a trigonometrical survey'. Scale ten miles to an inch, drawn by T.L. Mitchell, engraved by John Carmichael, Sydney. Republished in London in 1834.

15 D.N. Jeans, 'The impress of central authority upon the landscape: South-eastern Australia 1788–1850', in *Australian Space, Australian Time*, eds J.M. Powell and M. Williams, Oxford University Press, Melbourne, 1975, pp. 14–15; D. Jeans, 'Town planning in New South Wales, 1826–1842', *Australian Planning Institute Journal*, vol. 3, 1965, pp. 191–5.

16 Proudfoot, 'Town plans and their impact', Notes on surveyors.

17 R. Bunker, 'Process and product in the foundation and laying out of Adelaide', *Planning Perspectives*, vol. 13, 1998, pp. 243–53. A controversial analysis of the plan is D.L. Johnson and D. Langmead, *The Adelaide City Plan: Fiction and Fact*, Wakefield Press, Adelaide, 1986.

18 The papers of the Philosophical Society of New South Wales may be found in the *Sydney Magazine of Science and Art*, James W. Waugh, Sydney, vol. 1, 1858, and vol. 2, 1859. In Melbourne, the turbulent years of the early gold rushes had given impetus to the formation of the Philosophical Institute of Victoria, described by M.E. Hoare in his 'Learned societies in Australia: The foundation years in Victoria, 1850–1860', in *Records of the Australian Academy of Science*, vol. 1, no. 2, Canberra, 1967, pp. 7–29.

19 W.V. Aird, *The Water Supply, Sewerage, and Drainage of Sydney*, Metropolitan Water Sewerage and Drainage Board, Sydney, 1961; H. Proudfoot, *Exploring Sydney's West*, Kangaroo Press, Sydney, 1989.

20 M. Lewis, *Melbourne*, Melbourne City Council, Melbourne, 1995, pp. 41, 67–8.

21 Dan Huon Coward, *Out of Sight: Sydney's Environmental History 1851–1981*, Australian National University, Department of Economic History, 1988, p. 107.

22 C. Cunneen, 'Christopher Rolleston', *Australian Dictionary of Biography*, vol. 6, 1976, pp. 55–6. Rolleston enlarged on this theme the next year with another paper on sewage disposal, and he contributed monthly figures to the society's journal on the 'health of Sydney'. His *Annual Statistical Register* was published every year as a parliamentary paper.

23 W. Bland, *Sanitary Reform of Towns and Cities*, J. Cox, Sydney, 1857; Dr Evans, 'Obituary for Dr William Bland', *The Empire*, 21 January 1862.

24 D. Clark, 'Worse than physic: Sydney's water supply 1788–1888', in *Nineteenth Century Sydney*, ed. M. Kelly, Sydney University Press, Sydney, 1978, pp. 66–81.

25 *Sydney Morning Herald*, 7 October 1958.

26 W.S. Jevons, 'Remarks upon the social map of Sydney, 1858', manuscript held in the Mitchell Library, State Library of New South Wales; R.D. Collison Black and R. Konekamp, eds, *Papers and Correspondence of William Stanley Jevons*, vol. 1, Macmillan, London, 1972.

27 In a letter to A. Cuninghame, 29 February 1852, Cuninghame Papers,

A3180, Mitchell Library, State Library of New South Wales (information from Barry Dyster).
28 A.J.C. Mayne, *Fever, Squalor and Vice: Sanitation and Social Policy in Victorian Sydney*, University of Queensland Press, St Lucia, 1982.
29 E.E. Lampard, 'The urbanising world', in *The Victorian City*, vol. 1, eds H.J. Dyos and M. Wolff, Routledge & Kegan Paul, London, 1973, p. 9.
30 P. Spearritt, *Sydney since the Twenties*, Hale & Iremonger, Sydney, 1978, p. 2.
31 G. Davison, *The Rise and Fall of Marvellous Melbourne*, Melbourne University Press, Melbourne, 1979, pp. 7–9.
32 Davison, *Rise and Fall of Marvellous Melbourne*, pp. 7–9.
33 Jane Jacobs quoted by Gillian Tindal in 'Existential cities', in *Architecture of the British Empire*, ed. R. Farmor-Hesketh, Weidenfeld & Nicolson, London, 1986.
34 R. Freestone, *Model Communities: The Garden City Movement in Australia*, Thomas Nelson, Melbourne, 1989, pp. 51–6; J. Keily, 'Study on unity of design in planning new towns and new suburbs', *Transactions and Proceedings, Victorian Institute of Surveyors*, vol. 3, 1891, pp. 88–104; and J. Sulman, 'The laying out of towns' [1890] reprinted in J. Sulman, *An Introduction to the Study of Town Planning in Australia*, Government Printer of New South Wales, Sydney, 1921, pp. 214–16.
35 A.M.S. Roberts, 'City improvement in Sydney: Public policy 1880–1900', PhD thesis, University of Sydney, 1978.
36 Freestone, *Model Communities*, pp. 55–6.
37 H. Proudfoot, 'The history of Ku-ring-gai', in *Municipality of Ku-ring-gai Heritage Study*, eds R. Moore, P. Pike, H. Proudfoot and L. Tropman, Ku-ring-gai Shire Council, Sydney, 1987, pp. 33–99.

2 From city improvement to the city beautiful

1 *Congress of Engineers, Architects, Surveyors And Members of Allied Professions, to discuss Questions relating to the Laying Out and Building of the Federal Capital, and matters of Professional interest generally, held in Melbourne during the Commonwealth Celebrations*, May 1901.
2 R. Freestone, *The Federal Capital of Australia: A Virtual Planning History*, Australian National University, Urban Research Program Working Paper no. 60, June 1997.
3 C.C. Reade, 'Foreword', in *Official Volume of Proceedings of the First Australian Town Planning and Housing Conference and Exhibition Adelaide 1917*, Vardon & Sons, Adelaide, 1918, pp. 5–9.
4 A. Sutcliffe, *Towards the Planned City: Germany, Britain, the United States and France 1780–1914*, Blackwell, London, 1981.
5 W.H. Wilson, *The City Beautiful Movement*, Johns Hopkins University Press, Baltimore, 1989.

6 G.H. Knibbs, 'The theory of city design', *Journal and Proceedings of the Royal Society of New South Wales*, vol. 35, 1901, pp. 62–112.

7 G. Sydney Jones, 'Some thoughts concerning the federal city', in *Congress of Engineers, Architects, Surveyors*, pp. 22–5.

8 This chapter develops ideas first presented in R. Freestone, 'The city beautiful: Towards an understanding of the Australian experience', *Journal of Architectural and Planning Research*, vol. 15, 1998, pp. 91–108.

9 C. Bogue Luffman, 'The agricultural, horticultural, and sylvan features of a federal capital', in *Congress of Engineers, Architects, Surveyors*, p. 45.

10 R. Freestone and S. Veale, 'The street beautiful: Triumphal arches and urban improvement in Sydney 1888–1925', *Public History Review*, vol. 4, 1995, pp. 25–40.

11 H. Kent, 'City improvement', *Art and Architecture*, vol. 4, 1907, p. 128.

12 D. Brain, 'Discipline and style: The Ecole des Beaux-Arts and the social production of an American architecture', *Theory and Society*, vol. 18, 1989, pp. 807–68.

13 D.H. Burnham and E.H. Bassett, *Plan of Chicago*, 1909; facsimile edn, Princeton Architectural Press, New York, 1993.

14 R. Freestone, 'Planning for profit in urban Australia: A descriptive prolegomenon', *Antipode*, vol. 13, no. 1, 1981, pp. 15–26.

15 S. Petrow, 'Making the city beautiful: Town planning in Hobart c1915 to 1926', *Tasmanian Historical Research Association, Papers and Proceedings*, vol. 36, 1989, pp. 99–112.

16 Daniel Burnham quoted in 'Royal Commission for the Improvement of the City of Sydney and Its Suburbs', *New South Wales Parliamentary Papers*, vol. 4, 1909, p. xxiv.

17 D.M. Bluestone, 'Detroit's city beautiful and the problem of commerce', *Journal of the Society of Architectural Historians*, vol. 47, 1988, pp. 245–62.

18 J.D. Fitzgerald, 'Town planning and civic beautification', *The Lone Hand*, vol. 14, 1914, p. 448.

19 R.K. Clark 'The city beautiful: Promise and reality', *The Architect*, vol. 10, no. 2, 1969, pp. 40–4.

20 See respectively J. Barlow, 'The city beautiful', *Journal of the Institute of Architects of New South Wales*, vol. 1, 1904, pp. 7–9; R. Haddon, 'Melbourne of the future', *Journal of the Royal Victorian Institute of Architects*, vol. 5, 1907, pp. 90–3; John Sulman, *An Introduction to the Study of Town Planning in Australia*, Government Printer of New South Wales, Sydney, 1921, p. 173.

21 R. Freestone, 'Sulman of Sydney: Modern planning in theory and practice 1890–1930', *Town Planning Review*, vol. 67, 1996, pp. 45–63.

22 F. Somers, 'The life and works of John Bede Barlow', B. Arch. thesis, University of New South Wales, 1970.

23 G. Temple Poole, 'Perth City', *West Australian Mining, Building and Engineering Journal*, vol. 20, no. 509, 1912, p. 18; see also R. and J. Oldham, *George Temple Poole: Architect of the Golden Years 1885–1897*, University of Western Australia Press, Nedlands, 1980.

24 H. Edquist, 'Harold Desbrowe-Annear and the city beautiful', *Transition*, nos 59–60, 1998, pp. 46–57.
25 D. Rowe, 'John Smith Murdoch and the early development of Canberra', *Fabrications*, vol. 6, 1995, pp. 24–37.
26 R. Mackay, 'Robert Charles Given Coulter 1864–1956', B. Arch. thesis, University of New South Wales, 1971.
27 A.M.S. Roberts, 'City improvement in Sydney: Public policy 1880–1900', PhD thesis, University of Sydney, 1978.
28 P. Ashton, *The Accidental City: Planning Sydney since 1788*, Hale & Iremonger, Sydney, 1993, pp. 25–7.
29 J.M. Giles, *50 Years of Town Planning with Florence Taylor*, Building Limited, Sydney, 1959.
30 N. Selfe, 'Sydney: Past, present and possible', *Australian Historical Society, Journal and Proceedings*, vol. 1, 1906, p. 355–7.
31 J. Sulman, *The Improvement of Sydney*, John Sands, Sydney, 1908, p. 17.
32 N. O'Flanagan, 'The improvement of Sydney: Infrastructure and administration', PhD thesis, Australian National University, Canberra, 1990.
33 E. Irvin, *Sydney as It Might Have Been*, Alpha Books, Sydney, 1974, pp. 97–8.
34 Barlow, 'The city beautiful', p. 9.
35 An extended account of the Royal Commission is R. Gibbons, 'Improving Sydney 1908–1909', in *Twentieth Century Sydney*, ed. Jill Roe, Hale & Iremonger, Sydney, 1980, pp. 120–33.
36 'Editing a city: The report of the Royal Commission for Sydney improvement. How it can be made practicable', *Building*, July 1909, p. 35.
37 D. Winston, *Sydney's Great Experiment: The Progress of the Cumberland County Plan*, Angus & Robertson, Sydney, 1957.
38 E.C. Relph, *The Modern Urban Landscape*, Croom Helm, London, 1987.
39 A.R. Jemmett, 'The improvement of the city of Sydney and its suburbs', *Journal of the Royal Institute of British Architects*, vol. 17, 1910, pp. 533–40.
40 'Proposed reconstruction of Sydney', *The Bulletin*, 31 December 1908, p. 6.
41 J. Davis, 'Federal city for Commonwealth of Australia', 1906, Australian Archives, Series A 100/1, Item A1907/238.
42 The definitive investigation of this controversial competition and its outcomes is by J. Reps, *Canberra 1912: Plans and Planners of the Australian Capital Competition*, Melbourne University Press, Melbourne, 1997.
43 J. Weirick, 'Walter Burley Griffin, landscape architect: The ideas he brought to Australia', *Landscape Australia*, vol. 10, 1988, pp. 241–6, 255–6; P. Proudfoot, *The Secret Plan of Canberra*, University of New South Wales Press, Sydney, 1994; and A. Watson, ed., *Beyond Architecture: Marion Mahony and Walter Burley Griffin: America Australia India*, Powerhouse Publishing, Sydney, 1998.
44 Quoted in G.A. Taylor, *Town Planning for Australia*, Building Limited, Sydney, 1914, p. 35.

45 W.B. Griffin, *The Federal Capital: Report Explanatory of the Preliminary General Plan*, Government Printer, Melbourne, 1913, p. 5.

46 M. Manieri-Elia, 'Toward an "imperial city": Daniel H. Burnham and the city beautiful movement', in *The American City: From the Civil War to the New Deal*, eds G. Giucci, F. Dal Co, M. Manieri-Elia and M. Tafuri, Granada, London, 1980, pp. 1–141.

47 D. Van Zanten, 'Walter Burley Griffin's design for Canberra, the capital of Australia', in *Chicago Architecture 1872–1922: Birth of a Metropolis*, ed. J. Zukowsky, Art Institute of Chicago, Chicago, 1987, p. 335.

48 M.L. Peisch, *The Chicago School of Architecture: Early Followers of Sullivan and Wright*, Random House, New York, 1964.

49 K. Fischer, *Canberra: Myths and Models. Forces at work in the Formation of the Australian Capital*, Institute of Asian Affairs, Hamburg, 1984.

50 T. Adams, *Recent Advances in Town Planning*, J. and A. Churchill, London, 1932, pp. 159–61.

51 Taylor, *Town Planning for Australia*, pp. 56–68.

52 R. Freestone, 'The early twentieth century: Images of the formative years', *Australian Planner*, vol. 26, 1988, p. 16.

53 G. Stephenson, *The Design of Central Perth*, University of Western Australia Press, Nedlands, 1975.

54 Sulman, *Town Planning in Australia*, pp. 52–3.

55 W. Rybczynski, *City Life: Urban Expectations in a New World*, Scribner, New York, 1995.

56 'The city, town and village beautiful', *Shire and Municipal Record*, vol. 7, 1914, pp. 134–6.

3 Towards metropolitan organisation

1 E.C. Rigby and T.G. Ellery, 'The future of Australian cities', in *Official Volume of Proceedings of the First Town Planning and Housing Conference and Exhibition Adelaide 1917*, Vardon & Sons, Adelaide, 1918, p. 52.

2 V. Ryan, 'Method of laying out towns and suburbs', Circular dated 30 May 1913, State Records South Australia, GRG 35/1/1913/157.

3 C. Reade, 'Municipal town planning', in *Official Volume*, 1918 p. 94.

4 J. Fitzgerald, 'The president's address', *Volume of Proceedings of the Second Australian Town Planning Conference and Exhibition Brisbane 1918*, Government Printer, Brisbane, 1918, p. 27.

5 C. Reade, 'Town planning in Australasia: Problems and progress in the far Pacific', *Town Planning Review*, vol. 3, 1912, p. 10.

6 V. Ryan 'Draft circular', 1 February 1913, State Records South Australia, GRG 35/1/1913/157.

7 For a study of the development of the town planning movement in Britain see G. Cherry, *The Evolution of British Town Planning*, Leighton Buzzard, London, 1974, and for the United States see M. Scott, *American City Planning since 1890*, University of California Press, Berkeley, 1969.

8 T. Horsfall quoted in W. Ashworth, *The Genesis of Modern British Planning: A Study in Economic and Social History of the Nineteenth and Twentieth Centuries*, Routledge & Kegan Paul, London, 1954, p. 172.
9 R. Unwin, 'The city development plan', in *Transactions of the Town Planning Conference London 10–15 October 1910*, Royal Institute of British Architects, London, 1911, p. 247.
10 P. Spearritt, *Sydney since the Twenties*, Hale & Iremonger, Sydney, 1978, p. 12.
11 C. Purdom, ed., *Town Theory and Practice*, Benn Brothers, London, 1911, p. 247.
12 R. Unwin, *Nothing Gained by Overcrowding: How the Garden City Type of Development Might Benefit Both Owner and Occupier*, Garden Cities and Town Planning Association, London, 1912, p. 1.
13 Unwin, 'The city development plan', p. 250.
14 M. Miller, *Raymond Unwin: Garden Cities and Town Planning*, Leicester University Press, Leicester, 1992, p. 133.
15 P. Abercrombie, 'Study before town planning', *Town Planning Review*, vol. 6, 1916, p. 172.
16 C. Reade, 'Report on planning and development of towns and cities of South Australia', *South Australian Parliamentary Papers*, no. 63, 1919, p. 6.
17 J. Sulman, *Town Planning: A Sketch in Outline*, Government Printer of New South Wales, Sydney, 1919, p. 13.
18 H. Barwell, 'South Australia: Soldiers' settlements', in *Official Volume*, 1918, p. 65.
19 J. Laverty, 'Town planning in Brisbane, 1842–1925', *Royal Australian Planning Institute Journal*, vol. 9, 1971, p. 20.
20 J.C. Morrell, 'The town planning problem of metropolitan Melbourne', in *Official Volume*, 1918, pp. 104–5.
21 G. Poole quoted in R. and J. Oldham, *George Temple Poole: Architect of the Golden Years 1885–1897*, University of Western Australia Press, Nedlands, 1980, p. 141.
22 C. Reade, 'Greater Melbourne and town planning', *Town Planning and Housing Review*, 31 May 1915, p. 23.
23 Statistics from C. Reade, 'Practical town planning', in *Volume of Proceedings*, 1918, p. 11; and J. Sulman, *An Introduction to the Study of Town Planning in Australia*, Government Printer of New South Wales, Sydney, 1921, pp. 206, 211–12.
24 P. Morton, *After Light: A History of the City of Adelaide and Its Council, 1878–1928*, Wakefield Press, Adelaide, 1996, p. 68.
25 For an overview of municipal administration see L. Sandercock, *Property, Politics, and Urban Planning: A History of Australian City Planning, 1890–1990*, Part 1, Transaction Publishers, New Brunswick, 1990.
26 C. Reade, 'Town planning in Australasia', p. 2.
27 R. Freestone, *Model Communities: The Garden City Movement in Australia*, Thomas Nelson, Melbourne, 1989, pp. 62–3, 71–7.

28 Freestone, *Model Communities*, p. 70.
29 Laverty, 'Town planning in Brisbane', p. 24.
30 S. Petrow, 'Making the city beautiful: Town planning in Hobart c1915 to 1926', *Tasmanian Historical Research Association, Papers and Proceedings*, vol. 36, 1989, pp. 102–4.
31 J. Fitzgerald, 'The president's address', *Volume of Proceedings*, 1918, p. 26.
32 Rigby and Ellery, 'The future of Australian cities', pp. 52–3.
33 For a comprehensive survey of the tour see R. Freestone, 'An imperial aspect: The Australasian town planning tour of 1914–1915', *Australian Journal of Politics and History*, vol. 44, 1998, pp. 159–76.
34 C. Garnaut, 'Of passion, publicity and planning: Charles Reade and the Mitcham Garden Suburb', *Australian Planner*, vol. 32, 1995, pp. 183–4.
35 C. Garnaut, 'Model and maker: Colonel Light Gardens and Charles Reade', PhD thesis, University of South Australia, 1997, pp. 260–5.
36 Freestone, *Model Communities*, Chapter 4.
37 Freestone, *Model Communities*, p. 81.
38 R. Freestone, 'Exporting the garden city: Metropolitan images in Australia, 1900–1930', *Planning Perspectives*, vol. 1, 1986, p. 69.
39 G. Poole quoted in K. and J. Oldham, *George Temple Poole*, p. 145.
40 W. Bold, 'The distribution of parks, playgrounds and other open spaces', *Volume of Proceedings*, 1918, p. 154.
41 Ryan, 'Method of laying out towns and suburbs'.
42 Freestone, *Model Communities*, p. 210.
43 Reade, 'Towns and cities of South Australia', p. 13.
44 Freestone, 'Exporting the garden city', p. 75.
45 Sulman, *Town Planning in Australia*, p. 17.
46 I. Alexander, 'Land use and transport planning in Australian cities: Capital takes all?', in *Urban Planning in Australia: Critical Readings*, eds J.B. McLoughlin and M. Huxley, Longman Cheshire, Melbourne, 1986, p. 115.
47 Freestone, 'Exporting the garden city', p. 71.
48 J. Sulman, 'The planning of Sydney: Past, present and future', in *Report of the Eighty-fourth Meeting of the British Association for the Advancement of Science: Australia 1914*, John Murray, London, 1914, p. 480.
49 L. Stickells, 'Form and reform', *Firmness, Commodity, Delight?: Questioning the Canons. Papers from the Fifteenth Annual Conference of the Society of Architectural Historians of Australia and New Zealand, Melbourne, 1998*, Society of Architectural Historians of Australia and New Zealand, Adelaide, 1998, p. 361.
50 G. Poole, 'The metropolis of Western Australia', *Official Volume*, 1917, p. 129.
51 M. Webb, 'Urban expansion, town improvement and the beginning of town planning in metropolitan Perth', in *Western Towns and Buildings*, eds M. Pitt Morison and J. White, University of Western Australia Press, Nedlands, 1979, pp. 377–82.

52 R. Clark, 'The garden city movement and Western Australia', *The Architect*, vol. 10, December 1969, pp. 28–9; Freestone, *Model Communities*, pp. 205–7.
53 Webb, 'Urban expansion', p. 381.
54 Stickles, 'Form and reform', p. 362.
55 Freestone, *Model Communities*, p. 206.
56 M. Nankervis, 'History for the taking: The alienation of urban parkland in Australian cities', in *The Australian City—Future/Past: Proceedings of the Third Australian Planning History/Urban History Conference*, ed. T. Dingle, Monash University, Melbourne, 1997, p. 328.
57 Sulman, *An Introduction to the Study of Town Planning in Australia*, p. 106.
58 Freestone, *Model Communities*.
59 C. Garnaut, 'Transposing the model: Design sources for the Mitcham Garden Suburb', in *The Australian City—Future/Past*, pp. 11–20.
60 S. Cheney, 'Colonel Light Gardens, a unique suburb in Adelaide: Law shapes the urban environment', *Alternative Law Journal*, vol. 19, 1994, pp. 153–5.
61 The southern section of the original plan was altered in 1924 to accommodate Australia's first mass housing scheme, the Thousand Homes Scheme. See C. Garnaut, 'Remodelling a model: The Thousand Homes Scheme in Colonel Light Gardens', *Journal of the Historical Society of South Australia*, no. 23, 1995, pp. 5–35.
62 S. Ward, 'The garden city introduced', in *The Garden City: Past, Present and Future*, ed. S. Ward, E & FN Spon, London, 1992, p. 5.
63 Rigby and Ellery, 'The future of Australian cities', p. 52.
64 Morrell, 'The town planning problem of metropolitan Melbourne', *Official Volume*, 1917, p. 104.
65 *Report of the Metropolitan Town Planning Commission 1929*, Government Printer, Melbourne, 1929, p. 19.

4 From theory to practice

1 A. Hutchings, 'Conscious purposes', in *With Conscious Purpose: A History of Town Planning in South Australia*, eds A. Hutchings and R. Bunker, Wakefield Press, Adelaide, 1986, p. 4; A. Hutchings, 'The development of comprehensive town planning in South Australia: Its successes and failures', Master of Planning thesis, University of Adelaide, 1985, pp. 27–9. See also A. Sutcliffe, *Towards the Planned City: Germany, Britain, the United States and France 1780–1914*, Basil Blackwell, Oxford, 1981, pp. 202–9.
2 'Town Planning and Housing Bill', *South Australian Parliamentary Debates*, 1916, p. 1684.
3 J. Reps, *Canberra 1912: Plans and Planners of the Australian Capital Competition*, Melbourne University Press, Melbourne, 1997.
4 'Report of the Select Committee of the Legislative Council: Town Planning

and Development Bill', *South Australian Parliamentary Papers*, no. 69, 1920, p. 1.

5 P. Troy, 'Report on "Equity, environment, efficiency: Urban Australia" ', *Urban Futures*, no. 24, 1998, p. 11.

6 C. Vaughan, 'The South Australian Town Planning and Housing Bill', *Official Volume of Proceedings of the First Australian Town Planning and Housing Conference and Exhibition Adelaide 1917*, Vardon & Sons, Adelaide, 1918, p. 79.

7 A. Hutchings, 'Comprehensive town planning comes to South Australia', in Hutchings and Bunker, *With Conscious Purpose*, p. 65.

8 'Introductory number to the first edition', *The Light Journal of Town Planning and Housing*, South Australian Town Planning Association, Adelaide, 1919, p. 4.

9 B. Melotte, 'Planning in the Perth metropolitan region 1900–1970', *The Twentieth Century Urban Planning Experience: Proceedings of the Eighth International Planning History Society Conference and Fourth Australian Planning/Urban History Conference*, ed. R. Freestone, University of New South Wales, Sydney, 1998, p. 612.

10 *Town Planning and Development Act 1928* (WA), s. 6(2).

11 *Town Planning and Development Act 1928* (WA), s. 14.

12 *City of Perth Endowment Lands Act 1920* (WA), s. 40(2).

13 J.D. Fitzgerald quoted in P. Ashton, *The Accidental City: Planning Sydney since 1788*, Hale & Iremonger, Sydney, 1993, p. 32.

14 *The Local Authorities Acts Amendment Act 1923* (Qld), s. 33(1)(b).

15 M. Clark, *A Short History of Australia*, Macmillan, Melbourne, 1981, p. 202.

16 Department of Town Planning, *Report by the Acting Government Town Planner, William John Earle M.C. 1920–21*, Government Printer, Adelaide, 1921.

17 A. Hutchings, 'Visions for Adelaide: The persistence of planning ideas', *Urban Policy and Research*, vol. 6, 1988, pp. 136–7.

18 R. Freestone and M. Grubb, 'The Melbourne Metropolitan Town Planning Commission, 1922–30', *Journal of Australian Studies*, no. 57, 1998, pp. 131–2.

19 Freestone and Grubb, 'Melbourne Metropolitan Town Planning Commission', p. 128.

20 *Metropolitan Town Planning Commission Act 1922* (Vic), s. 10(1)(a) and (b).

21 Reps, *Canberra 1912*, pp. 330–1.

22 J.B. McLoughlin, *Shaping Melbourne's Future? Town Planning, the State and Civil Society*, Cambridge University Press, Melbourne, 1992, p. 34.

23 Freestone and Grubb, 'Melbourne Metropolitan Town Planning Commission', p. 134.

24 Ashton, *The Accidental City*, p. 54.

25 R. Freestone, 'Sulman of Sydney: Modern planning in theory and practice 1890–1930', *Town Planning Review*, vol. 67, 1996, pp. 45–63.

26 *The City of Brisbane Act 1924* (Qld), s. 36(2).

27 R. Stokes and R. Hill, 'The evolution of metropolitan planning in Western Australia', in *Urban and Regional Planning in Western Australia*, eds D. Hedgcock and O. Yiftachel, Paradigm Press, Perth, 1992, pp. 111–30.
28 Melotte, 'Planning in the Perth metropolitan region 1900–1970', pp. 611–12.
29 P. McManus and O. Yiftachel, 'Early Metropolitan Planning in Perth, Western Australia', *Planning History*, vol. 13, no. 3, 1991, p. 5.
30 R. Younger, *Australia and the Australians*, Rigby, Adelaide, 1970, p. 544.
31 L. Sandercock, *Property, Politics and Urban Planning: A History of Australian City Planning, 1890–1990*, Transaction Publishers, New Brunswick, 1990.
32 M. Grubb, 'A history of town planning in Victoria 1910–1944', Master of Town and Regional Planning thesis, University of Melbourne, 1976; R. Howe, 'F. Oswald Barnett: Social reformer and planner', *Planning History*, vol. 17, no. 1, 1995, pp. 19–22.
33 Sandercock, *Property, Politics and Urban Planning*, p. 133; P. Spearritt, *Sydney since the Twenties*, Hale & Iremonger, Sydney, 1978, pp. 72–5.
34 S. Marsden, *Business, Charity and Sentiment: The South Australian Housing Trust 1936–1986*, Wakefield Press, Adelaide, 1986, p. 15.
35 J. Minnery, 'Superman or public servant: The changing role and influence of the Queensland co-ordinator general', in Freestone, *The Twentieth Century Urban Planning Experience*, p. 640.
36 S. Petrow, 'Planning pioneer: R.A. McInnes and town planning in Queensland and Tasmania 1922–1956', *The Australian City—Future/Past: Proceedings of the Third Australian Planning History/Urban History Conference*, ed. T. Dingle, Monash University, Melbourne, 1997, p. 45.
37 *Queensland Parliamentary Debates*, VCLXVI, 1934, p. 888.
38 *Queensland Parliamentary Debates*, VCLXVI, 1934, p. 888.
39 J. Starke, *The Law of Town and Country Planning in New South Wales*, Butterworths, Sydney, 1966, p. 38.
40 Freestone, 'Sulman of Sydney', p. 61.
41 Sandercock, *Property, Politics and Urban Planning*, p. 7.

5 A new paradigm

1 See also S. Marsden, *Business, Charity and Sentiment: The South Australian Housing Trust 1936–1986*, Wakefield Press, Adelaide, 1986; R. Howe, ed., *New Houses for Old: Fifty Years of Public Housing in Victoria*, Department of Housing and Construction, Melbourne, 1988; C. Allport, 'The unrealised promise: Plans for Sydney housing in the forties', in *Twentieth Century Sydney: Studies in Urban and Social History*, ed. Jill Roe, Hale & Iremonger, Sydney, 1980.
2 P. Hall, *Urban and Regional Planning*, Penguin, Harmondsworth, 1974, pp. 99–125.
3 F.O. Barnett, W.O. Burt and F. Heath, *We Must Go On: A Study of Planned Reconstruction and Housing*, The Book Depot, Melbourne, 1944, p. 3.

4 R. Howe, 'Wanted a plan!: Vision and reality in planning post-war Melbourne, 1945–55', paper presented at the Second Planning/Urban History Conference, Australian National University, 1993; R. Howe, 'Housing and the church: A vision and a challenge', the Inaugural F. Oswald Barnett Oration, Ecumenical Housing Inc., Melbourne, 1993.
5 Howe, 'Wanted a plan!', p. 3.
6 P.N. Troy, ed., *Federal Power in Australia's Cities: Essays in Honour of Peter Till*, Hale & Iremonger, Sydney, 1978, p. 15.
7 H.C. Coombs, *Trial Balance*, Macmillan, Melbourne, 1991, pp. 58 and 66.
8 Commonwealth Housing Commission, *Final Report*, Department of Post-War Reconstruction, Canberra, 1944, p. 23.
9 Sandercock, *Cities for Sale*, p. 16.
10 J.S. Gawler, *A Roof over My Head: Housing, Town Planning and Local Government*, Lothian, Melbourne, 1963, pp. 63 and 65.
11 Coombs, *Trial Balance*, p. 69.
12 Gawler, *A Roof over My Head*, p. 21.
13 R. Howe, 'From rehabilitation to prevention: The war years', in Howe, *New Houses for Old*, pp. 45–68.
14 Marsden, *Business, Charity and Sentiment*, pp. 146ff.
15 P. Spearritt, *Sydney since the Twenties*, Hale & Iremonger, Sydney, 1978, p. 88.
16 S. Fitzgerald, *Sydney 1842–1992*, Hale & Iremonger, Sydney, 1992, p. 230.
17 S. Petrow, 'Planning pioneer: R.A. McInnis and town planning in Queensland and Tasmania 1922–1956', in *The Australian City—Future/Past: Proceedings of the Third Australian Planning History/Urban History Conference*, ed. T. Dingle, Monash University, Melbourne, 1997, pp. 43–52; G. Greenwood and J. Laverty, *Brisbane 1859–1959: A History of Local Government*, Council of the City of Brisbane, Brisbane, 1959, pp. 532, 543.
18 R. Blythe, 'Planning education: The establishment of town planning at the Hobart Technical College', in Dingle, *The Australian City*, p. 37.
19 Coombs, *Trial Balance*, p. 69.
20 P. Harrison, 'City planning', in *Australian Cities and Public Policy*, ed. P. Scott, Georgian House, Melbourne, 1978, p. 161.
21 Gawler, *A Roof Over My Head*, p. 94; R. Howe, 'The concrete house frontier and the planning of Melbourne in the 1940s and 1950s', in *The Cream Brick Frontier: Histories of Australian Suburbia*, eds G. Davison, T. Dingle and S. O'Hanlon, Monash Publications in History, no. 19, Melbourne, 1993, p. 77.
22 Harrison, 'City planning', p. 143; Fitzgerald, *Sydney 1842–1992*, p. 28.
23 B. Melotte, 'Planning in the Perth metropolitan region 1900–1970', in *The Twentieth Century Urban Planning Experience: Proceedings of the Eighth International Planning History Society Conference and Fourth Australian Planning/Urban History Conference*, ed. R. Freestone, University of New South Wales, Sydney, 1998, p. 613.
24 Harrison, 'City planning', p. 142.

25 Harrison, 'City planning', p. 141; S. Petrow, 'Against the spirit of local government: The making of town and country planning legislation', *Australian Journal of Public Administration*, vol. 54, 1995, pp. 205–18.
26 F. Heath, *Latrobe Valley Development: Regional Survey and Report*, State Electricity Commission of Victoria, Melbourne, 1948, p. 39.
27 Allport, 'The unrealised promise'; Howe, 'Wanted a plan!'.
28 Coombs, *Trial Balance*, p. 66.
29 Spearritt, *Sydney since the Twenties*, p. 86.
30 F.O. Barnett and W.O. Burt, *Housing the Australian Nation*, New Left Book Club Research Group, Melbourne, 1942; J.S. Gawler., *A Roof Over My Head*, Lothian, Melbourne, 1963; W. Bunning, *Homes in the Sun*, W.J. Nesbit, Sydney, 1945.
31 Spearritt, *Sydney since the Twenties*, p. 89; Harrison, 'City planning', p. 43.
32 M. Berry, 'To buy or rent? The demise of a dual tenure policy in Australia 1945–60', in Howe, *New Houses for Old*, pp. 98–100.
33 Howe, 'The concrete house frontier', pp. 78–83.
34 S. Marsden, 'Constructing Playford's city: The South Australian Housing Trust and the transformation of Adelaide, 1936–1966', PhD thesis, Flinders University, 1993, p. 288.
35 H. Stretton, *Ideas for Australian Cities*, Georgian House, Melbourne, 1970, p. 3.
36 D. Garden, *Builders of the Nation: The A.V. Jennings Story*, Melbourne University Press, Melbourne, 1992.
37 Spearritt, *Sydney since the Twenties*, p. 106.
38 Howe, 'Wanted a plan!', pp. 11–13; Gawler, *A Roof Over My Head*, p. 83.
39 Walkley quoted in S. Marsden, *Business, Charity and Sentiment*, pp. 145–6.
40 Harrison, 'City planning', p. 142.
41 S. Ward, 'Re-examining the international diffusion of planning', in Freestone, *The Twentieth Century Urban Planning Experience*, p. 937.
42 McInnis quoted in Petrow, 'Planning Pioneer', p. 43.
43 Howe, 'Wanted a plan!', pp. 6–7; R. Strauss, 'The Cumberland County Council Scheme: Sydney's green belt and the anti-urbanist imperative', in Freestone, *The Twentieth Century Urban Planning Experience*, pp. 881–5.
44 Spearritt, *Sydney since the Twenties*, pp. 96–8; B. Norman, 'Peter Harrison's early years in Canberra', in *The Australian Planner*, ed. R. Freestone, University of New South Wales, Sydney, 1993, pp. 223–4.
45 Howe, 'Wanted a plan!', pp. 13–14.
46 J.B. McLoughlin, *Shaping Melbourne's Future? Town Planning, the State and Civil Society*, Cambridge University Press, Melbourne, 1992, p. 39.
47 Howe, 'Wanted a plan!', p. 6; Blythe, 'Planning education', p. 35.
48 M. Grubb, 'The 1954 Melbourne and Metropolitan Planning Scheme: home grown product or American import?', in Dingle, *The Australian City*, p. 273; Howe, 'Wanted a plan!', pp. 1–2.
49 McInnis quoted in Petrow, 'Planning Pioneer', p. 43.

50 *Faithfull* quoted in Strauss, 'The Cumberland County Council Planning Scheme', p. 881.
51 N. Taylor, 'Paradigms and town planning theory since 1945', in *The Twentieth Century Urban Planning Experience*, p. 893.
52 Allport, 'The unrealised promise', p. 9. See also R. Freestone, 'The shattered dream: postwar modernism, urban planning, and the career of Walter Bunning', *Environment and Planning* A, vol. 28, 1996, pp. 731–52.
53 See, for example, P. Troy, *Federal Power in Australian Cities*.
54 See, for example, J. Kemeny, *The Privatised City: Critical Studies in Australian Housing and Urban Structure*, Occasional Paper, Centre for Urban and Regional Studies, University of Birmingham, Birmingham, 1983.
55 See, for example, F. Stilwell, *Australian Urban and Regional Development*, Australian and New Zealand Book Company, Sydney, 1974.
56 See, for example, C. Allport, *The Unrealised Promise*.
57 See, for example, R. Howe, 'Inner Suburbs: From Slums to Gentrification', in *Suburban Dreaming: An Interdisciplinary Approach to Australian Cities*, ed. L.C. Johnson, Deakin University Press, Melbourne, 1994, pp. 141–59.

6 The post-war city

1 For an elaboration of these themes, see S. Greive, 'Urban governance in Western Australia: The primacy of land and the emergence of growth coalitions', in *The Twentieth Century Urban Planning Experience: Proceedings of the Eighth International Planning History Society Conference and Fourth Australian Planning/Urban History Conference*, ed. R. Freestone, University of New South Wales, Sydney, 1998, pp. 271–6; and P. Freund and G. Martin, *The Ecology of the Automobile*, Black Rose Books, Montreal, 1993.
2 F. Stilwell, *Understanding Urban Policy*, Allen & Unwin, Sydney, 1993.
3 M. Webber and P. Rigby, *The Golden Age Illusion: Rethinking Postwar Capitalism*, Guildford Press, London, 1996, p. 16.
4 Tim Winton, *Cloudstreet*, Penguin Books, Melbourne, 1990.
5 M. Neutze, *Urban Development in Australia: A Descriptive Analysis*, 2nd edn, George Allen & Unwin, Sydney, 1981, p. 45.
6 Neutze, *Urban Development in Australia*, p. 9.
7 J. Rickard, *Australia: A Cultural History*, 2nd edn, Longman, London, 1996, p. 220.
8 I. Burnley, P. Murphy and R. Fagan, *Immigration and Australian Cities*, Federation Press, Sydney, 1997, p. 15.
9 S. Lees and J. Senyard, *The 1950s: How Australia Became a Modern Society and Everyone Got a House and Car*, Hyland House, Melbourne, 1987.
10 M. Wackernagel and W. Rees, *Our Ecological Footprint*, New Society Publishers, Gabriola Island BC, 1996.
11 Lees and Senyard, *The 1950s*, p. 94.
12 Stephenson quoted in I. Alexander and S. Greive, 'Modernist town planning

and metropolitan planning: Reflections from Gordon Stephenson', *Urban Policy and Research*, vol. 15, 1997, p. 229.

13 See I. Alexander, 'Post-war metropolitan planning: Goals and realities', in *Equity in the City*, ed. P.N. Troy, Allen & Unwin, Sydney, 1981, p. 147.

14 P. Harrison, 'Planning the metropolis: A case study', in *The Politics of Urban Growth*, eds R.S. Parker and P.N. Troy, ANU Press, Canberra, 1972, p. 68.

15 P. Harrison, 'City planning', in *Australian Cities and Public Policy*, ed. P. Scott, Georgian House, Melbourne, 1978, p. 155.

16 See T. Logan, *Urban and Regional Planning in Victoria*, Shillington House, Melbourne, 1981, p. 26, and J.B. McLoughlin, *Shaping Melbourne's Future?: Town Planning, the State and Civil Society*, Cambridge University Press, Melbourne, 1992, p. 44.

17 Whether local government provides democratic representation for the community is often blurred by conflicts of interest among councillors with land development interests. See, for example, I. Alexander, 'City centre planning: For public or private interest?', in *Urban and Regional Planning in Western Australia: Historical and Critical Perspectives*, eds D. Hedgcock and O. Yiftachel, Paradigm Press, Perth, 1992, pp. 79–92.

18 Harrison, 'City planning', p. 143.

19 L. Sandercock, *Cities for Sale: Property, Politics and Urban Planning in Australia*, Melbourne University Press, Melbourne, 1975, p. 180.

20 McLoughlin, *Shaping Melbourne's Future?*, p. 39.

21 R. Bunker and A. Hutchings, eds, *With Conscious Purpose: A History of Town Planning in South Australia*, Wakefield Press, Adelaide, 1986.

22 Harrison, 'City planning', p. 156.

23 M. Peel, *Good Times, Hard Times: The Past and the Future in Elizabeth*, Melbourne University Press, Melbourne, 1995, p. 50.

24 M. Clark, 'Metropolitan planning in Hobart', in *Spirited Cities: Urban Planning, Traffic and Environmental Management in the Nineties*, ed. R. Freestone, Federation Press, Sydney, pp. 180–5.

25 Rickard, *Australia*, p. 222.

26 S. Marsden, *A History of Australian Capital City Centres since 1945*, Australian National University, Urban Research Program Working Paper No. 61, 1997, p. 32.

27 I. Alexander, 'Land use and transport planning in Australian cities: Capital takes all?', in *Urban Planning in Australia: Critical Readings*, eds J.B. McLoughlin and M. Huxley, Longman Cheshire, Melbourne, 1986, p. 121.

28 M. Neutze, *Australian Urban Policy*, George Allen & Unwin, Sydney, 1978, p. 172.

29 P. Spearritt, *Sydney since the Twenties*, Hale & Iremonger, Sydney, 1978, p. 98.

30 M. Luccarelli, *Lewis Mumford and the Ecological Region: The Politics of Planning*, Guildford Press, London, 1995.

31 McLoughlin, *Shaping Melbourne's Future?*, p. 43.

32 O. Yiftachel 'The role of the state in metropolitan planning: The case of Perth', *Urban Policy and Research*, vol. 6, 1988, pp. 8–18.
33 H. Stretton, *Ideas for Australian Cities*, 3rd edn, Georgian House, Melbourne, 1975, p. 228; his text refers to reports such as A. Stevenson, E. Martin and J. O'Neill's *High Life*, Melbourne University Press, Melbourne, 1967.
34 Stretton, *Ideas for Australian Cities*, p. 228.
35 Alexander, 'Post-war metropolitan planning'.
36 Stephenson quoted in Alexander and Greive, 'Modernist town planning and metropolitan planning', p. 227.
37 D. Winston, *Sydney's Great Experiment: The Progress of the Cumberland County Plan*, Angus & Robertson, Sydney, 1957, p. 71.
38 C. Allport, 'Women and suburban housing in Sydney', in *Urban Planning in Australia*, p. 71.
39 Alexander, 'Post-war metropolitan planning'.
40 C. Marsh, 'Retailing', in *Western Landscapes*, ed. J. Gentilli, University of Western Australia Press, Nedlands, 1979, p. 450.
41 Spearittt, *Sydney since the Twenties*, p. 171.
42 Winston, *Sydney's Great Experiment*, p. 51.
43 P. McManus, The Automobile and Planning in Perth, Western Australia: Historical Evolution, Centre for Architecture and Planning Research, Curtin University of Technology, Perth, 1993.
44 Spearritt, *Sydney since the Twenties*, p. 170.
45 Quoted in McManus, *The Automobile and Planning in Perth*, p. 20.
46 I. Alexander and D. Houghton, 'New investment in public transport II: Evaluation of the northern suburbs railway in Perth', *Australian Planner*, vol. 32, 1995, p. 88.
47 Harrison, 'Planning the metropolis', p. 74.
48 Logan, *Urban and Regional Planning in Victoria*, p. 26; McLoughlin, *Shaping Melbourne's Future?*
49 See, for example, J. Kenworthy and O. Yiftachel, *Problems and Prospects in Planning of Metropolitan Perth*, Centre for Architecture and Planning Research, Curtin University of Technology, Perth, 1991.

7 The corridor city

1 *Population in Australia: A Demographic Analysis and Projection*, Australian Government Publishing Service, Canberra, 1975.
2 P. Harrison, 'Sydney twenty-five years on', *Royal Australian Planning Institute Journal (RAPIJ)*, vol. 9, 1971, pp. 123–6.
3 M. Neutze, *Urban Development in Australia: A Descriptive Analysis*, George Allen & Unwin, Sydney, 1977, p. 209.
4 N. Ashton, 'Plans and Administration', *Australian Planning Institute Journal (APIJ)*, vol. 3, 1965, pp. 69–71.
5 S. Hart, 'Report on metropolitan Adelaide', *APIJ*, vol. 2, 1963, p. 114.

6 D. Winston, 'Old cities and new: Problems of the twentieth century revolution', *APIJ*, vol. 2, 1963, p. 206.

7 C.D. Buchanan, 'Land use and traffic generation', *APIJ*, vol. 3, 1964, pp. 24–6. While president of the Royal Town Planning Institute in 1963, Buchanan pushed for wider membership, land use planning being part of the wider spectrum of social and economic planning. His proposal became Institute policy in 1972. See G.E. Cherry, ed., *Pioneers in British Planning*, Architectural Press, London, 1981, p. 218.

8 Roselands (Sydney 1965) had more community services than Southlands (Melbourne 1958).

9 P. Troy and M. Neutze, 'Urban road planning in theory and practice', *Journal of Transport Economics and Policy*, vol. 3, 1969, pp. 139–51; M. Neutze, *Australian Urban Policy*, George Allen & Unwin, Sydney, 1978, p. 128.

10 G. Walkley, 'Presidential message', *APIJ*, vol. 3, 1965, pp. 61–2.

11 Editorial, *APIJ*, vol. 3, 1964, pp. 35–6.

12 P. Troy, *The Urban Research Program 1966–1996*, Australian National University, Urban Research Program, Canberra, 1997.

13 P. Loveday, 'Citizen participation in urban planning', in *The Politics of Urban Growth*, eds, R.S. Parker and P.N. Troy, Australian National University Press, Canberra, 1972, p. 136.

14 'Urban planning gains federal advocate', *APIJ*, vol. 4, 1965, pp. 140–1 (report of Whitlam's speech in parliament, 18 March 1965); E.G. Whitlam, 'Federal responsibilities in housing', *APIJ*, vol. 5, 1967, pp. 47–9.

15 J. Overall, *Canberra: Yesterday, Today and Tomorrow. A Personal Memoir*, Federal Capital Press, Canberra, 1995, p. 53.

16 Sir William Holford, *Observations on the Future Development of Canberra*, Commonwealth Government Printer, Canberra, 1958.

17 National Capital Development Commission (NCDC), Annual Reports, Commonwealth Government Printer, Canberra, 1959–60 to 1962–63.

18 H.W. Wells, *Advisory Report on Some Economic Considerations in Connection with the Development of the National Capital*, NCDC, Canberra, December 1963.

19 E.N. Bacon, 'Canberra as a statement of world culture', *Architecture in Australia*, vol. 57, 1968, pp. 625–6. The development of central Canberra's landscape was guided primarily by the NCDC's Richard Clough and Richard Gray of Holford and Partners. The Australian Institute of Landscape Architects was launched in August 1996.

20 National Capital Development Commission, *The Future Canberra*, Angus & Robertson, Sydney, 1965, p. 57.

21 P. Harrison and G. Stephenson, 'Long term planning for Canberra', in *Canberra 1963*, ACT Division of RAPI, December 1973; also P. Harrison, 'Long-term planning for Canberra', *APIJ*, vol. 2, 1964, pp. 260, 263–4.

22 M. Simpson, 'Thomas Adams 1871–1940', in *Pioneers in British Planning*, p. 35. Lewis Mumford was Adams' strongest critic, calling his plan 'a

continuance of past mistakes': L. Mumford, *The Culture of Cities*, Secker & Warburg, London, 1948, p. 390.

23 National Capital Planning Commission and Regional Planning Council, *The Nation's Capital: A Policies Plan for the Year 2000*, Washington DC, 1961.

24 Alan M. Voorhees and Associates, *Canberra Land Use Transportation Study General Plan Concept*, Alan M. Voorhees and Associates, McLean, Virginia, January 1967, p. 7.

25 Voorhees and Associates, *Canberra General Plan Concept*; W.G. Hansen and I.W. Morison, 'Canberra: A study of land use and transport', *Proceedings, Fourth Conference of the Australian Road Research Board*, vol. 4, part 1, 1968, p. 60; K.F. Fischer, *Canberra: Myths and Models. Forces at Work in the Formation of the Australian Capital*, Institute of Asian Affairs, Hamburg, 1984, Chapters 4 and 5.

26 P. Harrison, 'Approach to a metropolitan plan', *Architecture in Australia*, vol. 57, 1968, pp. 630–4.

27 Overall, *Canberra*, p. 82. Prime ministers after Sir Robert Menzies retired in 1966: Harold Holt, 1966–67; John Gorton, 1968–71; and William McMahon, 1972.

28 National Capital Development Commission, *Tomorrow's Canberra*, Australian National University Press, Canberra, 1970, p. 234.

29 National Capital Development Commission, *Metropolitan Canberra: Policy Plan, Development Plan*, Canberra, July 1984; National Capital Planning Authority, *Submission to Commonwealth Grants Commission Inquiry into Financing the ACT*, National Capital Planning Authority, Canberra, September 1990.

30 P. Mees, '31 up: Canberra's Y-plan approaches middle age', unpublished paper, submitted to the Australian National University as an entry for the 1998 Peter Harrison Prize.

31 NCDC studies for Canberra's new towns expected up to 30 per cent local employment and a similar proportion of vehicle miles to be intra-town (Hansen and Morison, 'Canberra: A study of land use and transport', p. 52). An October 1995 Australian Bureau of Statistics survey of journeys to work, school and shops in the ACT showed 24 to 31 per cent local employment, and a 1995 ABS national survey of motor vehicle use showed that travel per capita in Canberra (7745 kilometres per year) was just below the metropolitan average (7811 kilometres) and 9 per cent lower than Perth (8545 kilometres).

32 J.B. McLoughlin, *Shaping Melbourne's Future? Town Planning, the State and Civil Society*, Cambridge University Press, Melbourne, 1992, p. 45.

33 The Whitlam family, after 21 years in western Sydney, had no piped sewerage, travelled 20 miles (32 kilometres) to the nearest high school, and lacked a municipal library and sealed local roads: L. Oakes, *Whitlam PM*, Angus & Robertson, Sydney, 1973, p. 183.

34 R.B. Lansdown, 'Some financial aspects of an Australian new town', *APIJ*, vol. 4, no. 4, 1966, pp. 174–80.
35 Town and Country Planning Board, *Organisation for Strategic Planning*, Melbourne, 1967. P. Whateley, 'Planning strategies for Melbourne and Sydney', *APIJ*, vol. 7, no. 2, 1969, p. 46–54. McLoughlin (*Shaping Melbourne's Future?*, p. 5) notes state government obsession with questions of a 'vital' central city rather than the metropolitan whole.
36 Melbourne and Metropolitan Board of Works, *Future Growth of Melbourne*, MMBW, Melbourne, 1967. Successive Victorian Governments kept the split in metropolitan planning responsibilities until a planning ministry and department were formed in 1980.
37 D. Morrison, 'Resort planning: Factions toy with Western Port plans', *RAPIJ*, vol. 17, no. 2, 1979, p. 152–5.
38 State Planning Authority of New South Wales, *Sydney Region Outline Plan*, 1968, p. 67.
39 R. Cardew, 'Corridors of planning: Recollections of the Sydney Region Outline Plan preparation', *The Twentieth Century Urban Planning Experience: Proceedings of the Eighth International Planning History Society Conference and Fourth Australian Planning/Urban History Conference*, ed. R. Freestone, University of New South Wales, Sydney, 1998, pp. 89–94.
40 P. Harrison, 'Planning the metropolis', in *The Politics of Urban Growth*, p. 90.
41 More than half the population increase in new suburbs in Sydney and Melbourne in the 1970s would be migration from older suburbs: Department of Environment, Housing and Community Development, 'Population change in major urban centres, 1971–1976', EHCD, Canberra, February 1977.
42 G. Stephenson and D. Carr, 'Planning for millions within the Perth region', paper to the Royal Australian Institute of Architects Convention, Perth, May 1966.
43 Metropolitan Region Planning Authority reports: *Perth Region and People*, August 1968; *The Corridor Plan for Perth*, November 1968; *Report on the Corridor Plan for Perth*, July 1972. See P. Harrison, 'Corridors of confusion: Policy conflicts in planning the Perth region', *RAPIJ*, vol. 10, 1972, pp. 97–9.
44 Cities Commission, *Annual Reports*, 1972–73 and 1973–74.
45 J. Paterson, 'Sydney's great experiment goes into mass production', *RAPIJ*, vol. 18, 1980, pp. 91–5.
46 Neutze, *Urban Development in Australia*, p. 230.
47 Neutze, *Urban Development in Australia*, p. 158.
48 H. Stretton, *Ideas for Australian Cities*, Georgian House, Melbourne, 1970.

8 Administrative coordination, urban management and strategic planning in the 1970s

1 This section and the next are based on M. Berry, 'The political economy of Australian urbanisation', *Progress in Planning*, vol. 22, no. 1, 1984, pp. 1–83;

C. Lloyd and P. Troy, *Innovation and Reaction: The Life and Death of the Federal Department of Urban and Regional Development*, George Allen & Unwin, Sydney, 1981; A. Parkin, *Governing the Cities: The Australian Experience in Perspective*, Macmillan, Melbourne, 1982; L. Sandercock, 'Urban policy', in *From Whitlam to Fraser: Reform and Reaction in Australian Politics*, eds A. Patience and B. Head, Oxford University Press, Melbourne, 1979, pp. 140–56; L. Sandercock and L. Orchard, 'Urban policies', in *From Fraser to Hawke: Australian Public Policy in the 1980s*, eds B. Head and A. Patience, Longman Cheshire, Melbourne, 1989, pp. 324–66.

2 Centre for Urban Research and Action (CURA), *The Displaced: A Study of Housing Conflict in Melbourne's Inner City*, CURA, Melbourne, 1977; A. Jakubowicz, 'The green ban movement: Urban struggle and class politics', pp. 149–66, and N. Wilkinson, 'Conflict over transport in Melbourne', pp. 204–22, in *Australian Urban Politics: Critical Perspectives*, eds J. Halligan and C. Paris, Longman Cheshire, Melbourne, 1984; P. Mullins, 'The struggle against Brisbane freeways: 1966–74', *International Journal of Urban and Regional Research*, vol. 4, 1980, pp. 342–52; P. Mullins, 'The "middle class" and the inner city', *Journal of Australian Political Economy*, vol. 5, 1982, pp. 13–16.

3 C. Baldock and B. Cass, eds, *Women, Social Welfare and the State in Australia*, George Allen & Unwin, Melbourne, 1983; M. Ferrier, 'Sexism in Australian cities: Barriers to employment opportunities', *Women's Studies International Forum*, vol. 6, no. 1, 1983, pp. 73–84; S. Young, '. . . you can't be in two places at once . . .', *Social Alternatives*, vol. 1, no. 8, 1980, pp. 17–22.

4 As well as the sources cited in Note 1, this summary of Whitlam's urban policies is drawn from: Halligan and Paris, *Australian Urban Politics*; M. Neutze, *Australian Urban Policy*, George Allen & Unwin, Sydney, 1978; L. Sandercock and M. Berry, *Urban Political Economy: The Australian Case*, George Allen & Unwin, Sydney, 1983; P. Scott, ed., *Australian Cities and Public Policy*, Georgian House, Melbourne, 1978; P. Troy, ed., *Federal Power in Australia's Cities: Essays in Honour of Peter Till*, Hale & Iremonger, Sydney, 1978. One of the most influential books of its time, and anecdotally known for having been central to the formulation of DURD's policies, is H. Stretton, *Ideas for Australian Cities*, Georgian House, Melbourne, 1970.

5 P. Groenewegen, 'Federalism', pp. 50–69, and L. Sandercock, 'Urban Policy', pp. 140–56, in Patience and Head, *From Whitlam to Fraser*.

6 C. Maher, 'Australian urban character: Pattern and process', in *Urban Planning in Australia: Critical Readings*, eds J.B. McLoughlin and M. Huxley, Longman Cheshire, Melbourne, 1986, p. 27.

7 B. Gregory and P. Sheehan, 'Poverty and the collapse of full employment', in *Australian Poverty: Then and Now*, eds R. Fincher and J. Nieuwenhuysen, Melbourne University Press, Melbourne, 1998, pp. 105–11.

8 P. Mullins, 'Hedonism and real estate: Resort tourism and Gold Coast development', in *Conflict and Development*, ed. P. Williams, George Allen & Unwin, Sydney, 1984, pp. 31–50.

9 Maher, 'Australian urban character', p. 29.

10 D. White, P. Sutton, A. Pears, C. Mardon, J. Dick and M. Crow, *Seeds for Change*, Patchwork C.C.V, Melbourne, 1978; C. Jay, *Towards Urban Strategies for Australia*, Australian Institute of Urban Studies, Canberra, 1978.

11 M. Daly, *Sydney Boom, Sydney Bust*, George Allen & Unwin, Sydney, 1982; L. Sandercock, *Cities for Sale: Property, Politics and Urban Planning in Australia*, Melbourne University Press, Melbourne, 1975; L. Sandercock, *The Land Racket*, Silverfish Books, Canberra, 1979.

12 See references in note 2, and also: M. and V. Burgmann, *Green Bans, Red Union: Environmental Activism and the New South Wales Builders Labourers' Federation*, University of New South Wales Press, Sydney, 1998; H. Kendig, *New Life for Old Suburbs*, George Allen & Unwin, Sydney, 1979; W. Logan, *The Gentrification of Inner Melbourne*, University of Queensland Press, St Lucia, 1985; R. Roddewig, *Green Bans: The Birth of Australian Environmental Politics*, Hale & Iremonger, Sydney, 1978.

13 I. Alexander, 'Land use and transport planning in Australian cities: capital takes all?', in McLoughlin and Huxley, *Urban Planning in Australia*, pp. 125–8; C. Forster and M. McCaskill, 'The modern period: Managing metropolitan Adelaide', in *With Conscious Purpose: A History of Town Planning in South Australia*, eds A. Hutchings and R. Bunker, Wakefield Press, Adelaide, 1986, pp. 91–3.

14 A. Skeffington, *People and Planning*, Report of the Committee on Public Participation, Her Majesty's Stationery Office, London, 1968; L. Sandercock, 'Citizen participation: The new conservatism', in Troy, *Federal Power in Australia's Cities*, pp. 117–32.

15 Sources for this section are: Alexander, 'Land use and transport planning'; P. Harrison, 'City planning', in *Australian Cities and Public Policy*, ed. P. Scott, Georgian House, Melbourne, 1978, pp. 141–73; T. Logan, 'Urban and regional planning in a federal system: New South Wales and Victoria', in *Urban Australia: Planning Issues and Policies*, eds S. Hamnett and R. Bunker, Mansell/Nelson Wadsworth, Melbourne, 1987, pp. 42–60; Neutze, *Australian Urban Policy*.

16 P. Wilenski, 'Sydney's urban management: A perspective from the late '70s', in his *Public Power and Public Administration*, Hale & Iremonger, Sydney, 1986, p. 239.

17 See M. Peel, *Good Times, Hard Times: The Past and Future in Elizabeth*, Melbourne University Press, Melbourne, 1995, for an excellent account of the SAHT's creation of the new town of Elizabeth.

18 Wilenski, 'Sydney's urban management', p. 240.

19 This debate took place both as a retrospective assessment of the planning issues of the 1970s and as different views of the future of planning for the 1980s and 1990s. Each side is succinctly argued in M. Neutze, 'Planning as urban management: A critical assessment', and J. Mant, 'The instruments of planning: urban management', in *Metropolitan Planning in Australia: Urban Management*, Australian National University, Urban Research Unit Working

Paper No. 6, 1988. Both Mant and Neutze were involved in the formulation of planning strategies in the 1980s, and Mant, in particular, was extremely influential in various planning agencies throughout Australia for more than two decades. Other aspects of this debate can be found in: M. Painter, 'Urban government, urban politics and the fabrication of urban issues', in Halligan and Paris, *Australian Urban Politics*, pp. 31–44; C. Paris and P. Williams, 'Planning, urban crisis and urban management', in McLoughlin and Huxley, *Urban Planning in Australia*, pp. 102–9.

20 C. Lindblom, 'Still muddling, not yet through', *Public Administration Review*, vol. 39, 1979, pp. 517–26.

21 J. Holmes, 'The Hamer government and urban planning in Victoria', in *Interest Groups and Public Policy: Case Studies from the Australian States*, ed. R. Scott, Macmillan, South Melbourne, 1980, p. 202.

22 This section is based on I. Alexander, 'Post-war metropolitan planning: Goals and realities', in *Equity in the City*, ed. P. Troy, George Allen & Unwin, Sydney, 1981, pp. 145–71; Alexander, 'Land use and transport planning'; Harrison, 'City planning'; and Wilenski, 'Sydney's urban management'.

23 Wilenski, 'Sydney's urban management', p. 247.

24 Sources for this discussion are: Holmes, 'The Hamer government and urban planning'; B. Logan, 'The shape of Melbourne: A political geography of Melbourne's planning in the 1970s and 1980s', in McLoughlin and Huxley, *Urban Planning in Australia*, pp. 131–56; T. Logan, *Urban and Regional Planning in Victoria*, Shillington House, Melbourne, 1981; T. Logan, 'Urban and regional planning in a federal system'; J.B. McLoughlin, *Shaping Melbourne's Future? Town Planning, the State and Civil Society*, Cambridge University Press, Melbourne, 1992.

25 Holmes, 'The Hamer government and urban planning', p. 202.

26 Holmes, 'The Hamer government and urban planning', pp. 213–18; T. Logan and E. Ogilvy, 'The statutory planning framework', in *Equity in the City*, ed. P. Troy, George Allen & Unwin, Sydney, 1981, pp. 190–2; L. Sandercock, *The Land Racket*.

27 See, for example, McLoughlin, *Shaping Melbourne's Future?*; Neutze, *Australian Urban Policy*; Paris and Williams, 'Planning, urban crisis and urban management'; L. Sandercock, 'A socialist city in a capitalist society?', in Sandercock and Berry, *Urban Political Economy*.

28 This outline of planning for Adelaide in the 1970s is based on C. Forster, 'Managing metropolitan Adelaide: Past performances and present issues', *Urban Policy and Research*, vol. 2, 1984, pp. 40–3; Forster and McCaskill, 'The modern period'; Harrison, 'City planning'; Mant, 'The instruments of planning'.

29 Mant, 'The instruments of planning'.

30 Examples of studies of central–local relations, in general, and the sacking of the Melbourne City Council, in particular, can be found in: Halligan and Paris, *Australian Urban Politics*; T. Logan, *Urban and Regional Planning*

in Victoria; W. Logan, 'The shape of Melbourne'; McLoughlin, *Shaping Melbourne's Future?*; Parkin, *Governing the Cities*; P. Saunders, 'The crisis of local government in Melbourne: The sacking of the City Council', in Halligan and Paris, *Australian Urban Politics*, pp. 88–109.

31 O. Yiftachel and J. Kenworthy, 'The planning of metropolitan Perth: Some critical observations', in *Urban and Regional Planning in Western Australia: Historical and Critical Perspectives*, eds D. Hedgcock and O. Yiftachel, Paradigm Press, Perth, 1992, pp. 131–48.

32 Wilenski, 'Sydney's urban management', p. 248.

33 The actions of the Kennett Liberal–National Coalition Government in Victoria since coming to power in 1992 have illustrated the strength of political will and the parliamentary majority required to effect fundamental change to the structures of government, including local government. More change to local government and the planning system has taken place in the last six years than in the previous two decades. The effects of this on metropolitan development are only just becoming evident. See L. Johnson, C. Long and W. Logan, 'Jeff Kennett's Melbourne: Postmodern city, planning and politics', in *The Twentieth Century Urban Planning Experience: Proceedings of the Eighth International Planning History Society Conference and Fourth Australian Planning/Urban History Conference*, ed. R. Freestone, University of New South Wales, Sydney, 1998, pp. 436–41.

9 The revival of metropolitan planning

1 C. Forster and M. McCaskill, 'The modern period: Managing metropolitan Adelaide', in *With Conscious Purpose: A History of Town Planning in South Australia*, eds A. Hutchings and R. Bunker, Wakefield Press, Adelaide, 1986, p. 106.

2 L. Orchard, 'National urban policy in the 1990s', in *Australian Cities: Issues, Strategies and Policies for Urban Australia in the 1990s*, ed. P. Troy, Cambridge University Press, Melbourne, 1995, pp. 65–86.

3 Department of Health, Housing and Community Services, *Better Cities: National Developments 1991–92*, Australian Government Publishing Service, Canberra, 1992. See also G. Campbell, 'The Better Cities Program: A catalyst for urban reform', in *Spirited Cities: Urban Planning, Traffic and Environmental Management in the Nineties*, ed. R. Freestone, Federation Press, Sydney, 1993, pp. 267–79.

4 Department of Health, Housing and Community Services, *Building Better Cities Information Kit*, Goals and Objectives, DHHCS, Canberra, 1991, p. 3.

5 For example, see I. Alexander, 'DURD revisited?: Federal policy initiatives for urban and regional planning 1991–94', *Urban Policy and Research*, vol. 12, 1994, pp. 6–26.

6 B. Badcock, 'The urban program as an instrument of crisis management in Australia', *Urban Policy and Research*, vol. 11, 1993, pp. 72–80.

7 A. Beer, 'Never mind the content, let's understand the process: An alternative perspective on recent federal urban initiatives', *Urban Policy and Research*, vol. 13, 1995, pp. 107–12.

8 Alexander, 'DURD Revisited?', p. 23.

9 See, for example, S. Hamnett, 'The multi-function polis: 1987–1997', *Australian Planner*, vol. 34, 1997, pp. 225–30; W. Hamilton, *Serendipity City: Australia, Japan and the Multi-Function Polis*, ABC Books, Sydney, 1991; and M. Castells and P. Hall, *Technopoles of the World: The Making of 21st Century Industrial Complexes*, Routledge, London, 1994.

10 S. Holliday, 'Metropolitan planning and demography: Sydney as a case study', in *The Twentieth Century Urban Planning Experience: Proceedings of the Eighth International Planning History Society Conference and Fourth Australian Planning/Urban History Conference*, ed. R. Freestone, University of New South Wales, Sydney, 1998, pp. 364–9.

11 M. Berry and M. Huxley, 'Property development, capital switching and state intervention: Studies of Melbourne, Australia', paper to the International Sociological Association, Urban and Regional Development Research Committee Conference, University of Hong Kong, August 1985.

12 D. Wilmoth, 'Urban consolidation policy and social equity', in *Urban Consolidation: The Equity Issue*, ed. L. Sandercock, Macquarie University, Sydney, 1982, p. 17.

13 S. O'Toole, 'The states and territories: New South Wales', in *Metropolitan Planning in Australia*, Australian Urban and Regional Development Review, Workshop Paper No. 3, Melbourne, 1994.

14 J. Forbes, 'Metropolitan planning in Perth', in *Metropolitan Planning in Australia*, pp. 120–8.

15 D. Hedgcock, 'Planning the outward growth of Australian capital cities: Perth', *Urban Policy and Research*, vol. 12, 1994, p. 125.

16 R. Bunker, 'State planning operation', in Troy, *Australian Cities*, p. 162.

17 Quoted in National Capital Planning Authority, *National Capital Plan: Principles, Policies and Special Requirements. Draft Proposals*, vol. 2, Australian Government Publishing Service, Canberra, 1989, p. 20.

18 J. Conner, 'Canberra: The lion, the witch and the wardrobe', in Freestone, *Spirited Cities*, pp. 225–36.

19 K. Seibert and V. Sposito, *Strategic Planning for Metropolitan Melbourne*, Report prepared for Metropolis '93, World Association of Major Metropolises, Montreal, 23 April 1993, p. 20.

20 J.B. McLoughlin, *Shaping Melbourne's Future? Town Planning, the State and Civil Society*, Cambridge University Press, Melbourne, 1992.

21 J.B. McLoughlin, 'The case for a legal basis for land-use planning systems', *Built Environment*, vol. 18, no. 3, 1992, pp. 217–18.

22 Sarkissian Associates, with W. Bell, *Future Development Options for Metropolitan Adelaide: A Social Impact Evaluation*, Report for the South Australian Department of Environment and Planning, Adelaide, 1987.

23 H. Stretton, 'Urban consolidation: Who consolidates who?' *Adelaide Review*,

no. 55, 1988, pp. 4–6; H. Stretton, 'Urban consolidation: What if it doesn't work?' *Adelaide Review*, no. 56, 1988, pp. 6–9; B. Badcock, 'Metropolitan planning in South Australia', Australian National University, Urban Research Unit Working Paper No. 10, 1989.

24 Badcock, 'Metropolitan planning in South Australia', p. 12.

25 M. Neutze, 'Planning as urban management: A critical assessment', in *Metropolitan Planning in Australia: Urban Management*, Australian National University, Urban Research Unit Working Paper No. 6, 1988, p. 14.

26 R.J. Stimson, 'A place in the sun? Policies, planning and leadership for the Brisbane region', *Urban Futures*, vol. 2, 1992, pp. 51–2.

27 R.J. Stimson, *Brisbane—Magnet City: A Report on Strategies for the Development, Growth and Management of Brisbane City into the 21st Century*', Brisbane City Council, Brisbane, September 1991 (widely referred to as the 'Stimson Report').

28 S. Hamnett and S. Parham, '2020 vision: A planning strategy for metropolitan Adelaide', *Urban Futures*, vol. 2, 1992, p. 85.

29 G. Scott, 'Economic policy', in *The Bannon Decade: The Politics of Restraint in South Australia*, eds A. Parkin and A. Patience, Allen & Unwin, Sydney, 1992, p. 88.

30 M. Peel, 'The urban debate: From "Los Angeles" to the urban village', in Troy, *Australian Cities*, p. 52.

10 The late 1990s

1 See R. Cardew and P. Williamson, 'Residential construction on Melbourne's urban fringe', *Urban Futures*, vol. 4, 1994, pp. 31–9; P. Williamson and R. Cardew, 'Housing growth in metropolitan Perth', *Urban Futures*, no. 18, 1995, pp. 47–52; and S. Holliday, 'Metropolitan planning and demography: Sydney as a case study', in *The Twentieth Century Urban Planning Experience: Proceedings of the Eighth International Planning History Society Conference and Fourth Australian Planning/Urban History Conference*, ed. R. Freestone, University of New South Wales, Sydney, 1998, pp. 364–9.

2 See, for example, B. Jessop, 'The entrepreneurial city: Re-imaging localities, redesigning economic governance, or restructuring capital?', in *Transforming Cities: Contested Governance and New Spatial Divisions*, eds N. Jewson and S. MacGregor, Routledge, London, 1997, pp. 28–41.

3 M. Peel, 'The urban debate: From "Los Angeles" to the urban village', in *Australian Cities: Issues, Strategies and Policies for Urban Australia in the 1990s*, ed. P. Troy, Cambridge University Press, Melbourne, 1995, p. 39.

4 P. Healey, *Planning for the 1990s*, University of Newcastle upon Tyne, Department of Town and Country Planning Working Paper No. 7, 1989, p. 2.

5 L. Sandercock, *Towards Cosmopolis: Planning for Multicultural Cities*, John Wiley, Chichester, 1998, p. 197.

6 G. Davison and R. Fincher, 'Urban studies in Australia: A road map and ways ahead', *Urban Policy and Research*, vol. 16, 1998, p. 189.
7 L. Orchard, 'Shifting visions: National urban and regional policy in Australia since the 1940s', in Freestone, *The Twentieth Century Urban Planning Experience*, p. 22.
8 J. Howard and S. Duggan, *The Australian Urban System: Trends and Prospects*, Report by Cooper and Lybrand Consultants for the Australian Urban and Regional Development Review, Canberra, 1994, p. 3.
9 P. Keating, Opening Address to the Australia/OECD Conference, Cities and the New Global Economy, Melbourne, November 1994.
10 Prime Minister's Urban Design Task Force, *Urban Design in Australia*, Australian Government Publishing Service, Canberra, 1994.
11 Prime Minister's Urban Design Task Force, *Urban Design*, p. 24.
12 L. Neilson, 'Partnerships in Australian urban management', paper to the Australian Institute of Urban Studies/Royal Australian Planning Institute Conference, *Planning in Victoria*, Bendigo, 12 October 1995.
13 Neilson, 'Partnerships', p. 13.
14 Neilson, 'Partnerships', p. 16.
15 Questions have been raised about the continuation of arrangements for fiscal equalisation between states as part of the Howard Government's proposals to overhaul the national taxation system, while decisions about extensions to the national rail system, and the long-awaited rail connection to Darwin in particular, are dependent upon private investment, rather than on any vision for national infrastructure development.
16 Orchard, 'Shifting visions', p. 26.
17 In 1995, the Council of Australian Governments (CoAG) agreed on a set of 'Competition Principles' which required legislation to be reviewed to see whether it restricts competition and, if so, whether this can be justified. On consequential changes to planning legislation in New South Wales, see A. Conway, 'Integrated development assessment: NSW Environmental Planning and Assessment (Amendment) Act 1997', paper to the Royal Australian Planning Institute conference in Brisbane, 8 July 1998, p. 2.
18 C. Knowles, 'The NSW state government's urban management', *Australian Planner*, vol. 33, 1996, p. 67.
19 K. Yearbury, 'Planning for the new millennium: Draft Integrated Planning Bill', address to the Queensland Environmental Law Seminar, 27 September 1997, Brisbane, p. 19.
20 Western Australian Planning Commission, *State Planning Strategy: Final Report*, WAPC, Perth, December 1997, p. 22.
21 R. Maclellan, Victorian minister for planning, 'Planning a better future for Victorians', public address delivered at the Royal Exhibition Building, Carlton, Victoria, 13 August 1993, p. 1.
22 It was claimed that the government had reduced the number of zones to 25 from a former figure of 2871 zones.

23 Property Council of Australia—Victorian Division, *Submission to City Plan '97*, unpublished, September 1997 (available through Property Council of Australia, Victorian Division, Level 7, 136 Exhibition Street, Melbourne, Victoria 3000).
24 E. Ogilvy, 'City Plan '97 and the death of planning control', in *Planning Practice 1998: The Best and Worst Examples of City Planning and Development*, ed. K. Shaw, People's Committee for Melbourne, North Melbourne, July 1998, p. 39.
25 S. Moseley, 'Sydney's new metropolitan strategy', *Australian Planner*, vol. 32, 1995, p. 134.
26 New South Wales Department of Urban Affairs and Planning, *A Framework for Growth and Change: The Review of Strategic Planning*, DUAP, Sydney, 1997.
27 See especially New South Wales Department of Urban Affairs and Planning and Department of State and Regional Development, *Sydney as a Global City*, DUAP/DSRD, Sydney, 1996.
28 New South Wales Department of Urban Affairs and Planning, *A Framework for Growth and Change*, p. 19.
29 Council of the City of Sydney, *City Plan*, Council of the City of Sydney, Sydney, 1996.
30 G.H. Searle, 'Regime, regulation and two decades of central Sydney development', in Freestone, *The Twentieth Century Urban Planning Experience*, p. 810.
31 South-East Queensland Regional Co-ordination Committee, *South-East Queensland Regional Framework for Growth Management 1998*, Queensland Department of Local Government and Planning, Brisbane, 1998, p. 17.
32 Brisbane City Council, *The Brisbane 2011 Plan: The Livable City for the Future*, Brisbane City Council, Brisbane, 1996.
33 Government of Victoria, *A Place to Live, Urban Development 1992–2031: Shaping Victoria's Future*, Department of Planning and Housing, Melbourne, 1992.
34 J. Reynolds, 'Shaping Victoria's future: A place to live—Victoria's long term urban development strategy', *Urban Futures*, vol. 2, 1992, p. 74.
35 Government of Victoria, *Creating Prosperity: Victoria's Capital City Policy*, Department of Planning and Development, Melbourne, 1994.
36 Government of Victoria, *Living Suburbs: A Policy for Metropolitan Melbourne into the 21st Century*, Department of Planning and Development, Melbourne, 1995.
37 Government of Victoria, *Living Suburbs*, p. 5.
38 Department of Infrastructure, *From Doughnut City to Café Society*, Department of Infrastructure, Melbourne, 1998.
39 K. O'Connor, 'Understanding metropolitan Melbourne ... without being confused by coffee and doughnuts', *Urban Policy and Research*, vol. 16, 1998, pp. 139–45.
40 City of Melbourne, *CityPlan*, Melbourne City Council, Melbourne, 1998.

41 C. Long, 'The Melbourne Docklands', in Shaw, *Planning Practice 1998*, p. 51.
42 R. Bunker and A. Hutchings, 'South Australia in the 1990s: A review of urban development, planning and policy', in *South Australia in the 1990s*, ed. S. Hamnett, South Australian Planning Papers No. 6, Planning Education Foundation of South Australia, Adelaide, 1997, p. 56.
43 Bunker and Hutchings, 'South Australia in the 1990s', p. 46.
44 Bunker and Hutchings, 'South Australia in the 1990s', p. 48.
45 Adelaide 21 Steering Committee and Project Team, *Adelaide 21: City Centre Strategy for the New Era*, Council of the City of Adelaide/Government of South Australia, Adelaide, 1996.
46 S. Hamnett, 'The Multi-Function Polis: 1987–1997', *Australian Planner*, vol. 34, 1997, pp. 225–30.
47 Australian Capital Territory Government, *Canberra: A Capital Future*, ACT Government, Canberra, December 1996. Part 2: *Strategies for a Viable, Sustainable Future—The Right Image for Canberra*, p. 7.
48 Western Australian Planning Commission, *Draft State Planning Strategy*, WAPC, Perth, 1996, p. 75.
49 Western Australian Planning Commission, *State Planning Strategy: Summary of Discussion Papers*, WAPC, Perth, 1996.
50 M. Painter, 'Urban government, urban politics and the fabrication of urban issues: The impossibility of urban policy', *Australian Journal of Public Administration*, vol. 34, 1979, p. 346.
51 M. Neutze, 'Planning as urban management: A critical assessment', in *Metropolitan Planning in Australia: Urban Management*, Australian National University, Urban Research Unit Working Paper No. 6, 1988, p. 11.
52 Bunker and Hutchings, 'South Australia in the 1990s', p. 54.
53 J. Borja and M. Castells, *Local and Global: Management of Cities in the Information Age*, United Nations Commission for Human Settlements/ Earthscan, London, 1997, p. 155.
54 Western Australian Planning Commission, *State Planning Strategy Final Report*, WAPC, Perth, 1997, p. viii.
55 M. Peel, 'The urban debate', p. 42.
56 C. Long, 'Of edifice complexes, credit card consumers, sports stadia and marinas: Melbourne's Docklands as symbol of late 20th century urban development', in Freestone, *The Twentieth Century Urban Planning Experience*, p. 540.
57 D. Harvey, 'Contested cities', in Jewson and MacGregor, *Transforming Cities*, p. 20.
58 J. Sulman, *An Introduction to the Study of Town Planning in Australia*, Government Printer of New South Wales, Sydney, 1921, p. 213.
59 Advertising leaflet, Master of Social Science, Environment and Planning, Facilty of the Constructed Environment, Royal Melbourne Institute of Technology, September 1998.
60 N. Taylor, 'Paradigms and town planning theory since 1945', in Freestone, *The Twentieth Century Urban Planning Experience*, p. 892.

61 M. Jacobs, 'Sustainability and community', *Australian Planner*, vol. 32, 1995, p. 111.

62 W. Sarkissian, 'With a whole heart: Nurturing an ethic of caring for nature in the education of Australian planners', PhD thesis, Murdoch University, Perth, 1996.

Index